The Continuing Purpose

The Continuing Purpose

*A History of the National Trust,
its Aims and Work*

Robin Fedden

Longmans

LONGMANS, GREEN AND CO LTD
48 Grosvenor Street, London W1
*Associated companies, branches and representatives
throughout the world*

© *Robin Fedden 1968*
First published 1968

To the Committees, Staff, and Members of
the National Trust

Printed in Great Britain by
Spottiswoode, Ballantyne & Co. Ltd., London and Colchester

Contents

Illustrations

Foreword

by the Earl of Antrim, Chairman of the National Trust

The National Trust is based upon the vision of three people who saw that the twentieth century would be careless of much that it inherited. Octavia Hill, Sir Robert Hunter and Canon Rawnsley started the National Trust in the last years of the nineteenth century and all who love the natural appearance of the country and how man built in it must be forever grateful to them.

Mr Fedden, in this admirable and admirably-written book, shows how a brilliant idea has been made to live; he tells of changes of opinion in the National Trust itself; he describes the difficulties that have been faced; and he gives an excellent description of what the National Trust has achieved.

There is one aspect of the National Trust that I want to emphasise. The Trust would have had little success if it had not been given property, possessions and money, by all sorts of people who believed in its aims. It would also have achieved little if many generous men and women had not worked without material reward to further these aims. All who have given their riches or their time have done so because they were determined that at least some fine country or some splendid building should survive the demands of the philistine age in which we live.

The National Trust is a peculiarly English institution in that it fulfils a national need without being in any way part of the State. It offers a complete contrast to the formal organisations that preserve the great buildings of France and it is at times difficult for those who are unfamiliar with the National Trust to understand how it is financed, directed and staffed. Mr Fedden tells this complicated story in a way which will explain to those who are interested how this great organisation serves the country.

Preface

The main sources for the history of the Trust are Annual Reports and Committee Minutes. The early files were consigned to the flames at the beginning of the last war, a conflagration shrouded in mystery as deep as that which attended the burning of the Alexandrian library. Detailed records for most properties thus exist only from the forties.

Miss Dorothy Hunter's notes for a biography of her father, projected many years ago, have thrown valuable light on early years. So too have the published biographies of Octavia Hill and Canon Rawnsley; and, for a later period, a private memoir by Ronald Norman. Books by, or about, John Bailey, G. M. Trevelyan, and Lord Zetland, have enabled me to understand something of their attitude and the role they played. I have also drawn on *The National Trust: A Record of Fifty Years' Achievement*, and Mr B. L. Thompson's *The Lake District and the National Trust*. As important as any publication has been the memory of those who worked for the Trust before the last war. My title, *The Continuing Purpose*, is with permission taken from a speech by Lord Wemyss, Chairman of the National Trust for Scotland.

Where my text deserts fact for opinion the views expressed are my own and do not necessarily reflect those of the Council and Executive Committee.

I owe a debt gratefully acknowledged to members of the Trust's committees and staff, both past and present. Many of them read parts of my typescript, supplied information, and corrected errors. Their help was essential. I wish in particular to thank Miss Isolde Wigram who deciphered my handwriting and made valuable suggestions.

R.F.

November 1967

Part One

The History

Chapter 1

The Founding Fathers

In September 1884 a remarkable address was delivered in Birmingham to the annual congress of the National Association for the Promotion of Social Science. Having summarised the progress of the battle to save common lands, a battle conducted by the Commons Preservation Society since its foundation in the winter of 1865–6, the speaker deplored the fact that the Society had no power to acquire land, and that even the purchase of common rights was impossible for an association without corporate existence. He then proceeded to advocate the creation of a special body, incorporated under the Joint Stock Companies Acts, to buy and hold, for the benefit of the nation, land and buildings and more particularly land to which common rights were attached. He outlined in some detail the functions of such a body, 'existing primarily for the purpose, not of putting money into the pockets of its shareholders, but of advancing objects they have at heart'. The central idea, he said, 'is that of a Land Company formed . . . . with a view to the protection of the public interests in the open spaces of the country'. The conception was novel.

The address was given by Robert Hunter, who had for many years been honorary solicitor to the Commons Preservation Society, and it sketched for the first time the form and purpose of a body like the National Trust. In connection with the work of the Kyrle and Commons Preservation Societies, he had looked carefully into the state of the law and was convinced of the need for a statutory body, as distinct from a merely voluntary association, with power to buy or accept gifts of land and buildings in order to administer them in the public interest. The Birmingham proposals found ready support among some of Robert Hunter's friends. From one quarter came the offer of £100 to launch the scheme, and James Bryce (later Lord Bryce) thought the proposals important enought to warrant the reprinting of the address by the Commons Preservation Society.[1] But it was in Octavia Hill, whom Robert Hunter had first met in connection with the fight for common land, that he found the most active ally. She immediately saw the value of his conception and gave it determined support. In February 1885

3

she wrote of the difficulty of finding a short expressive name for the 'new Company', and stated her preference for the word 'Trust', adding: 'You will do better, I believe, to bring forward its benevolent than its commercial character. People don't like unsuccessful business, but do like Charity where a little money goes a long way because of good commercial management.' At the head of this letter Robert Hunter pencilled with a query the words 'National Trust'.

Though a name had been found, it was some years before the new organisation took shape. Progress was slow, depending as it did wholly on Robert Hunter and Octavia Hill, both already deeply immersed in other public activities. Further, in the most likely quarter, there was not the ready support that might have been expected. The prestige of the Commons Preservation Society was already considerable but it was not immediately placed behind Robert Hunter's proposals. The Chairman of the organisation, Shaw Lefevre (later Lord Eversleigh), apparently feared that the creation of a holding company would adversely affect the Commons Preservation Society and divert funds elsewhere. As late as 1889 Octavia Hill lamented to Robert Hunter that 'Mr. Shaw Lefevre does not rise to the idea of the new Society.'

Unexpected help came from the North. Hardwicke Rawnsley, a man of dynamism, had been introduced to Octavia Hill by Ruskin when working as a priest among the poor in Seven Dials. It was the start of a lifelong friendship. In 1883, when he accepted the living of Crosthwaite near Keswick and assumed the role, which he enjoyed, of foremost defender of the Lake District, a projected railway Bill which would have ruined the seclusion of Derwentwater and Borrowdale brought him into contact with Robert Hunter and the Commons Preservation Society. Robert Hunter was among those who guaranteed a fund to fight the Bill, but passionate local opposition, well organised by Canon Rawnsley, led to its withdrawal. Soon after Robert Hunter's cooperation, and his skill in drafting appeals, were invoked in connection with another projected lakeside railway along Windermere. By 1885 he had joined Canon Rawnsley's Lake District Defence Society, and in the same year he and Octavia Hill gave strong support to the Canon's successful fight, famous in its day, to maintain two important rights of way in the Keswick area.

In immediately succeeding years, when Robert Hunter and Octavia Hill were trying to gain support for their projected 'National Trust', little contact seems to have been maintained with the champion of the Lake District. Then, in 1893, several properties of importance in the area, including the celebrated Falls of Lodore, came into the market, and

The Clergy House, Alfriston, Sussex. The Trust's first building

Great Langdale, Lake District. Most of the important daleheads are now in Trust ownership

Tarn Hows, Lake District. Given in 1930

Canon Rawnsley realised with dismay that, even if such places could be bought by public subscription, there existed no body capable of holding them for the benefit of the nation. He turned to the two friends whom he had found valuable in his earlier battles for the preservation of the Lakes, and who for many years had been advocating the creation of just such a body. His approach was more than welcome. He shared their energy and public spirit, but could also provide an emotive rallying cry. The Lake District was in danger. This was a cause that appealed to a wide public and for which the shades of Wordsworth and Coleridge could be enlisted to do battle. Almost overnight the long-cherished aim to create a 'National Trust' seemed realisable.

GROSVENOR HOUSE

Henceforth Robert Hunter, Octavia Hill and Hardwicke Rawnsley acted in concert. They were a formidable team. Over their signatures a printed notice was sent in the autumn of 1893 to likely supporters. Headed 'National Trust for Historic Sites and Natural Scenery', it was an invitation to a preliminary meeting on November 16th at the office of the Commons Preservation Society to discuss the formation and constitution of a responsible body 'to act as a Corporation for the holding of lands of natural beauty and sites and houses of historic interest to be preserved intact for the nation's use and enjoyment.' The meeting was well reported in the press. Mr Ruskin, the *Daily News* said 'would have been spared many a mournful page', if a body such as the proposed National Trust had existed earlier, and *The Times* in its enthusiasm surprisingly envisaged 'a future neither dim nor distant [when] the association may possibly go so far as to seek powers of compulsory purchase in cases where the public interest is clearly involved'. It saw no reason why 'a bit of beautiful scenery should not be the subject of a forced sale under equitable conditions just as much as a bit of ugly country for a railway'.

Following the November meeting a statement of the objects of the association, drafted by Robert Hunter, with a list of those who had consented to serve on the provisional Council, was issued over Canon Rawnsley's signature. The first name on the provisional council was that of the Duke of Westminster. Though now chiefly remembered as the owner whose horses four times won the Derby, he was a many-sided man, a philanthropist, an amateur of painting, and a liberal and enlightened landlord. As *The Times* quaintly put it, the first Duke could 'pass from a racecourse to take the chair at a missionary meeting without incurring the censure of the strictest'. He had been quick to respond to the idea of a National Trust, and in the following summer (1894) he offered the hospitality of Grosvenor House for a constituent meeting. The Trust was thus born in a splendid room off Park Lane, a surprisingly gilded cradle for an organisation which has always been poor.

The meeting was held on July 16th with the Duke of Westminster in the chair, and its purpose was to approve the draft constitution which the promoters had drawn up. After Hardwicke Rawnsley had spoken in general terms of the need for a National Trust and of the role which it could fill, two resolutions of moment were passed. They mark the inception of the Trust. First Octavia Hill moved 'that it is desirable to provide means by which landowners and others may be enabled to dedicate to the nation places of historic interest or natural beauty, and that for this purpose it is expedient to form a corporate body, capable of holding land, and representative of national institutions and interests'. Sir Robert Hunter, as by this date he had become, then moved the resolution 'that this meeting approves generally of the proposed constitution of the National Trust for Places of Historic Interest or Natural Beauty, as explained to the meeting, and authorises the necessary steps to be taken to procure the legal incorporation of the Trust'. The most sanguine supporters can hardly have envisaged what the acceptance of these resolutions was to mean.[2]

The resolutions of the meeting of July 16th were given effect in a Memorandum and Articles of Association, no doubt mainly drafted by Sir Robert Hunter, and issued over the names of nine signatories.[3] The articles were approved with negligible modification by the Board of Trade and the infant association was registered under the Companies Acts on January 12th 1895 as 'The National Trust for Places of Historic Interest and Natural Beauty'. On the grounds that the Trust was a non-profit making body, licence was obtained from the Board of Trade to omit the word 'Limited' from the title.[4]

THE TRINITY

Members of the Trust have been taught to revere the trinity which brought it into being: properly so, for they were remarkable. In distinguishing the persons of this trinity, it is not necessary to elevate one above another. All possessed in unusual degree the mixture of idealism and commonsense, of vision and determination, which is the hallmark of the successful reformer. That they were in other respects different yet complementary ensured fruitful cooperation.

6

Though Robert Hunter (1844–1913) made a distinguished career as solicitor to the Post Office, a position which he held for thirty years under thirteen postmasters-general, he was more than an able and conscientious civil servant. Pre-eminently he was the servant of public causes. In 1868 at the age of twenty-four he became honorary solicitor to the Commons Preservation Society and brilliantly conducted the series of complicated suits which culminated in the victory that saved six thousand acres of Epping Forest in 1874. The success of the Commons Preservation Society in its fight against enclosures was largely due to his knowledge and acumen. Though he also played a comparable role in the fortunes of Hampstead Garden Suburb, of which he was Chairman, the National Trust, his personal conception, remains his best memorial.

His character presents something of a paradox. Though retiring and self-effacing almost to a fault, he showed extreme pertinacity; though modest and reserved, he found no project too difficult and no problem too disconcerting. This quiet man left his mark on every enterprise with which the new organisation was associated. As Chairman of the Executive Committee from its first meeting in 1895 until his death in 1913 he firmly but unobtrusively directed and coordinated policy. He was the backbone of the Trust, as Octavia Hill was its inspiration and Hardwicke Rawnsley its advocate.

Octavia Hill (1838–1912) is above all associated with housing reform, and her pioneer work in that field, which began as early as 1864, is her outstanding achievement. It was in connection with housing that she came to realise the importance of open spaces and the necessity for their preservation. When her sister Miranda Hill in 1875 launched the Kyrle Society with the object of bringing some grace and beauty into the houses of the poor, Octavia Hill set up an Open Spaces Sub-Committee and persuaded her friend Robert Hunter to act as honorary legal adviser. 'Open air sitting rooms for the poor' were her objective. In the face of apathy and even hostility she worked over the next few years to save small plots of land in the metropolitan area. Some were vested in the appropriate local authority, others were incorporated in schemes of improved housing. Here and there disused and derelict burial grounds were reclaimed and turned into small but pleasant public gardens. More ambitious enterprises, such as the preservation of Parliament Hill and the Hilly Fields, near Lewisham, were carried against all odds to a successful conclusion by her energy and her extraordinary power of appealing both to purse and conscience. For these two open spaces £95,000 was required and was raised. When it came to the creation of a National Trust her role was invaluable. Her name was already nationally known, her contacts were innumerable (it was she who brought in the Duke of Westminster), and above all she possessed a power of inspiring devotion and loyalty to the causes in which she was selflessly interested. Perhaps something of a saint, she was the most complex and the most sensitive of the trinity which founded the Trust. She provided its aura.

It would be difficult to think of a greater contrast to these two than Hardwicke Rawnsley (1851–1920), the vicar of Crosthwaite and Canon of Carlisle. An athlete at Balliol and 'the troubadour of the college', he was a man of ardour and eagerness and always a colourful figure. His interests were legion. One year would see him in Moscow reporting the coronation of the Czar, and another in Athens attending an International Archaeological Conference. The day that found him on Helvellyn watching the sunrise might well see him launching the Keswick School of Industrial Arts, setting up a memorial to the Venerable Bede, concerning himself with the improved production of Cumberland butter, sitting on the committee of the National Association for the Prevention of Consumption, or giving battle for the preservation of Thirlmere. As we have seen, it was in connection with the Lakes that he came to share in the founding of the Trust, and neither the Lake District nor the Trust has had a more active advocate. Jowett of Balliol paid tribute to his hold as a preacher over his congregation, and when not in the pulpit his eloquence and his ready pen were constantly at the service of the Trust. Articles, sonnets, telegrams, letters to the press, poured out year after year. When he was not lecturing in America, he was talking in England; and his theme was always the same—the threat to the countryside and the importance of the role of the Trust. If his enthusiasm sometimes outran his judgment, as when he pressed the Trust to support the Plumage Bill or to make representations to Convocation to prevent clergy selling church plate, Robert Hunter's sobriety put things right. A natural orator endowed with unnatural energy, he was a propaganda machine in himself and he spread the Trust's gospel with force.

Chapter 2

The Early Years

The history of the Trust divides conveniently and realistically into six periods; these roughly correspond with the tenures of the first six chairmen of its Executive Committee. The early years are associated with the guidance and the policy of Sir Robert Hunter. They are also marked by an evangelical enthusiasm. Few people were involved, yet their achievement was extraordinary. Of the many appeals launched, all were successful. Membership was never more than 700, yet on the Chairman's death in 1913 sixty-two properties had been acquired, and the lines of future development were firmly set.[1]

The Executive Committee met for the first time in February 1895 at 1 Great College Street in the Trust's office, rented for the sum of £6 15s. a year.[2] Robert Hunter was in the Chair, and the members of the Committee included the Duke of Westminster, who had accepted office as President of the Trust; Canon Rawnsley, honorary secretary (a post he was to fill until his death twenty-five years later); and Harriet Yorke, honorary treasurer. The last was the lady who had lived with Octavia Hill in perfect understanding since 1880, a relationship, as Octavia Hill's biographer says 'peculiarly characteristic of English spinsters'. To their friends they were known as the Keeper and the Lion, and it was due to Octavia Hill that the Keeper also kept the accounts of the Trust. She did so until 1924. Octavia Hill herself, though regular in attendance at Executive Committee meetings, held no office. The first secretary was Lawrence Chubb (later Sir Lawrence Chubb) who after four years left to become Secretary of the Commons Preservation Society. From 1901 to 1911 the office was filled by Nigel Bond, who later served for many years on the Trust's Committees.

EARLY ACQUISITIONS

The first meeting of the Executive was no formality. Response to the creation of a National Trust had been immediate and there was business to transact. Some time earlier Canon Rawnsley, as ever persuasive, had been staying with a friend at Barmouth, Mrs F. Talbot. Hardly had the

Articles of Association been approved when this first of many generous donors bought and presented a property to the Trust. It was Dinas Oleu, four and a half acres of cliffland near Barmouth overlooking the great arc of Cardigan Bay. There could have been no happier acquisition, for in its proximity to a seaside town the land was inevitably threatened. 'We have got our first piece of property', wrote Octavia Hill. 'I wonder if it will be the last.'

The fear was unjustified. The Trust gave corporate form to ideas already in the air. It was safely launched and its aims made an appeal to a small but dedicated following. The Executive Committee was soon considering the acquisition of the Trust's first historic building, the clergy house at Alfriston. A half-timbered and thatched parish priest's house built in the mid-fourteenth-century, and one of the few surviving ecclesiastical buildings of its type, it was bought for £10 in the following year, a virtual gift. Its repair presented an immediate problem. 'It is to be hoped', the Report of 1896 stated, 'that the supporters of the Trust will not allow its first purchase to be rendered abortive through lack of funds to carry out the necessary work of maintenance.' This was the first of many appeals for funds to which members have generously responded. The money was subscribed and the clergy house duly repaired.

Dinas Oleu and Alfriston were small properties, and so were most of those acquired for many years to come. The Trust had resources only for modest purchase, and the time was still remote when large estates would be offered. Income by 1913 was only £2,063. In the circumstances it is astonishing, and contrasts with the more cautious use of funds in later years, how often the Trust stepped in to buy a small building or a small piece of land. Of the sixty-two properties acquired before the First World War, twenty-eight came by gift, twenty-one were bought, and thirteen acquired by public appeal. It speaks for the intimate nature of the Trust in this period, for the eloquence of a message personally carried, that so many of the new properties were either in Kent and Surrey or in the Lake District, the areas where Octavia Hill, Robert Hunter, and Canon Rawnsley lived and with whose preservation they were associated. Something of the sort is still true of the Trust. Personal recommendation—its best advocates are the donors who know its methods—continues to play a large part in the extension of its work, particularly where this may be easily identified as in the Lake District and Cornwall. In such areas every dale and headland point a moral.

The early years ensured the preservation of five important stretches of the Lake District (Brandelhow and Grange Fell on Derwentwater, Gowbarrow Park on Ullswater, Queen Adelaide's Hill on Windermere, and Borrans Field near Ambleside); of Barras Head at Tintagel, the first of the Cornish properties; of two nature reserves (part of Wicken Fen and Blakeney Point); and of the nucleus of large open spaces acquired later at Minchinhampton Commons, Hindhead, and Reigate. All but three of these were the subject of appeals to the public. In the light of the support given later by the Trust's provincial centres it is significant that the Gowbarrow appeal owed much of its success to the work of Committees in Manchester and Liverpool. Historic buildings included Joiner's Hall at Salisbury (sixteenth-century), Winster Market House (late seventeenth-century), Long Crendon Courthouse (fourteenth-century) and Buckingham Chantry Chapel (mainly fifteenth-century). The only large building to be acquired was Barrington Court, one of the best preserved country houses of the early sixteenth-century. It is interesting that the Executive Committee in 1912 considered the acquisition of an unspoilt English village, and the secretary was sent to look at Pollington in Yorkshire. His report was unfavourable, but the idea materialised twenty-two years later with the purchase of West Wycombe village. At this period the Trust whenever possible appointed local committees to administer newly acquired properties. The first, the Hindhead Committee (1906), remains sixty years later one of the most active and enterprising. On the outbreak of war the Trust's properties totalled some 5,500 acres.

ANCILLARY ACTIVITIES

The Trust was uniquely constituted to acquire land and buildings by gift or purchase. Unlike other amenity societies, it was a holding rather than a propaganda body. Yet the Trust at the start, and indeed long after, assumed the role of national watchdog, and regarded any issue affecting unspoilt country or good buildings as its natural concern. Threats to property that did not belong to the Trust, and was never likely to do so, formed the subject of constant and energetic intervention. This policy was affirmed in the first leaflet published by the Trust, *Its Aims and Its Work*.

The National Trust [it reads] is not only a holder of natural scenery and ancient buildings, but it also does what it can to promote local interest in the preservation of any worthy historical object or natural beauty.

Whether it be a waterfall destroyed as in the case of Foyers, or an old bit of Sir Christopher Wren's London, the Trinity Almshouses,

Whitechapel, that is threatened, or the quietude of Kynance Cove and the destruction of the rocks off the Cornish foreshore, near the Lizard, or the alteration of the line of the shore at Chelsea that is brought under its notice, or the need of obtaining such a pleasure ground as Churchyard Bottom Wood for the people, the Trust, working sometimes alone, at other times in conjunction with kindred societies brings its influence to bear in the direction and spirit of its promoters.

It helps when necessary to stimulate and promote legislation upon matters cognate to its aims and intention.

When only two years old the Trust was advising the London County Council on the listing of historic buildings and a year later was making representations about Peterborough Cathedral, St Cross Almshouses at Winchester, and the Chelsea Embankment. In 1899 it was actively opposing no less than three schemes for light railways, in addition to developments at Albury and Bromley. In the first decade of the century the Trust intervened as a propagandist in such diverse matters as the condition of Stonehenge, the proposed Snowdon railway, encroachment on Hampstead Heath, and threats to Basingwerk Abbey, Whitgift Hospital, the town walls of Berwick-on-Tweed, and Georgian streets in Westminster and Bath. It even issued a circular on the importance of the preservation of yew trees in churchyards.

A wish to unite all bodies concerned with conservation was a related feature of early policy. In 1900 archaeological societies and field clubs were invited to affiliate with the Trust. By 1903 eighteen had done so and the number rose to over eighty. This association, so sensible in theory, seems to have produced few results. In 1940 the affiliated societies disappear without trace, and their loss is unsignalled in the minutes of the Trust (see Chapter 14).

Between the two world wars propagandist interventions grew less frequent. Though in 1925 the Trust joined in the impassioned debate on the destruction of Waterloo bridge and was concerned even after the Second World War with such questions as the preservation of the Regent's Park terraces, there was a gradual disengagement from issues in which it was not directly involved. A first indication of this change of policy appears as early as 1919 when the Executive Committee discussed at length 'how far the Trust should engage in work of a militant character, as opposed to its functions as a holding body'. Though in 1930 the Council was still referring to the Trust as 'a national institution to which the public at large looks for guidance and assistance whenever any question is raised of the preservation of places of historic interest or natural beauty', and though in the same year the Trust became responsible for a Cathedral Amenities Fund whose income was to be devoted to the improvement of the setting of English cathedrals, a change of major significance was taking place. It can be illustrated by the Trust's attitude towards the City churches. In 1897 on the invitation of the Bishop of London it readily took part in a movement for their better preservation; forty-four years later it declined to be represented on the Committee concerned with the rebuilding of the same churches after the Second World War. Buildings which it would never own seemed no longer a proper matter for intervention. This change of policy, curiously enough, was not the result of an Executive Committee decision, and it has never received formal recognition. No doubt it was prompted by the increasing number of Trust properties, and by the belief that intervention with government, local authorities, and the public, would be more effective if limited to the cases with which the Trust was directly concerned and on which it could speak not only with knowledge but with the authority deriving from the ownership of inalienable property of national importance.

The change of policy has probably owed something to the emergence of a new amenity front. In 1895 few people were worried about landscape and historic buildings, and there were few societies to fight for them. The position has now changed. Many organisations, ranging from national bodies, such as the Council for the Preservation of Rural England and the Georgian Group, to local societies, such as the Weald of Kent Preservation Society and the Bath Preservation Trust, are now actively concerned with, and assume responsibility for, specific sectors of the field of preservation. These bodies were created for propaganda purposes and exist to marshal opinion and fight battles. In their hands the Trust now tends to leave issues in which it is not directly concerned. When members of the public write, as they continually do, calling attention to the proposed demolition of an historic building or to danger threatening a stretch of countryside, they are usually referred to the appropriate propaganda organisation. Thus the Trust in the fulness of time has emerged as the holding body envisaged in its original Articles of Association. Specifically constituted to save land and buildings by acquisition, it now concentrates on this primary task.

THE TRUST OUTSIDE ENGLAND

The scope of the Trust's early interventions in England was paralleled by the sweep of its geographical ambitions. At a date when the sun never set on the Empire and seemed unlikely to do so, the Executive Committee in 1909, on enquiry from the Colonial Office, expressed their readiness to hold the splendid twelfth-century keep of the Templars at Kolossi in Cyprus, and at one time there was talk of a property in the West Indies. Fortunately negotiations were abortive. The Trust in early days was also surprisingly sensitive to the achievements and importance of the New World. Probably this is to be accounted for by the prestige of the Trustees of the Reservations of Massachusetts. Founded in 1891 to hold land in the public interest, it was the senior body of its sort and its constitution influenced that of the Trust. Canon Rawnsley went to the United States to lecture in 1899 and was followed by another committee member in 1900. In the latter year an honorary organising secretary was appointed in Concord, and of the seventy-six corresponding members listed in the Report of 1902–03 fifteen were in the United States. They included Frank Lloyd Wright and Charles Eliot Norton. Curiously enough in 1903 Sulgrave Manor, the Northamptonshire home of the Washington family, was offered to the Trust and unfortunately turned down on grounds of cost (£5,500).[3] A year later, with the examples of Yellowstone and Banff in mind, the Annual Report proposed the creation of a national park in the Lake District.

In 1899 a threat to Killarney led to the establishment of a Joint Anglo-Irish Sub-committee, and a motion was passed, seconded by Octavia Hill, that 'it is desirable that branches of the National Trust be established in Ireland and Scotland'. The Trust's single Irish property was acquired in the following year. This was Kanturk Castle, a sixteenth-century ruin in County Cork. It is now let on long lease to the Irish National Trust and is under the guardianship of the National Monuments branch of the Irish Office of Works. In 1903 'Mr Yeats of the Irish Literary Society' attended a meeting of the Executive Committee of the Trust to give his views on the preservation of the Hill of Tara. Unfortunately no record of those views has been preserved.

It was purely by chance that the Trust did not also acquire property across the Border before the foundation of the National Trust for Scotland in 1931. The first Report of the Provisional Council in 1895 referred to the Trust's efforts to save the Fall of Foyers, and in 1900 the Trust was among the bodies which vainly opposed a railway along the foreshore of the Firth of Forth. Scottish matters continued to occupy the Trust in early years and in 1908 it was decided to hold a meeting in Glasgow. At the request of the Lord Provost 'in consequence of the amount of distress caused by unemployment', the venue was changed to Edinburgh where Canon Rawnsley addressed a large gathering. A few years later (1914) at the request of Lord Bryce, one of the Trust's vice-presidents, he again visited Scotland 'to initiate a movement for the organisation of a branch of the National Trust for Scotland'. The motion seconded by Octavia Hill in 1899 had borne no practical fruit.[4]

The strong representation of the arts and literature in the early counsels of the Trust calls for mention. It was to be expected. Men such as Ruskin and Morris had dominated, and indeed created, the movement to save buildings and the countryside. In 1900 three of the Trust's four vice-presidents, among them Watts and Herkomer, were members of the Royal Academy; two painters were on the Executive Committee, and Sir Edward Poynter, President of the Royal Academy, was to join the Committee in 1904. Among the distinguished writers who served on the Committee in its first years were Sidney Colvin, St Loe Strachey, and John Bailey. These painters and writers surely made a special contribution to the imagination and zest which characterised the Trust's early undertakings.

Chapter 3

The First World War and After

The Earl of Plymouth, Chairman: 1914–1923

The death of Octavia Hill in 1912, of Sir Robert Hunter in the following year, and of other pioneers such as Briscoe Eyre, marked the passing of the first generation. Something of 'glad confident morning' went with it. Though Canon Rawnsley was to remain active in the Lake District for another seven years, the Trust would be different, for it had been both inspired and dominated by the personalities of its founders. Without them it was a more prosaic instrument. A new era presented a new problem which does not seem to have been immediately apparent: the fulfilment, through better organisation and with a wider popular support, of the destiny the founders had planned, yet without the loss of their crusading spirit. In the event it was many years before the Trust acquired either a greater degree of organisation or an appreciable increase in membership.

THE FIRST WORLD WAR

Lord Plymouth, one of the vice-presidents, became chairman on Sir Robert Hunter's death. It was a further link with the arts, for he was a competent painter, the author of a work on John Constable, a trustee of the National Gallery, and chairman of the trustees of the Tate Gallery. He had also been a distinguished First Commissioner of Works to whose imagination the country owed the preservation of the Crystal Palace and the creation of the Mall as a processional avenue. He had not long succeeded when war broke out. Though the dislocation at headquarters and the interruption of committee work was not comparable to that which occurred in 1940, the war had a marked influence on the activity of the Trust. This was partly because it possessed little formal organisation and almost no staff. Its progress in the past had been due to the personal efforts of a limited number of enthusiastic members. After 1914 their energies were largely directed elsewhere. A disproportionate burden fell on the shoulders of S. H. Hamer, who had become secretary in 1911 and was to hold the post until 1933. The Council also thought it proper to discontinue in wartime the many appeals for new properties which had earlier proved so successful.

Achievement was limited. Nineteen-sixteen, an exceptionally disappointing year, saw the acquisition of only one property. When a chain of bonfires was lit on Trust lands from Cornwall to Cumberland in celebration of peace, membership income was less than in 1914. Moreover the repair and upkeep of properties had suffered during the war, and (as in 1945) the Trust was faced with a backlog of maintenance. In 1918 a vain approach for help was made to the Carnegie Trust. By 1920 the annual accounts showed the then unprecedented deficit of £600.

POSTWAR DEVELOPMENTS

One of the immediate tasks of the postwar years was to build up membership and thus strengthen the Trust's financial position. Yet on Lord Plymouth's death in 1923 the high-water marked reached in 1914 had been passed by a mere hundred members (825). Though the Council in its Annual Reports repeatedly referred to the need for increased membership, and in 1922 invited every member to enrol another in the course of the year, few practical steps were taken. Articles in the press and a series of lectures arranged at University College were clearly inadequate; nor was the publication of monographs on properties, for which a sub-committee was set up in 1920, likely to produce a marked influx of members. In view of the Trust's finances, the lack of positive action to attract members between 1918 and 1928 is puzzling. Perhaps at heart the Trust still paid tribute to the idea of a small band of devoted workers. If Octavia Hill and a handful of friends had accomplished so much, was there really need for a large impersonal membership? Moreover the small band, whose numbers in 1918 were no more than those of a London club and who shared a pleasant community of interests and outlook, could be relied upon to make a generous financial contribution. Its members were always dipping into their pockets and were particularly ready to do so in a crisis. The same individuals repeatedly proved generous benefactors. In 1920 of the 730 members of the Trust 85 were Honorary Members, donors of £100 or more (or of property of an equivalent value), and 183 were Life Members, donors of £20 or upwards. Of the 460 ordinary members only 128 paid the stipulated subscription of ten shillings; most of them paid at least a pound and 58 paid two guineas or over.[1]

Such figures give rise to the suspicion that when the Council spoke of the urgent need for support they had an eye as much on increased donations from existing benefactors as on the recruitment of new members. The figures also go far to explain the financial viability of the Trust over the long period, more than thirty years, when its members numbered less than a thousand.

During the war a single appeal had been issued by the Trust. In conjunction with other societies concerned for the preservation of the countryside, it had urged both individuals and public authorities to consider the acquisition of open spaces as war memorials. The Council felt that 'no more fitting form of memorial could be found to commemorate those who had fallen in the war than to dedicate to their memory some open space, some hilltop commanding beautiful views, some waterfall or sea-cliff, which could be enjoyed for all time by those who survived'. As a result, several properties came to the Trust. The most notable were Scafell Pike, in memory of the men of the Lake District; Great End and Great Gable, with nearly 1,200 acres of the Scafell massif, in memory of members of the Fell and Rock Climbing Club; St Catherine's Point in memory of the men of Fowey; and Castle Crag on Derwentwater.

With the coming of peace, appeals were once again set on foot, often four or five of them running at the same time. In 1921 Lyveden New Bield, that curious and beautiful Jacobean building symbolising the Passion, was finally acquired as the result of an appeal first launched before the war, and in the following year a major appeal, raising £8,000, was organised by Country Life to secure for the Trust a vital area on Box Hill where the Trust had gained a substantial footing in 1914. Other valuable gifts or purchases during the period 1914 to 1923 were the Dodman (145 acres) on the Cornish coast; Waggoner's Wells linking the Trust's Bramshott and Ludshott Commons properties, bought as a memorial to Sir Robert Hunter; St Boniface Down (221 acres), a stretch of downland which includes the highest point in the Isle of Wight; and not least Scolt Head, 1,620 acres of sand dunes, salt marshes, and shingle beach, with a rich marine flora and bird life, acquired with funds raised by the Norfolk Naturalists' Trust. In 1921 the acquisition of Chartwell was considered, which must then have looked very different and was of particular significance as adjoining the Trust's Mariners' Hill property. Negotiations fell through, and it was bought in the following year by a politician in eclipse. Having acquired a new importance and a new lustre, it was made over to the Trust in 1946 as a memorial to a statesman—Sir Winston Churchill.

At the end of 1923 there were 102 properties. This was forty more than on the outbreak of war. Yet the Trust had been in existence nearly thirty years, and the increase was not as satisfactory as it seemed at the time. The rate of growth had declined. During the first ten years of the Trust's existence properties came in at the rate of one or two a year; each new acquisition seemed an achievement and was a cause for rejoicing. Then suddenly in 1906, possibly as a result of the national appeals for Brandelhow and Gowbarrow Park, the Trust's first big properties, the rate increased. Until 1914 there was an average of five new properties a year. Over the following decade, partly as a result of the war, the average dropped to four. The Trust was still making headway, but it was slower than might have been hoped.

Chapter 4

Change and Reform

John Bailey, Chairman: 1923–1931

On the death of Lord Plymouth in 1923, John Bailey (1864–1931) was elected chairman of the Executive Committee. The choice was wise. As one of the surviving pioneers, he could recall the first battles of the Trust and the spirit that informed them. He had taken the chair at a meeting of the Executive as early as 1902 and had often done so from 1918 onwards. Having also been chairman of both the General Purposes and Estates Committees, he knew the workings of the Trust intimately. No one was in a better position to remedy its weaknesses. Among the sanest critics of his day, he exhibited the same force and sense in his management of the Trust's affairs as in his literary judgments. He was responsible for firmly stating the cardinal principle, always implicit in the Trust's work, that preservation is its first task and must always take precedence over public access. 'Preservation', he said, 'may always permit of access, while without preservation access becomes for ever impossible.' Not his least service to the Trust was the introduction to its counsels of two close friends who for many years played a decisive role in its affairs: R. C. Norman, who was to be Chairman of the London County Council, and G. M. Trevelyan, the historian. These became chairmen respectively of the General Purposes and Estates Committees. They were, as Trevelyan wrote, a band of brothers, and the work prospered in their hands.

FINANCIAL REORGANISATION AND CHANGING STANDARDS

During the eight years when Bailey's influence was paramount membership, which had been virtually stationary since 1914, nearly trebled. It was the beginning of an upward trend that only the Second World War temporarily checked. In the same period properties began to come in at the average rate of over ten a year, double that of the previous decade. It is possible to distinguish some of the causes which contributed to this renewed and increased vitality.

In the first place a tighter and simpler control was placed on expenditure from 1925. Annual estimates thereafter were prepared

Park Head, St. Eval, Cornwall. One of the many stretches of coastland acquired through Enterprise Neptune

Appledore, Kent. Three and a half miles of the Royal Military Canal were given in 1936

Looking towards Blakeney Point, one of the Trust's nature reserves. Given in 1912

On the Farne Islands. Acquired by public appeal in 1925

by the Estates Committee for properties and by the General Purposes Committee for other matters. After the examination of the Estates Committee figures by the General Purposes Committee, both sets of estimates were submitted to the Executive Committee for approval. The sub-committees were then authorised to spend the sums approved without further reference to the Executive. The system established at this time is, subject to minor modification, still in force.

Measures were also taken to build up the general fund of the Trust. As early as 1910 Mrs John Lowe had bequeathed £200, which the Executive Committee decided should be 'invested separately, to form the nucleus of an emergency fund, the income from which might be used for the purposes of the Trust'. From this modest start has grown the General Fund which at the end of 1967 amounted to £470,000 and constitutes its free working capital. Though after 1910 sums received were from time to time allotted to the fund, its growth was slow. It stood in 1927 at some £5,500. A more substantial reserve was needed to give the Trust a safe financial margin. In 1927 it was decided to raise an endowment fund of £25,000. Though money at first came in sparingly—only £1,400 was subscribed in the next two years—this was an important step, and in 1931 with a grant of £6,000, the first of many generous benefactions from the Pilgrim Trust, the fund was firmly established.

To strengthen the central finances of the Trust, an attempt was made in 1927 to persuade local committees to make a contribution from their funds towards the cost of head office management. It was just that they should do so, since the services provided by head office directly contributed to the efficient management of local properties. The response was not encouraging, and it was only after the Second World War that a fixed percentage of most local committee funds was channelled into the head office accounts. A start at least was made, and the Executive Committee's request reflected an understanding that, with increasing growth, a more coordinated system of finance was necessary. The informal organisation of the Trust dating from its early days, and the administration of innumerable small properties by innumerable small committees with little central supervision, was becoming inappropriate.

Before the end of the first war the Estates Committee had been concerned at the inadequate supervision of many properties and at the excessively remote control from London. Though circumstances in wartime were partly responsible, many properties tended to go their

3

own way—it was often a good one—managed by two or three local supporters. Though these supporters were enthusiastic and well-intentioned, it would have been surprising if all had been equally efficient. The Trust's properties had increased in number, and were continuing to increase, yet no proper machine existed to administer them. A single secretary in London was responsible for properties, different in character and presenting different problems, scattered across the country from Cumberland to Kent and from Cornwall to Northumberland. Only the voluntary labours of local committees and individual supporters kept the machine going. Surprisingly for ten years after the war nothing was done to increase the head office staff. Lack of money, the chronic ailment of the Trust, was no doubt the reason. It is significant that the belated appointment of an assistant-secretary in 1929 followed the appeal for a substantial reserve fund. From this date a more regular inspection and control of the Trust's work in the provinces became possible. It was still inadequate and over a decade passed before the Trust set up a provincial administration. But again a start had been made.

In another direction a necessary definition of policy occurred. In early days the Trust had welcomed any gift. An inconsiderable fragment of medieval masonry, the smallest plot of attractive country, seemed acceptable. Anything that would extend the influence of the Trust, any tangible exemplar of its aims and purposes, appeared worth holding. With the passage of time it became evident that a number of its properties were of local rather than national importance and that the imposition of stricter standards of selection was necessary. The Trust was also beginning to learn that, unless control could be exercised over their surroundings, the acceptance of small parcels of land, however beautiful, was rarely wise. The lesson took surprisingly long to learn. Maggotty's Wood, once a delightful small copse in Cheshire, situated in country no less delightful, was accepted as late as 1935. It now stands forlorn on the boundary of a housing estate. Many years were also to pass before higher standards were consistently imposed. But again a start was made in the twenties, and no doubt Bailey was responsible. In 1919, when in the chair at the Executive Committee, he had spoken at length on this problem, suggesting that the Trust should exercise a greater discretion in the acceptance of properties, and that it should arrive at a clear understanding of the type of property worth preserving. Too often, he said, the Trust in the past had been looked upon by improvident owners as a means of hiving off financial liabilities in the form of unproductive land or old buildings.

PUBLIC RELATIONS AND AWAKENING PUBLIC INTEREST

No less important was the concession to the spirit of the age which led in 1928 to the formation of a publicity committee. That this step was long delayed must reflect a reluctance to resort to marketing methods, a reluctance understandable in those who had preached a personal message and whose ardent converts had most often been made by the spoken word. The distrust of formal publicity was not without foundation and it can be argued that over-concentration on publicity has been known to alter the character of societies such as the Trust. However by the late twenties publicity was inevitable; the scale of the Trust's activities called for it, and results soon justified it. Lectures were organised, G. M. Trevelyan produced an eloquent pamphlet, public dinners were arranged, and the B. B. C. devoted its Week's Good Cause to the work of the Trust. By 1930 there were 2,000 members. In the following year the activities of the new committee had so far increased that an assistant for publicity was appointed to the staff. Again it was only a start, but from the decision of 1928 the present publicity and public relations organisation of the Trust derives.

These developments, which might collectively be described as a first step in bringing the Trust up to date, were important in themselves but they derived an added importance from their timing. The conservation of buildings and landscape was belatedly becoming a topic of national interest. New forces had been stirring for some time and new influences were at work. The years 1930–31 saw the amendment of the Ancient Monuments Act of 1913, the introduction of the first Town and Country Planning Bill, the anxiously awaited report of the Addison Committee on the formation of National Parks, the creation of an Amenities Group in the House of Commons, and not least the Finance Act which exempted from death duties property given or devised to the Trust. These were important developments, all germane to the Trust's work. In so far as the Addison Committee on National Parks was concerned not only had the chairman given evidence, but the Executive Committee had turned down the proposal of the Local Authorities Association that the Trust should be the body to administer National Parks. The Committee did so in the conviction that the Trust must remain an unofficial body and that only as such could it effectively carry out its aims. An era was beginning in which the Trust need no longer maintain almost singlehanded the struggle to protect the best of the countryside. It was providential that at this time the Trust's finances were overhauled, its administration strengthened, and the rudiments of a publicity machine created. New possibilities lay ahead.

EXPANSION

Many important properties came to the Trust between 1923 and 1931. Among open spaces were Hatfield Forest, one of the few surviving royal forests of East Anglia, where vast hornbeams are a feature of the chases; Great Langdale, perhaps the sternest and most impressive of the wilder Lakeland dales; the bulk of the Ashridge estate with its ancient woods; Stonehenge Down, surrounding the great Neolithic monument for whose protection the Trust had first been concerned in 1900; Dover's Hill, a natural amphitheatre on the edge of the Cotswolds overlooking the Vale of Evesham; Dunkery Beacon, the summit of Exmoor, with the most extensive view in the west country; Bolt Head and Bolt Tail, a rugged stretch of cliff and coast in Devon extending nearly six miles (and for many years the longest continuous stretch of coast in the protection of the Trust); and the remote Farne Islands with their grey seals and bird colonies, then the only breeding ground of the Eider duck in England. The last five were bought with money raised by public appeal.

The buildings acquired in this period were for the first time as important as the open spaces, thus marking a change of emphasis in the Trust's activity that was later to become pronounced. Bodiam and Tattershall castles (1925–1926) are among its most imposing medieval buildings, the former perhaps the most romantic English castle of its period. They were the gift of Lord Curzon who meticulously restored them, and he devised them to the Trust in the conviction that 'beautiful and ancient buildings, which recall the life and customs of the past, are not only a historical document of supreme value, but are a part of the spiritual and aesthetic heritage of the nation, imbuing it with reverence and educating its taste'. By 1931 Bodiam was already attracting 10,000 visitors a year. Montacute in Somerset, one of the loveliest late sixteenth-century houses in England, and the Assembly Rooms in Bath, designed by John Wood at the height of the town's fashionable ascendancy, though both acquired in 1931 through the Society for the Protection of Ancient Buildings, were in effect the gift of Ernest Cook.[1] (Among the most generous of the Trust's many benefactors, he subsequently gave the Coleshill and Buscot estates, and made the general fund the largest donation ($£100,000$) it has received). Two important Roman buildings also came to the Trust in this period: Chedworth Villa, a well-preserved example of a Roman country residence, and Housesteads Fort and adjoining stretches of Hadrian's Wall, a moving and dramatic survival of the Imperial occupation. Notable among smaller buildings, and in scale more characteristic of the Trust's earlier acquisitions, was Paycocke's at Coggeshall in Essex, a half-timbered merchant's house dating from about 1500. On John Bailey's death in 1931 the Trust owned close on two hundred properties. In less than a decade the number had nearly doubled.

From this period also dates the decision (1926), following Irish independence, to operate in Ulster. Though the first property there was not acquired for a decade, this was another decision of importance. It led in due course to the development of a thriving and semi-independent branch of the Trust which, with the active cooperation of the Northern Ireland government, has done great things.

ANOTHER PICTURE

The annual reports of the Trust year by year and the minutes of its Committees, while telling of achievement, record also in sombre detail the fateful appearance of developments inimical to the countryside. Everything that has affected the landscape, from motor rallies on the South Downs and the threat of hydroplanes on Windermere, to pylons, advertising, river pollution, litter, new highways, caravan camps, and the block planting of spruce finds a melancholy place in the records of the Trust. It usually does so before 1930. Sometimes Trust intervention was able to achieve prohibition or improvement; often it was in vain.

In 1897, and again in 1905 at Grasmere, consideration of telegraph poles comes as a first premonition of the grim wirescapes of the future. In 1906 the Trust was invited by the Postmaster General to comment on the draft of the Telegraph (Construction) Bill, and a special sub-committee made recommendations. Two years later the Trust called a conference 'to consider the question of the disfigurement of roads by telephone and telegraph posts'. The importance of better routing was emphasised, and protests were made to the Postmaster-General. After the First World War the problem of wirescape took on a new dimension with the laying of high tension cables for electricity, and in 1922 the Trust made its first intervention on this score in connection with the Grampians electricity scheme. By 1926 the problem had grown so grave that the Trust made a general representation to the government on the indiscriminate siting of high-power standards; in 1929 a Trust deputation again waited on the minister responsible.

The first sign of concern for advertising in the countryside came in 1909 when the Trust pressed the Lancashire and Cumberland County Councils to control advertising in the Lake District, and made strong representations to the Michelin Tyre Company about a particularly offensive advertisement, which the company were good enough to withdraw. Over twenty years later the Trust was still fighting advertisements in the countryside, though times had changed and the occasion of their protest to the Home Secretary in 1932 was sky-advertising from aeroplanes.

The traffic problem as reflected in road-widening and the need for new roads and bridges appears as early as 1907 in the Lake District, when the Trust urged the Cumberland County Council to replace bridges in native stone. To the Minister of Transport, soon after the First World War, letters were addressed about arterial roads, and the first intervention in connection with the new bypasses was at Conway in 1937. With the building of motorways the difficulty of reconciling traffic and amenity, and the consequent threat to Trust land, has further increased (see Chapter 16).

Roads bring tourism and its related problems. The Trust was in touch with the Cyclists Touring Club in 1902, and the increase in camping led to the consideration of camp sites on Trust land some fifteen years later. Then as now the decision was that no general permission could be given for camping, but that applications would be treated on their merits. Oddly enough the litter menace, now so grave a problem, does not seem to have been serious enough to engage the attention of the Trust until 1924.

As a Government timber policy developed it inevitably involved the Trust. The importation of fifteen hundred lumberjacks from Canada in 1916 elicited a plea that measures 'should be taken to avoid destruction of timber which is a characteristic feature of the natural beauty of the country'. The Office of Woods and Forests, surprisingly perhaps in wartime, promised as far as possible to respect timber 'which forms a feature of the landscape'. With the creation of the Forestry Commission the block planting of spruce became a major preoccupation, and led to a Joint Conference with the Commission in 1932. The record of the first thirty-five years is one of intensifying threats to the landscape.

Chapter 5

The Country House Scheme and the Second World War

The Marquess of Zetland, Chairman: 1932–1945

In 1932 R. C. Norman declined an invitation to become chairman. He foresaw the day when large estates might be given to the Trust and he thought that the new chairman should be a great landowner in touch with the potential donors of such estates. He undertook to find the right man and finally approached the Marquess of Zetland. The latter had been Lord Curzon's secretary and was his official biographer; Norman thus stressed Curzon's interest in, and his generous benefactions to, the Trust. The association was enough. Though without previous experience of the Trust, Lord Zetland accepted. This distinguished public servant, who had already been governor of Bengal and was to hold ministerial office, threw himself into the new task. Soon after, when offered the post of British representative on a League of Nations commission, he refused it as incompatible with his responsibilities to the Trust. He had been the readier to assume these responsibilities by reason of his confidence in the men most closely concerned with its work: R. C. Norman, G. M. Trevelyan, and Lord Esher. Many years later he paid tribute to the role they played in the framing of policy and the control of administration during the fourteen years he served as chairman.

If Lord Zetland did not react with marked sensibility to landscape or architecture, his eminence, his knowledge of men, and his capacity for affairs, enabled him to do great things for the Trust. Even when Secretary of State for India (1935–40) its affairs received his close attention. During this period the Trust's secretary was summoned regularly to the India Office where the agendas of Executive Committee meetings were discussed in the minutest detail.

The death of John Bailey, and the resignation early in 1934 of S. H. Hamer, who had been secretary since 1911, marked a break almost as clear as that of 1913–14. A period was opening in which the Trust was in broad outline to assume its present organisation and in which, though its aims remained unchanged, its activities were to be dramatically extended. In retrospect the period tidily ends with the termination of the Second World War and the resignation in 1945 both of Lord Zetland and of D. M. Matheson, who succeeded Hamer in the secretaryship. By that date three important developments had occurred: a Country House Scheme was fairly launched; the Trust had emerged as a considerable landowner; and an administrative organisation had been set up in the provinces.

COUNTRY HOUSES

The danger in which many country houses stood became generally apparent, and in dramatic fashion, only after the outbreak of the Second World War. It had long been foreseen by a minority. Even in the twenties their uncertain future in a rapidly changing economy gave concern. As early as 1923 the Trust had in vain pressed the Chancellor of the Exchequer to introduce legislation whereby the owners of historic buildings should receive tax concessions to enable them to meet the high costs of maintenance. Ten years later at a National Trust dinner, Professor W. G. Constable, Director of the Courtauld Institute, speaking after Lord Grey of Fallodon, pleaded that positive steps should be taken, and in time, to ensure the preservation of the most important country houses. He suggested that the finest examples should be granted preferential rating and taxation.

The Professor's theme was taken up in the following year by a more powerful advocate and proclaimed from a wider stage. At the Annual General Meeting in 1934 the Marquess of Lothian, in moving the election of the Council, asked that the Trust should extend its protecting arm in a definite and considered manner to the historic country houses of England. Characteristic of this country and unrivalled in any other, they were, he said, under sentence of death by taxation and estate duty. In a reasoned speech, he suggested measures to save them. The first step, and a prerequisite to all else, was a survey of the ground. Until the extent of the problem was known, remedies could not be intelligently applied. The best country houses should be scheduled, and these, he recommended, should be subject to four types of fiscal relief. Firstly, houses and gardens of national importance should be eligible for exemption from death duty in precisely the same way as works of art had been since 1910. The parallel between houses and chattels was exact, and the different treatment illogical (see Chapter 7). If pictures in a great house deserved exemption so did their splendid architectural setting. Secondly, the exemption from death duty accorded to a house and its contents should remain in force even if they were sold, provided — and the proviso was important—that after sale they were preserved as an entity and public access was given. This controversial idea, which, even in its application to chattels, was foreign to the Finance Act of 1910, appeared to Lord Lothian the only certain method of blunting 'the abhorred shears of taxation' and of keeping houses and their contents intact for the nation when they came on the market. Thirdly, the owners of scheduled houses should be permitted to include in their tax claims all sums spent on the upkeep, restoration, or embellishment of such houses, provided their historic and artistic character was strictly preserved. Fourthly, such houses should be derated.

Even if these fiscal reliefs could be obtained, Lord Lothian recognised that many houses would inevitably pass out of private ownership and must cease to exist as family homes. It was therefore imperative, he said, to find new uses for old houses, so that they might fulfil a creative role in a changing world. Finally, and here Lord Lothian specifically addressed his appeal to members, the Trust should equip itself to hold large properties, bequeathed, given, or bought, and so gradually draw within its orbit a number of historic furnished houses, together with the land or monetary endowment sufficient to maintain them.

RESULTS OF LORD LOTHIAN'S INITIATIVE

At the time Lord Lothian's speech was startling. He had proposed action both by the government and by the Trust. It was to the possibility of government action through fiscal channels that the Trust first turned its attention. Early in 1936 a meeting was held in the rooms of the Royal Geographical Society at which the Duc de Noailles described the work of the Demeure Historique for the preservation of châteaux, and explained the tax concessions and other advantages which the French government extended to the owners of historic buildings. A special committee was formed soon after to invite the cooperation of the owners of important country houses in the preparation of a scheme which would adapt French principles to English conditions. It was hoped that government might be sympathetic, for the First Commissioner of Works addressing the Annual Meeting of the Trust in the year after Lord Lothian's speech stressed the importance of preserving houses intact with their contents. This course, he pointed out, was preferable to waiting until they became ruins and could be scheduled by his department as Ancient Monuments. By the end of 1936 Lord Zetland, acting as honest broker for all the great houses of England, was in a position to open conversations with the Chancellor of the Exchequer. He outlined a scheme which would enable country house owners to obtain tax concessions similar to those enjoyed in France, provided their houses were open to the public at a small charge. It was coldly received. Government opinion and interest lagged behind the Continent. Not until 1947 was the statutory listing of historic buildings undertaken—it had started in France over a century earlier—and not until 1953 with the passing of the Historic Buildings and Ancient Monuments Act did inhabited buildings become eligible for repair and maintenance grants. No fiscal concessions have yet been extended to the private owner.

In 1937 the Council reported the failure of any general scheme for the preservation of country houses in private ownership. On the other hand the Chancellor, it was stated, viewed with sympathy Lord Lothian's proposal that the Trust should be equipped to preserve them. In the same year a new National Trust Act included a special clause enabling the Trust to acquire and hold land or investments, in order to provide from rents and other income for the maintenance and conservation of property. This made feasible a Trust 'Country House Scheme' and several owners were ready to consider this as an alternative to the general scheme which had perforce been abandoned. The Country House Scheme is discussed in detail in Chapter 12. Essentially it enables an owner to endow and transfer to the Trust an historic country house with the contents that contribute to its atmosphere and interest, while permitting him and his assigns to remain in occupation, subject to public access on specified days. The arrangement, while ensuring the permanent preservation of the house and its contents, can sometimes offer a donor financial advantages, since the endowment in the hands of a charitable trust pays no tax.

The results of Lord Lothian's initiative were highly important. The launching of the Country House Scheme in 1937 foreshadowed a marked extension of the Trust's work. To save the Alfriston Clergy House and Buckingham Chantry Chapel had no doubt been valuable; to preserve a Knole or a Petworth was another and a greater matter. The Trust in its new role was to become the surveyor of vast mansions, the curator of extensive collections, and the foremost gardener in the country. The Lothian scheme also meant that the Trust would no longer be associated predominantly with open spaces. In future the two purposes for which it had been created—the preservation of land and of buildings—were to be of equal importance.

This, as will be seen in Chapter 6 led to fundamental changes in its administration.

BLICKLING AND THE COUNTRY HOUSE SCHEME

It was fitting that Blickling in Norfolk, one of Lord Lothian's family seats, should be the first great house to come to the Trust under the new scheme. Though his germinal speech in 1934 had been prompted by the secretary of the Trust, Lord Lothian himself had good reason to appreciate the threat to country houses that taxation presented. In 1930 on the death of his predecessor, the 10th Marquess, a vast sum had been exacted in estate duty. In order to raise the money it had been necessary to sell abroad many of the rarest volumes from the Blickling library, thus partially depleting a family collection of great interest. He was determined that this should not happen a second time and that on his death Blickling and its contents should be preserved in their entirety. So it came about that in 1940 this beautiful Jacobean house with nearly everything in it, and an estate of some 4,500 acres, were left to the Trust. The terms of Lord Lothian's bequest indicate the public spirit which inspired it. He stipulated that subject to some regular access by the public it should be let 'as a family residence to a person who will love, appreciate and respect Blickling Hall and will use it not only as a private residence but as a place from which public or intellectual or artistic activities go forth and in which persons or conferences of persons interested in such things are entertained'.

The Country House Scheme was novel and response was not immediate. But Lord Lothian's example proved that it was viable and gave owners confidence. Sir Charles Trevelyan's gift of his Wallington estate followed. It comprised nearly 13,000 acres and the seventeenth-century house whose grave exterior provides so satisfactory a foil to the rococo plaster-work of its state rooms. By 1943 the scheme had caught on. In that and the succeeding year a dozen houses were transferred. Among them were the Astor mansion at Cliveden (a gift directly inspired by Lord Lothian's example); Polesden Lacey with its collection of Dutch and English masters and its fine French furniture; Great Chalfield, a moated manor and a picturesque survival of the domestic architecture of the late fifteenth century; West Wycombe Park with its porticos and painted ceilings, and its memories of the Hell Fire Club; Speke Hall, the largest of the surviving black-and-white houses of the sixteenth-century; Gunby Hall, Tennyson's 'haunt of ancient peace', whose orderly façade and mellow brick exemplify the sobriety of the country building of 1700; and Lacock Abbey whose character derives from the mixed and happy marriage of thirteenth-century cloisters, early renaissance features, palladian drawing-rooms, and the best gothick hall in England.

Such houses are a brief epitome of the history of architecture in this country. They were precisely the type of building which the Country House Scheme had been designed to save. Whether the Trust was well advised to accept the endowment of such houses in the form of agricultural estates is open to question. The question was not posed at the time. The improvement of many such estates later called for large capital expenditure (see Chapter 11). Their acceptance also meant, as did acceptance of agricultural estates not given for endowment, such as the Dolaucothi property, that the Trust came to hold a considerable acreage to which only limited access could be given. This later led to criticism, since it was not always easy to explain to the general public the Trust's obligations towards its farm tenants and the necessity to restrict access in the interests of farming.

FERGUSON'S GANG

It was not only in the preservation of country houses that the Trust's work was expanding. In the twenties there had been some ten new properties a year. From 1932 to 1944 the number rose to an average of nearly thirty, and in 1938 reached fifty-nine. Acquisitions have never been more exciting or more rapid. Moreover they were sometimes cloaked in mystery, for these years saw the maximum activity of Ferguson's Gang. Elected by secret ballot, the members of this saintly mafia were anonymous to the world and assumed such colourful pseudonyms as Sister Agatha, Kate O'Brien, the Nark, Bill Stickers, the Bloody Bishop, and Red Biddy. They swore to follow their leader Ferguson in preserving England and in frustrating the monster described by Clough Williams-Ellis in his book *England and the Octopus*. Having decided that the Trust was the best instrument for its purpose, the Gang repeatedly gave it beneficent attention. A first contribution was made to the secretary on 30 December 1930. Like those that followed in subsequent years it was delivered in notes and coin by a masked member of the Gang. The secretary observed that the coin was usually Victorian and it later transpired that members were expected to save for the Trust all Victorian coinage that came into their hands. The largest sum delivered in this way was £2,000. No questions were asked, much less answered. But the Gang did more than hand over swag. In 1932 they presented Shalford Mill, an eighteenth-century watermill on the Tillingbourne, where subsequently their secret meetings were held. Other properties followed: the early eighteenth century town hall of Newtown (this rotten borough in the Isle of Wight returned among other distinguished members of parliament Marlborough and Canning), which had been restored by the Artichoke, a distinguished architect who has not been permitted to reveal his name; the medieval remains of Steventon Priory; and Trevescan Cliffs and Mayon, a fine example of a Cornish cliff fortification.

The constitution of Ferguson's Gang states that active membership is 'terminable only by death; but [that] this is not so difficult as might be supposed'. Time indeed has reduced the membership and the activity of the Gang, but it celebrated its fortieth anniversary in 1967 and its members still preserve their anonymity. Ferguson's sex is among the few facts that have been firmly established. The masked leader visited Broadcasting House in 1935 and the voice that listeners heard dispelled rumours that Ferguson was a lady. His appeal brought 600 new members and £900, a considerable sum at the time.

VILLAGES AND THE COUNTRYSIDE

Among the properties which came to the Trust during this period were three villages: West Wycombe, bought from the Royal Society of Arts in 1934; Styal, a rare example of 18th century industrial planning, given in 1939; and Lacock, a 'wool' village and one of the most beautiful in England, given in 1944. This was an important development. The Trust's experience has shown that the preservation of a single cottage, or even of a group of cottages, is of questionable value when no control can be exercised over adjoining buildings. A large and self-contained unit such as a village is another matter. The Trust is well equipped to manage such a unit and, while undertaking modernisation, to ensure that its architectural character remains unchanged.

In the same period the Trust acquired a cross-section of the best English and Welsh landscape scenery. Among the finest open spaces were Buttermere in the Lakes, parts of Dovedale in Derbyshire, the Sugar Loaf in Monmouthshire, the Dolaucothi estate in Carmarthenshire, Drovers in Sussex, Pentire Head in Cornwall, and the Holnicote and Killerton estates in Somerset and Devon, the last two given by Sir Richard Acland.

Many of these are large properties (Holnicote 12,420 acres, Killerton 5,020 acres, Dolaucothi 2,398 acres, Sugar Loaf 2,130), and with the estates accepted as endowments under the Country House Scheme (Wallington 12,992 acres, Blickling 4,436 acres, Gunby, 1,423 acres), they profoundly altered the nature of the Trust's responsibilities. In the course of a decade its holding more than tripled and it became one of the largest landowners in the country. It suddenly found itself dealing with dozens of farm tenants, and problems of estate management became paramount. As the owner of large woodlands, it was brought into close contact with the Forestry Commission, with whom cooperation and methods had been exhaustively discussed at a joint conference as early as 1932. As the owner of large tracts of land in areas such as the Lake and Peak Districts, it was intimately involved in the considerations and proposals that were later to lead to the creation of National Parks. As the owner of areas of special ecological interest, it shared the preoccupations, and required the advice, of the natural history societies. The change in the scope of the Trust's responsibilities was as unexpected as it was sudden. It called for drastic reorganisation.

ADMINISTRATION

By 1940 the Trust owned some four hundred properties. How could they be best administered in accordance with its purposes? There were two alternatives. The first was to employ local firms of land agents, each firm managing the properties in its immediate neighbourhood, under close supervision and policy control from headquarters. This system was already in operation at certain properties. The second was to appoint a staff of agents who should be the fulltime employees of the Trust. After some hesitation the latter alternative was preferred. The decision was perhaps wise; it was also surprising. At a time when even private landowners with compact estates were tending to put their affairs into the hands of professional firms, the Trust took the opposing course. After the war it was to be the only public body with large holdings of agricultural land, other than the Agricultural Land Commission, that relied for the management of its estates exclusively on its own agents.

In 1940 it was argued, and no doubt rightly, that a Trust staff would better appreciate the essential aims of the organisation than professional firms. Its members would feel a greater loyalty and a greater responsibility. There were none the less disadvantages. The number of wholetime agents the Trust could afford to employ was limited. Thus the area in the care of each would be large. There would consequently be much travelling and high transport costs. In certain parts of the country where properties were few and widely scattered, an agent would have to cover distances that made effective day to day management difficult. On the other hand it was maintained that, as the number of Trust properties increased, the work of management would justify the appointment of more agents and thus the creation of smaller and more efficient areas. This to some extent has occurred, but there are still (1967) one or two agents who look after properties more than a hundred miles apart.

Though an agent had been appointed to the head office of the Trust as early as 1935, it was not until the end of the war that the new system of estate management was fully in operation, with the country divided into eight areas each under the control of an agent. General supervision was exercised from London by a Chief Agent, appointed in 1942, and a Deputy Chief Agent. The same system exists today, though as was foreseen the Trust has fortunately been able to create more and smaller areas. There are now (1967) sixteen areas and twenty-four agents and subagents. Further administrative problems which first became apparent in the period under review (1932–45), and which in part directly relate to the method of estate management then set up, are referred to in Chapter 6.

THE TRUST IN WARTIME

In 1914 the Trust held 63 properties and controlled 5,814 acres. On the outbreak of war in 1939 the comparative figures were 410 properties and 58,900 acres. It had become a large organisation and disruption was correspondingly great. The system of control by committees meeting in London had to be modified and for a time abandoned. The London office was at first moved with a reduced staff to West Wycombe Park, and Lord Esher, chairman of the General Purposes Committee, who lived nearby at Watlington Park, for months directed policy almost alone. There were occasions when no other members of the Executive Committee was able to attend meetings. Business was none the less pressing. In 1940 income from membership subscriptions fell; visitors were few and properties such as Bodiam Castle, where income was largely dependent on admission fees, were severely affected; money could no longer be raised by appeal, since the Trust thought it improper to make demands on the public in wartime. Loss of staff led to administrative difficulties, and the creation of the new network of area agents had to be postponed from year to year. Positive and sometimes unpopular action was necessary to ensure that historic buildings should be requisitioned only for suitable purposes, and that wartime installations on Trust land should be allowed only when absolutely necessary and should do minimum damage. Not least there was the bombing of Trust property. The Bath Assembly Rooms were burnt in 1942, and Kent houses such as Stoneacre and Owletts were damaged by flying bombs.

In spite of all this, the Trust miraculously prospered. Membership dropped from 7,100 in 1939 to 6,500 in 1942, but land and buildings continued to accrue. Acquisitions in 1943 and 1944 were as important and varied as any in the Trust's history. It can even be argued that the threat of invasion made many people better appreciate their countryside and opened blind eyes to the necessity for its preservation from enemies within as well as without. Even membership was to recover, and increase, far more rapidly than after the First World War. In these years the National Trust Act of 1937, which enabled local authorities to contribute to the work of the Trust, began to bear fruit in maintenance grants and donations. A Woodlands Fund was set up for postwar planting, and in 1942 an accumulated surplus enabled the Trust to go into the market and buy five properties. Though the financial position was less sound than appeared, as little was spent, or could be spent, on repair and maintenance, 1945 found the Trust poised for further advance.

ULSTER AND WALES

The advance was to occur both in England and across the Irish Channel. In 1936 a Regional Committee had been set up for Ulster and the recruitment of members was started on the understanding that their subscriptions should be used only for expenses in Northern Ireland. The first property, Killynether Castle, was given in 1937 and the fine expanse of beach at White Park Bay followed almost at once. In the same year the Ulster parliament brought their legislation into line with Westminster, including a provision in the Finance Bill to exempt property given or devised to the Trust from estate duty. In 1943 the Northern Ireland Committee, expressing a native spirit of independence, asked for autonomy. The Trust, whose primary concern is conservation, has never wished to create an *imperium*, but the request placed headquarters in a difficult position. So long as the Northern Ireland Committee remained a branch of the National Trust it was necessary that central policy decisions should be respected locally. If the Trust was to be ultimately responsible for the actions of the Committee it must exercise ultimate control. Autonomy within the framework of the Trust was refused, but it was made clear that the Trust would raise no objection, and would withdraw from the area, if Northern Ireland

Clumber Park, Nottinghamshire, perhaps the most visited of the Trust's properties. 3,784 acres bought in 1946 by public subscription and managed jointly by the Trust and Local Authorities

Clent Hills, Worcestershire. 355 acres maintained with the support of 20 local authorities

Bredon Tithe Barn, Worcestershire. A XIV century tithe barn acquired as a gift and with a grant from the Pilgrim Trust in 1951

wished to establish its own organisation, provided a distinctive name was adopted for the new preservation society.

In the event a separate body was not set up, and with the accession of Lord Antrim to the chairmanship of the Northern Ireland Committee in 1945 a period of sustained achievement and cooperation began. For convenience it may be considered at this point. In 1948 a paid secretary was engaged and an administrative office established. The following decade witnessed the preservation of some of the finest houses and gardens in the Six Counties: among them Castlecoole, James Wyatt's grave and elegant masterpiece; Florence Court, with its fluid eighteenth-century plasterwork, set in a wild landscape of romantic beauty; Castleward on Strangford Lough, combining curiously the classical and gothick styles; and the gardens of Mount Stewart and Rowallane with their profusion of tender and exotic plants. This achievement owed much to the enlightened policy of the Ministry of Finance in Northern Ireland, which wisely applied the Land Fund (see Chapter 7) both to the acquisition and endowment of these and other properties, and to the chairman of the Trust's Northern Ireland Committee who effectively brought to the attention of the government the urgency and the necessity of conservation.

The spirit of independence which stirred Ulster in 1943 found expression in Wales in the same year. The Merioneth County Council proposed the creation of a separate National Trust for Wales. It is a proposal that has since been made more than once. The character of the principality, its vigorous and separate cultural tradition, appear to favour such a development. The Trust certainly would not oppose it. However in 1943 there existed in Wales neither sufficient public interest nor financial backing to support an effective and independent Trust. There is little evidence that things have changed, for even today the total Trust membership in Wales barely exceeds 2,500. If a separate organisation as suggested by the Merioneth County Council was premature, it was time that a special branch of the Trust should be established in Wales. An Advisory Committee was accordingly set up in 1945. This body meets alternately in North and South Wales. With the development of a policy of decentralisation, the Committee for Wales ceased to be advisory in 1955 and its chairman since 1965 has a seat on the Executive of the Trust in London.

PRINCESS LOUISE

Reference at this point must be made to Princess Louise, Duchess of Argyll. President of the Trust since 1902, she died in the first year of the war. Throughout her long tenure of office she was actively concerned to follow and even to guide policy. For many years she presided at the Annual General Meetings and to the last she was accustomed to summon the secretary to hear and discuss the Trust's most recent initiatives. The Presidency remained vacant until Queen Mary in 1944 accepted the office. She in turn was succeeded in 1953 by H. M. Queen Elizabeth the Queen Mother, whose support and active interest are of great value to the Trust.

Chapter 6

The Postwar Years:
Change and Development within the Trust

The Earl of Crawford and Balcarres, Chairman: 1945–1965

In the postwar period the Trust adjusted its views and its aims to profound change, both economic and social, and it was drawn more and more, in an era of planning, into contact with government and government agencies. It will be convenient in this chapter to review these years in terms of the Trust's internal development and the extension of its activity in new fields, leaving for the succeeding chapter consideration of its role in the planned society of postwar Britain.

At the end of the war Lord Zetland had been chairman for thirteen years, Cecil Lubbock honorary treasurer for twelve, and D. M. Matheson secretary for eleven. In 1945, the year of its jubilee, the Trust acquired a new chairman, a new treasurer, and a new secretary, and moved into new and larger offices at Queen Anne's Gate. Once again the appointment of a Chairman coincided with the beginning of another era. After 1945 growth, both as to property and membership, was to be accelerated, problems were confronted such as its founders never envisaged, and a more complex structure and organisation were developed.

It was to be a period of gain, but also, in one sense, of loss. Size and a more formal administration meant that the Trust became less personal and contacts with donors and tenants less intimate. As properties came in rapidly, often through the machinery of government legislation, there was not always the sense that each acquisition was an achievement, and often a testimony both to the donor's love of the English countryside and his confidence that it could be saved only by the Trust. A dedicated and amateur group, quixotic and sometimes haphazard, was replaced by an organisation. This change to meet changed circumstances was necessary, but all those who served the Trust before the war recognise that something was lost. They would echo the sentiments of someone who worked for the Trust with little consideration of personal reward for over twenty years: 'The times when things were smaller, more amateur, more voluntary, produced a wonderful feeling . . . . there was a bond between everyone concerned.' This is true. Big and small organisations differ in more than size.

None the less, a marked feature of the Trust is the degree in which the spirit of its founders—enthusiasm, flexibility, and the absence of formal rules—has survived in a large corporate body. There can be few organisations of comparable size which remain, after a life of seventy years, so human, so little rigid, and with so many valuable illusions. The Trust's informality may sometimes exact a price in terms of strict efficiency, but it brings its own rewards.

THE NEW CONTROL

In 1945 the chairmanship was again offered to Ronald Norman and once again he declined the office. Lord Crawford was, he felt, the right chairman by reason of his scholarship, his appreciation of the aesthetic issues central to the work of the Trust, his prestige, and his qualities of character; moreover like his father he had been closely connected with the Trust. When Lord Crawford accepted office, Norman remarked, with characteristic modesty, that his own outstanding service to the Trust had been his role in the choice of two ideal chairmen.

Lord Crawford directed the affairs of the Trust for twenty years. He did so for the greater part of this time in consultation with Lord Esher, chairman of the General Purposes and Historic Buildings Committees. Theirs was a fruitful division of labour, Lord Crawford exercising control in matters of high policy and Lord Esher effectively supervising its detailed execution. The latter had won a position of unique influence in the Trust. During the war he had often directed its activities almost singlehanded, he was in close touch with the staff, and he knew its properties better than any other member of its committees. He was also able and willing to devote unlimited time to its problems. Not least he was one of the most persuasive chairmen of his generation. In reviewing the postwar period it must be seen in the light of the guidance of these two men, at first seconded particularly by G. M. Trevelyan and Ronald Norman and then by Lord De La Warr, Lord Rosse, and the treasurer, Edward Holland-Martin. The Trust was also fortunate in its secretary, J. F. W. Rathbone. From the date of his appointment in 1949 until his retirement nearly twenty years later, his single-minded devotion made an immense contribution to its work.

The basic achievement of the twenty years of Lord Crawford's chairmanship may be shown by three comparisons. In 1945 the Trust owned 112,000 acres and 93 historic buildings, its outlay ran to

£111,529, and it enjoyed the support of 7,850 members. In 1965 there were 328,502 acres and over 200 historic buildings, an outlay of £1,864,083, and a membership of over 157,000. It was moreover an encouraging portent that the increase in membership became particularly marked from 1958 onwards.

In earlier chapters the acquisition of an important new property was an event that sometimes merited special notice. After 1945, with properties sometimes coming in at the rate of over thirty a year, individual mention is hardly feasible. Acquisitions such as Knole (1946), Petworth (1947), Waddesdon (1957), Hardwick (1959), Wasdale (1959), Brownsea Island (1962) become no more than landmarks, though important ones, charting progress. The preservation of houses and fine landscape must be taken for granted. It is the Trust's primary work and it prospered.

IMPROVEMENTS TO AGRICULTURAL ESTATES

The maintenance of the properties acquired in early days, for the most part stretches of down, moor, coast and woodland, or small buildings, was not difficult or costly. Only since the early forties had the Trust become the owner of agricultural estates, responsible for dozens of farms and hundreds of cottages. During the war lack of labour and materials held up repairs and improvements. As a result the Trust's budget yearly showed a modest surplus, but with a return to normal conditions deferred repairs called for urgent attention. Furthermore, ideas as to the farm buildings and services that farmers and cottagers had a right to expect from their landlord had radically changed. The last thing for which the Trust's estates had been chosen was their modern equipment and agricultural efficiency. Even in 1940 some of them were hardly up-to-date by the easy standards of that time. For the Trust to fulfil its duties as an enlightened landlord and give its tenants the buildings and services that came to be regarded as normal after the war, a vast programme of farm and cottage improvement was necessary.

In 1945, the year of the Trust's jubilee, an appeal was launched to meet some of the cost. £123,000 was raised of which Dr Dalton, on behalf of the Exchequer, guaranteed pound for pound subscribed by the public up to a total of £60,000. This served to initiate a programme which is not yet completed and which has imposed a severe strain on the finances of the Trust.

Improvements, mainly to farms and cottages, have since the war cost the Trust £1,700,000, and in 1967 the allocation for this purpose alone amounted to £205,000 (see Chapter 11). This expenditure has meant that in almost every year the budget has shown a deficit which has only been covered by legacies and donations, by money in fact which might otherwise have been deployed to save new land and buildings. Ironically it has come about that large estates given to the Trust prior to 1947, often to support a great house, and then believed to be valuable assets, have proved liabilities. Blickling (1940), Killerton (1942), Holnicote (1944) and Stourhead (1946), all Special Trusts (see page 178), showed respectively by 1965 accumulated deficits of £61,000, £88,500, £26,500 and £36,000. It is true that such liabilities can be regarded as temporary by a continuing body like the Trust, since these are fundamentally sound agricultural estates. After improvements have been carried out, rents can be raised. None the less, in the short term, modernisation has presented a financial problem which at times has assumed an aspect almost of crisis. The work is yet far from complete. But it has been tackled and much progress has been made. As a result the Trust should be able to look forward to a time when its agricultural properties are the most satisfactory feature of its economy.

The postwar period, while posing this new financial burden, produced challenges that prompted the extension of the Trust's work in four different ways.

COUNTRY HOUSES AND GARDENS

The danger in which many country houses stood was evident even before 1939 and the Country House Scheme had been devised to combat it. By 1945 the danger seemed a matter of national concern. For the Trust it was the major preoccupation of the immediate postwar years. It could not then be foreseen that the adaptability of owners to changed conditions, a buoyant stockmarket, and government intervention (see Chapter 7) would give many buildings a temporary reprieve. One house after another was abandoned. In 1943 a letter had appeared in *The Times* over the signatures of the chairmen of the Trust and the National Council for Social Service pleading that the authorities should take steps to use unwanted country houses for adult educational colleges. It was pointed out that in Denmark sixty such colleges existed and in England only nine. Early in 1945 the chairman wrote again to *The Times* advocating the use of such houses for educational purposes. The response was disappointing, though at Attingham in 1953 the Trust and the Shropshire County Council were to demonstrate how successfully and appropriately a country house could be adapted for precisely such a purpose.

The pressing nature of the country house problem led in 1945 to the establishment of the Trust's Historic Buildings Committee, under the chairmanship of Lord Esher, replacing a Country Houses Committee and with wider terms of reference. Its work brought it into close contact with Government departments and is thus discussed in Chapter 7, while the detailed procedure for the rescue of historic buildings is dealt with in Chapter 12.

The same combination of social and economic circumstances which threatened houses was, it soon appeared, likely to be fatal to many famous gardens. Previously the Trust had been little concerned with the preservation of gardens on their own account. It had acquired them almost by chance as part of the setting of great houses. When it became clear that something must also be done for gardens of outstanding horticultural interest that were not so situated, the Trust, as far as it could, stepped into the breach. In cooperation with the Royal Horticultural Society, a Gardens Scheme, comparable to the Country House Scheme, was evolved in 1948. This extension of the Trust's aims led subsequently to the preservation of such important gardens as Hidcote, Bodnant, Nymans, and Sheffield Park. The work and problems of its Gardens Committee are discussed in Chapter 13.

INDUSTRIAL MONUMENTS

The phrase 'of historic or architectural interest' as applied to buildings calls for reinterpretation by the Trust as tastes change and as styles of architecture, which may once have commanded little esteem, are seen to have merit. Some degree of reinterpretation occurred in the twenties with an increased appreciation both of Palladian and Baroque, and in the thirties when the acceptance of Wightwick Manor, a notable example of the influence of William Morris, indicated a new regard for the achievements of the Victorians. In the period 1945–65 a reinterpretation altogether more fundamental was required in respect of buildings which are the concern of industrial archaeology. These have been defined as 'any building or fixed structure—especially of the period of the Industrial Revolution—which either alone or in association with plant or equipment, illustrates or is significantly associated with the beginnings and evolution of industrial and technical processes'. Britain is incomparably richer in such buildings than other countries and, as the first great industrial power, possesses in its early factories, mills, bridges and canals a mixed treasure that is of great historic interest and often of considerable beauty.

43

The appreciation of these buildings with their stately machinery, and of our canals and early aqueducts, some of them not unworthy successors to the Pont du Gard, was strangely delayed. It was only after the war, when many had disappeared and more were threatened, that interest was tardily aroused. A change of outlook owed much to the Council for British Archaeology which in 1960 appointed a Research Committee on Industrial Archaeology and later, with the cooperation of the Ministry of Public Building and Works, launched a national survey of industrial monuments. Where canals were concerned the propaganda of the Inland Waterways Association played a valuable role.

In the late fifties it became evident that the Trust ought to be concerned in the preservation of these monuments and that the time had come to include them in the scope of its work. The Trust had taken over industrial monuments in the past but they had been usually of a picturesque and architecturally conventional character. Such were the attractive eighteenth-century lime kilns on the sands at Beadnell in Northumberland; the cotton mill and adjoining village at Styal in Cheshire, an early example of industrial planning; the medieval bridge at Eashing in Surrey; and a number of wind and watermills, the last usually accepted after consultation with the Wind and Watermill Section of the Society for the Protection of Ancient Buildings. The adoption of a more positive attitude towards a wider range of industrial monuments was both necessary and overdue, and it bore its first fruit in an agreement, concluded with the Transport Commission in 1959, to lease the southern section of the Stratford-on-Avon canal for five years. This section of the eighteenth-century canal, some thirteen miles long, with thirty-six locks and twenty bridges, had been abandoned for a generation. The formidable task of dredging and repair took over four years and the canal was reopened to traffic in 1964. The Trust has since acquired the freehold.

The year in which the Stratford Canal was opened saw the acquisition of some fifteen miles of the River Wey Navigation, dating from the mid-seventeenth century. In 1966 and 1967 four of the famous Cornish beam-engines, associated with the old tin-mining industry, came to the Trust, as did Thomas Telford's splendid suspension bridge over the Conway River. The latter would have been demolished, but for the intervention of the Trust. Almost unthinkable twenty years earlier would have been the acceptance in 1962 of covenants over the Middleton Colliery Railway situated in the most rebarbative quarter of Leeds, but probably the oldest (1758) rail transport in the world and retaining some of its original stone sleepers. To advise the Trust in the difficult and largely unfamiliar field of the preservation of industrial monuments, Rex Wailes, the foremost expert on the subject, accepted the appointment of Honorary Adviser in 1964. The intractable financial problems associated with the preservation of industrial monuments are referred to in Chapter 12.

Transport—such things as sailing and steam vessels, carriages, locomotives, and motor cars—do not strictly form part of the matter of industrial archaeology as defined above. But such objects are often of great interest and may sometimes be works of art. In the period under review, the Trust decided to extend its protection to these in the same way as to the contents of houses, and to apply the same criteria, historic interest and aesthetic appeal. Collections of carriages, motorcars, and industrial locomotives, have been established respectively at Arlington Court, Tatton Park, and Penrhyn Castle.

COASTAL PRESERVATION

Special mention in this period must be made of the coast. In certain inland areas, notably in the Lake District (where the Trust with strong local support was to succeed in preserving the heads of most of the central dales), the defence of the countryside had not been unsuccessful. The coast was in different case. Human erosion was unceasing and several miles a year were being lost to development. Pressure on some of the remoter coastal areas, still relatively unspoilt, was bound to increase dramatically with the building of new motorways and in particular with the completion of the long-awaited Severn Bridge. By the mid-fifties protection of the coastline had become in the Trust's view its most pressing task. Of the 3,080 miles of English coast only some 900 remained worth preserving, and of these the Trust controlled only about a hundred and twenty-five. Some people thought a problem of such magnitude beyond the powers of a private organisation and believed that only direct government action could be effective. However in 1957 a Cornish Coast Advisory Committee was appointed to coordinate efforts within the county, to alert local opinion, and to demonstrate to owners that the surest safeguard for their coastal land was inalienable ownership by the Trust. In the next eight years many properties in Cornwall, totalling some forty miles of coast, came to the Trust, mostly by gift. This was encouraging progress; yet key properties, wonderful headlands or fine unspoilt bays, were from time to time lost for lack of money to buy them. Without a substantial coastal fund there was a strict limit to preservation even within a single county.

In 1962 a local appeal was made by the Trust's Northern Ireland Committee to save stretches of the Ulster coast. Some £10,000 was raised, fifteen miles came into the guardianship of the Trust either by gift, purchase, or deed of covenant; and the first links in an imaginative coastal path, destined it is hoped to stretch twenty miles from Runkerry to Ballycastle, were acquired.

Encouraged by the success of these regional ventures, the Trust concluded that action on a nationwide scale was possible, and must be taken quickly if the threat to the best of England's remaining coastland was to be averted. It was decided to launch a national appeal for money to buy the finest coastland as it came on the market, and simultaneously to appeal to well-disposed owners to transfer their coastlands into the safe keeping of the Trust or to secure their relative protection by the gift of covenants (see p. 167).

As a preliminary step the Trust carried out in 1962–63 a detailed survey of the coast to identify the best stretches and to establish what was still worth preserving, and also to discover which of these stretches were in the greatest danger of development. Thus an overall picture of the shores of England, Wales and Ulster emerged and priorities were established. The survey revealed—the figure has already been quoted—that only some 900 miles of coast which could be classified as of outstanding natural beauty remained undeveloped.

A second essential preliminary to a national campaign was the support of the government and of the voluntary societies associated either with the preservation of amenity or with access to the countryside. A statement of purpose and policy was drawn up and, after consultations over a period of months, twenty-one Ministries and government agencies and sixty-three national voluntary societies pledged their active support and cooperation. The stage was now set. In May 1965 the appeal—which had been appropriately christened 'Enterprise Neptune'—was officially launched under the patronage of Prince Philip, Duke of Edinburgh, at a luncheon given by the Lord Mayor at the Mansion House. It is among the most ambitious conservation projects ever undertaken in Britain.

The Treasury, in token of government support, gave £250,000 to the appeal fund. From local authorities the Trust asked the equivalent of a 2d rate. The response was encouraging. By the end of the year 227 local authorities had contributed, and in one case the donation was the equivalent of 10·7 pence per ratepayer. Some authorities in lieu of money offered gifts of coastland. Material support came from other official quarters. The Ministry of Defence undertook to notify the Trust whenever a stretch of coast was no longer required by the Services so that, if desirable, Enterprise Neptune could take steps to acquire it. The Crown Estate Commissioners and the Duchy of Cornwall, owners of two-thirds of the foreshore in England and Wales, agreed to offer leases of foreshore adjacent to the Trust's coastal holdings.

Appeal was made to the general public through the press, which gave generous coverage, and through an elaborate canvassing organisation. Responsible to a Neptune Committee in London, a Campaign Director and six Regional Directors were appointed. These in turn controlled county commissioners, from whom depended district supervisors. Action Committees were set up in the counties and in the larger cities. Thus an appeal network covered the whole country. In December 1967 there were 20 county commissioners, 87 district supervisors, 18 action committees, and over 300 voluntary canvassers.

Two and a half years after the launching of the campaign, over a million pounds had been raised. Seventy-eight coastal properties, representing seventy-five miles of coast, had been acquired or protected by covenant (10,928 acres owned, 3,688 acres under covenant). Of these properties twenty-four were *gifts*. Negotiations were also well advanced for the acquisition of a further thirty-eight miles of coast. £820,200 had been spent or provisionally allocated from Enterprise Neptune funds for properties acquired by purchase or under negotiation.

Enterprise Neptune continues, and a target of two million pounds is the Trust's objective. The results so far are encouraging, but they would certainly have been better had not the campaign coincided with a period of economic depression. The latter accounts for the somewhat disappointing response from big business and industry. Yet the conservation of seventy-five miles of coast over two and a half years, with a further thirty-eight miles in prospect, is a notable achievement, If the 175 miles acquired (or protected by covenant) during the previous seventy years are added, the National Trust now controls development over some 250 miles of the finest coast in England, Wales and Ulster. Not least, Enterprise Neptune has awakened the public to the urgency and importance of coastal preservation.

PROBLEMS OF ACCESS

An earlier generation would have been hard put to conceive one of the increasingly difficult problems of the postwar period. Visitors once had to be lured to Trust properties. Since 1945 their arrival in ever greater numbers has sometimes tended to destroy the beauty of the very things they come to see and at certain properties to render nugatory the careful work of preservation carried out by the Trust. The Council in the Annual Report of 1947 first drew attention to the issues raised by increasing numbers of visitors. As the Report pointed out 'the mere presence of too great numbers may well spoil the peace and solitude which is the chief charm [of the Trust's open spaces]'. A decade later this postwar phenomenon had assumed more serious proportions. There were soon (1959) to be over a million visitors a year to the Trust's houses, and at one open space, Clumber Park, it was calculated that at a bank holiday weekend over 100,000 people, mainly coming in motorcars, flooded into the park. The Annual Report for 1958 forcefully expressed the Trust's concern for the effects on open spaces of such invasion:

'The care of open spaces has, in particular, called for a change of approach. At one time the Trust was concerned to expose an in-different public to the impact of the countryside, to induce thousands from the towns to discover the beauty of the moors, the fens, and the coastland under its protection. The Trust, aided by circumstances and the motor car, has achieved its object only too well. As a result, the Trust today is more and more concerned with the reverse process— the impact of the public on the countryside. All too often the public spoil the open spaces saved for their enjoyment by the Trust and private generosity. .... Numbers in themselves create a problem. A given area *cannot* properly support more than a given number of visitors, without strict control. Innocent summer walkers if they come in crowds will wear away the turf so that the autumn rains will scour into a torrent the track which they have worn down. The Trust's duty becomes one of control rather than inducement. Inevitably, this brings unpopularity in certain quarters. It is an unpopularity the Trust unhesitatingly accepts in confining the public to footpaths on agricultural land, in strictly limiting caravans, tents and car-parks to appropriate sites, and generally in regulating access to its open spaces. The Trust's responsibility is not only to make these areas accessible today, but to preserve them unspoilt for future generations.

This theme to which the Council reverted yet again in the Annual Report of 1961 finds its aptest and saddest illustration in such areas as the Lake District in summer. Nothing is better calculated to delight than the shores of Ullswater, provided they are not lined with parked motorcars. Nothing is likelier to raise jaded spirits than a walk over Helvellyn, provided it does not turn out to be a shuffle in a queue. The control of crowds, the Trust has discovered, raises complex issues. With visitors increasing every year, it may eventually become necessary at certain open spaces to devise some form of rationing by numbers, allowing access to stretches of country, as to houses, by ticket and limiting the number of tickets issued in any one day. Meanwhile the Trust does what it can. Wardens are employed to prevent fires and damage to trees and plants, and to carry out the perpetual and disheartening collection of litter. Car parks are provided, carefully sited and screened, as are lavatories and other buildings which the public require (see Chapter 9).

The view that the Trust should transform its open spaces, and in particular its coastline, into popular playgrounds is myopic. To the critics who reiterate that the Trust should everywhere provide marinas in its coves, and caravan camps on its headlands, that the public should be able to buy ices from kiosks on its sands, and find tarmac car parks beside its beaches, there are two simple and wholly convincing answers. First, this is not the Trust's primary business. The essential purpose for which it was created, and which parliament has approved, is different. Secondly, these things may be readily provided, and no doubt should be provided, on the 2,800 miles of coastline with which the Trust is not concerned. The 250 miles of coast which the Trust controls, most of it wild and of great beauty, must be preserved as far as possible in their natural state. They are held in trust for future generations and must not be sacrificed to short-term pressures. The same is true of the dales of the Lake District or the Peak, and indeed of all open spaces whether they have been saved by private generosity or public appeal. The principle established by John Bailey still stands: preservation, which is preservation for all time, must come first, and access, which is merely access at a brief moment in time, must be placed firmly second. This is not to imply that the Trust should not, and does not, create camp sites, temporary caravan parks, and car parks, where these can be suitably sited and contrived without damage to a landscape whose care is its special charge.

Houses, whose atmosphere is equally susceptible to destruction by overcrowding, present similar problems. The Council gave warning of this danger in 1947 when there were less than half-a-million paying visitors to the Trust's historic buildings. As we have seen, rather over a decade later they exceeded a million. By 1966 they were over two million. The numbers rise yearly. Though control is sometimes easier at houses than in the open country, there are none the less buildings where 'preservation' seems in danger of sacrifice to 'access', and where numbers destroy any sense of a house as a home, and make almost impossible creative contact with the past and with the art, and the art of living, that a house enshrines. The preservation of the character of a house, no less than of the beauty of a landscape is mandatory on the Trust.

At the same time it is the Trust's constant concern to increase the number of open days at some of its houses where access seems inadequate and is restricted by agreements with the donors. Without such agreements the houses could usually not have been preserved, but where they are in force time is a ready ally. Donors are mortal, circumstances change. No year passes without improved access to one or more such houses. By publicity and other means, the Trust also does everything possible to attract people to its less visited houses. There are a number, of great historic and architectural interest, which could without loss of character give pleasure to many more people. It is the Trust's wish that they should do so.[1]

ADMINISTRATION

The extension of the Trust's work in many directions made the recasting of administration among the most urgent issues of postwar years. Since 1895 growth had been uninterrupted, yet for almost fifty years there had been little change in the methods of administration. In 1939 on the outbreak of war the Trust was already the owner of many buildings and broad acres, yet its affairs in the field were still largely the concern of voluntary workers, often having extraordinary devotion but little time. The permanent staff was embryonic, and both then and for some time to come gave their services, because they believed in the cause, for a small wage. In 1917 a staff of two administered 6,275 acres and eleven historic buildings. Twenty years later (1937) a staff of twelve in London and the provinces administered, in happy but somewhat haphazard fashion, 51,449 acres and forty-five historic buildings. Soon after, the creation of the Country House Scheme, and the acquisition of the large estates that great houses brought as endowment, made an effective regional organisation imperative. The Trust needed a new machine.

Reference has been made in the previous chapter to the Trust's wartime decision to dispense with firms of professional land agents, and to appoint its own qualified agents. The Annual Report for 1945 was able to state that 'the system of regional offices with regional agents under a chief agent' was taking shape. It referred to the duties of these agents in terms which deserve quotation in view of subsequent developments. 'These Area Agents', the Report states, 'will have no easy task. Their responsibilities will inevitably extend beyond the mere management of the Trust's existing properties. They will become the *representatives* of the Trust over a very wide area and must strive to make themselves the central driving force, under the general guidance of Head Office, for *all* the Trust's activities in that area.'[2]

This liberal conception of the duties of the Trust's agents had the marked advantage of ensuring control by a single officer in each area. On the other hand it imposed heavy burdens on land agents which their technical training did not necessarily equip them to carry. It was also open to question whether land agents, whose duty by definition is to increase rents and manage land, were the persons best situated to preach the Trust gospel to tenants and prospective donors and to further its cause. At all events the system had hardly been introduced before it was changed. Within two years three regional representatives and five honorary regional representatives having special responsibility for 'aesthetic, architectural, and artistic matters.' were appointed to ease the burden of the area agents. The creation of this new type of official reflected Lord Esher's conviction that many of the problems of the Trust, as the owner of historic houses and great collections, did not fall within the experience of the average agent, and that the Trust's overriding responsibility for the maintenance of aesthetic standards, both where houses and landscape were concerned, called for another type of administrator.

The wish to supplement the technical knowledge of the agents was understandable, but the dual control set up by the appointment of representatives had serious disadvantages. From the start it proved impossible to draw a firm line between the respective spheres of representatives and agents, and it became evident that aesthetic considerations in an organisation such as the Trust's must affect all aspects of land management. The disadvantages of dual control were increased by the fact that representatives were responsible, in the first instance, through the Historic Buildings Secretary, to the Historic Buildings Committee, and agents through the Chief Agent to the Estates Committee. Thus parallel administration in the areas was reflected at committee level. That a system without a unified chain of command, and one in which spheres of responsibility were so loosely defined, worked, and continued to work, is a tribute to the spirit that informed the staff of the Trust and the readiness of representatives and agents to cooperate.

Though the drawbacks of dual control in the areas were soon recognised, it proved peculiarly difficult to find a satisfactory alternative. The matter recurrently preoccupied those responsible for the direction of the Trust, and a special sub-committee was set up in 1956 to consider both this problem and the decentralisation which the growth of the Trust seemed to require. Two years later the sub-committee made a number of recommendations. The most important of these were that representatives should be superseded by regional secretaries who should be generally responsible for administering their areas, and that the Estates and Historic Buildings Committees should be amalgamated.[3] In the event only one regional secretary was appointed and it proved impracticable to amalgamate the committees. After more than a decade, dual control in the areas, and in the committees concerned, had become so established a feature of the Trust's administration that it was perhaps not readily susceptible to treatment along the lines proposed. The solution ultimately found is described in Chapter 8.

Hardwick Hall, Derbyshire. Transferred through the Treasury in 1959

The Vyne, Hampshire. The classical portico (*Circa* 1654) is the earliest in England on a country house. Bequest 1956

Mussenden Temple, County Londonderry. Given in 1949

Ickworth, Suffolk. Begun about 1794 by the eccentric Earl-Bishop of Bristol.
Transferred through the Treasury in 1956

Chapter 7

The Postwar Years:
The Trust and Planned Conservation

The Earl of Crawford and Balcarres, Chairman: 1945–65

In a Utopia where a perfect sense of values prevailed there would be no place for a National Trust. In the society of the late nineteenth-century it filled a necessary role. Individuals undertook a task that government would not shoulder, and could not have attempted in the face of public indifference. After 1945, when a national conscience in the matter of the preservation of buildings and landscape tardily awoke and government began to take a hand, the awakening was bound to have a profound effect on the Trust. Government intervention might well have reduced its work, and in many countries it is plausible to argue that it would have done so. However in Britain the voluntary society is a traditional and important strand in the social pattern, and there is also a grounded, and possibly well grounded, prejudice against anything that resembles a Ministry of Fine Arts. Thus the postwar legislation, which to its credit sometimes anticipated rather than followed public opinion, tended to use the existing machinery of the Trust for its purposes. They were purposes to which the Trust had devoted itself for half a century, and its machinery offered considerable saving to the tax-payer. With limited resources, and accustomed to stringent economy, the Trust, as experience has shown, can manage a property on a smaller budget than official bodies find necessary.

The cooperation of the Trust with the Government was among the most important developments of the postwar period and gave its work an unforeseen impetus. The fact that government placed its confidence in the Trust was a recognition of its achievement, but it came both as an accolade and a challenge. It brought new fields of expansion but, no less, new problems. Among these the foremost was independence. The Trust's driving force had always been the dedication of a minority with an informed sense of, and sensibility to, the problems of the protection of landscape and buildings. The loyalty and drive of such a minority can rarely be harnessed to an organisation that is an appendage of government. Moreover the conservation of something as elusive as the flavour of a stretch of countryside or the spirit of a country house cannot easily be achieved by the formal methods of government departments. Thus the Trust, while welcoming the confidence of successive governments, has been concerned to preserve its autonomy. This is not because it is jealous of control, but because it knows that its aims and the type of preservation with which it has long been concerned can rarely be achieved by the necessarily standardized approach of a bureaucracy.

THE NATIONAL LAND FUND

While useful legislation, including such measures as Ancient Monuments Acts and the Finance Act of 1910, dates from an earlier period, it may be said that the financial cooperation of government in the rescue of land and buildings of national importance begins with the establishment in 1946 of the Land Fund by Dr Hugh Dalton. The creation of the Land Fund was an original and imaginative departure. It was also decisive. It committed government to the battle of conservation, a battle which almost for the first time it was proposed to carry into the wide territory that lay beyond the limited preserve defended by the Ancient Monuments Boards.

In his budget speech of April 9th 1946 the Chancellor announced his intention of creating, as 'a thank-offering for victory', a National Land Fund of £50 million, the money to be derived from the sale of surplus war stores and to be used for acquiring and preserving property in the national interest. Since Lloyd George's Finance Act of 1910 the Revenue had possessed powers to accept land and buildings, instead of cash, in payment of death duties; only twice in thirty-six years had these powers been invoked, and then for the conveyance of trivial properties to the Post Office and a local authority. It was the Chancellor's intention that in future they should be used more often. The primary purpose of the Land Fund, as stated by the Chancellor, was to enable the Treasury to reimburse the Revenue for properties offered in lieu of death duties and to transfer them to non-profit-making bodies such as the Trust, which lacked the resources to pay for them. 'We regard', the Chancellor said, such bodies 'as friends of the public interest and we desire to help them', and he stated his intention to take counsel with the Trust and with other organisations. This was very welcome.[1].

Early in 1944 the Trust had submitted a memorandum to the Deputy Prime Minister on the financial problem posed by the rescue of threatened houses and on the possibility of government help. Later, shortly before the budget of 1946, the secretary of the Trust had prepared for the

Chancellor a further memorandum stating that the Trust was concerned to preserve its independence and thus would not wish to ask for grants for its administrative organisation, but that the useful development of its work would be severely restricted if financial help in some form were not forthcoming. The memorandum solicited support for the maintenance and improvement of existing properties, and for the acquisition of land and country houses in which the donors retained no interest. Though there was more than one view in the Trust as to the wisdom of accepting an annual subvention, it was proposed that a sum should be included each year in the vote of the then Ministry of Town and Country Planning to assist the purchase by the Trust of land of outstanding national importance, and in the vote of the Ministry of Works for the purchase of historic buildings. Help in the form suggested did not materialise, but within a week of the Chancellor's budget speech the Minister of Town and Country Planning had told the Trust informally that the Chancellor in setting up the Land Fund had in mind to further its work in three ways: by transferring to the Trust, after acceptance in payment of death duties, historic buildings, stretches of beautiful open country, and lastly agricultural land in an area such as the Cotswolds where it seemed desirable to build in a local tradition. In May it was made clear to the Trust that the Chancellor was not prepared to go beyond this or to provide a direct annual subvention from the Land Fund. His decision seems, in retrospect, to have been in the best interests of the Trust, as was recognised by the Executive Committee at the time and particularly by the chairman who had throughout been opposed to the idea of a regular subsidy. In July, when the method of operation of the Land Fund as it affected the Trust had been clarified, he expressed in an appreciative letter to the Chancellor the Trust's thoughts on an annual grant. 'I feel', he wrote, 'that the independence of the Trust is of the greatest importance, and fear that, were we to accept a regular annual subvention from Parliament, a measure of State Control might result.'

The important thing in 1946 both for the nation and the Trust was that a Land Fund had been established, that the Finance Act of 1910 was to be implemented, and that government was committed to cooperation with the Trust in the preservation of land and buildings. Much that followed was implicit in the initiative taken by the Chancellor in 1946, not least the establishment in Northern Ireland of a separate land fund, set up by the Ulster Land Fund Act of 1949. The fund has been imaginatively used, and Castlecoole in 1951 was the first property to be acquired under the Act.

PROPERTIES AND CHATTELS ACCEPTED IN PAYMENT
OF DEATH DUTIES

When addressing the Annual General Meeting of the Trust in 1947 Dr Dalton was able to refer to acquisitions under his new Land Fund scheme. Hartsop in the Ullswater valley, 1,854 acres of farmland and fell, was the first open space passed to the Trust in this way, and Cotehele, a romantic late medieval house on the banks of the Tamar, was the first great house. Some fifty properties, distinguished either scenically or architecturally, have since come to the Trust in the same fashion, among them are Abinger Roughs, Croft Castle, Farnborough Hall, Hardwick Hall, Ickworth, Melford Hall, the Penrhyn estate, Shugborough Park and Sudbury Hall.[2]

The operation of the Land Fund has meant that fewer houses and estates have come by way of gift in an owner's lifetime or as a devise on his death. This trend is likely to become more pronounced. There is an important difference in the relationship between the Trust and a donor who has given a property, and an heir whose trustees have offered it in payment of death duties. The Trust has not necessarily an obligation to the latter, since the transfer of his property is purely the satisfaction of a tax obligation, and the Trust cannot, for instance, allow him to live in his family house otherwise than at a rackrent, unless he contributes at least the equivalent of such a rent by way of endowment or by gift of the contents of his house.

In 1953 legislation, for which the Trust had pressed, enabled the Revenue to accept chattels offered in payment of death duty in the same way as property, provided they had normally been kept in a house offered to the Trust. This legislation meant that the outright gift of the contents of great houses, such as the Blickling, Upton, Polesden Lacey, and Stourhead collections, was likely to become infrequent. The value of the 1953 Act was none the less immense. It offered a clear inducement to executors to keep collections intact in the houses of which they were an integral part. Great collections which have come to the Trust in satisfaction of death duties since 1953 include those at Ickworth with its splendid eighteenth century silver, Petworth with its Turners and classical marbles, Hardwick with its unique collection of tapestries and needlework, and the collections at Saltram, Shugborough, and Sudbury.

Chattels acquired by the Treasury in this way (under the Finance Act of 1953), if offered to the Trust for retention in their house of origin, are subject to the terms of an agreement with the Treasury. Chattels of lesser importance are given outright on the understanding that they are not removed, except for repair or temporary exhibition. More valuable objects remain Treasury property and are loaned for varying periods. They enjoy special safeguards. The Trust must display them as part of the setting of an historic country house, in a manner appropriate to such a setting, and not as if they were 'the contents of an art gallery or museum'. Treasury experts have the right to inspect them from time to time and to recommend their return to the Treasury if the Trust appears unable to ensure their proper conservation. The Trust, for its part, has the obligation to submit periodical reports, giving particulars of repairs or restorations carried out and specifying the insurance and security precautions in force.

ENDOWMENTS AND CHATTELS EXEMPTED FROM DEATH DUTIES

Since 1931 land and buildings given or devised to the Trust, provided they are declared inalienable, have been exempted from death duties. The Finance Act of 1949 extended this exemption to land or securities given as endowment by the donor of a property, and in 1951 the Chancellor saw reason to afford the same exemption to any objects associated with a building given to the Trust. Whereas the Act of 1949 greatly facilitated the provision of endowments, the Act of 1951 was responsible for the preservation of further private collections of national importance which might otherwise have been dispersed.[3]

Such collections (and also collections acquired by gift before 1951 but not necessarily exempt from duty, or acquired after 1953 in lieu of death duty), preserved in their original setting and in their historic context, have particular significance. So preserved, they are the faithful expression of the taste and outlook of successive generations living in a single house; when dispersed they can be appreciated only as art objects. Thus, to take only three examples, the Waddesdon Collection, expressive of the wealth, the flair, and the exotic tastes of the English Rothschilds, the Blickling Library, evoking the interests of Sir Richard Ellys, among the most active of early eighteenth-century bibliophiles, and the contents of Stourhead, largely a memorial to Sir Richard Colt Hoare, one of the foremost antiquarians of his day and a patron of the younger Chippendale, would lack a dimension and lose something of their interest in any context but their own. The taste of those who admired Netherlandish decoration in the second half of the seventeenth century, or of those who later went on the Grand Tour, was not always judicious, and their purchases were not always wise, but the things they acquired, seen in their houses, and often in the very places first chosen for them, have a significance lost in museums or in the interiors of contemporary collectors. They retain the erratic beat of the pulse of history. The Trust has always recognised that to save a house without its contents is unsatisfactory. Life ebbs from empty rooms. The preservation of a shell can only be justified by its extreme architectural importance. Even a Montacute, which the Trust has carefully and gradually furnished, must remain a museum piece, lacking the personal touch, the casual yet significant accretions of time, which make a house live.

In the twenty years following the Second World War the Trust, largely due to the government measures mentioned above, became a curator of great collections with a responsibility not only to maintain works of art but to conserve the atmosphere of the past which they invoke in the rooms where their owners placed them. Something is said in Chapter 12 of the Trust's attitude towards the acquisition of country houses and their contents, and of the processes involved. It can be said at this point that the Trust has no wish to create an architectural empire or to amass collections of works of art. It believes that houses are usually best looked after by private owners, and that something of atmosphere and of authenticity is lost when they come into the keeping of even the most sympathetic organisation. Thus the Trust has for many years wished to see legislation promoted which would tend to preserve houses 'at source' and in private ownership. In 1923 and in 1936 it put to the Chancellor the case for tax concessions to the owners of houses of outstanding historic or architectural interest, and in 1949, when submitting evidence to the Gowers Committee (see below), it again urged such concessions. For political and fiscal reasons, governments have refused to alter the tax structure in this sense.

One concession enjoyed by the owners of works of art of national importance, the Trust has long felt, should be extended to the owners of important buildings. Since the Finance Acts of 1910 and 1930 such works of art have been exempted from death duty unless sold. It seems to the Trust that similar exemption should be granted to houses of national importance with their gardens and parks, which are no less works of art than the pictures, furniture, and porcelain they contain. Legislative discrimination against works of art because they happen to take the form of architecture or find expression in the idyllic creations of a Brown or a Repton, seems unaccountable. Logic if nothing else demands that buildings and gardens, if works of art, should receive the same treatment as chattels. A measure for the relief of country houses on these lines seems as simple as it is reasonable. The Trust gave it particular thought in the late fifties, and in 1961 the Chairman submitted a memorandum on this and other legislative matters to the Chancellor. Up to the present time, much to the Trust's regret, no action has been taken to remedy a curious legislative anomaly.

THE HISTORIC BUILDINGS AND ANCIENT MONUMENTS ACT

Though successive governments showed no sign of introducing direct tax concessions to help fine houses, the appointment of the Gowers Committee in 1948 was welcome proof that they had the problems of the conservation of historic buildings in mind. The terms of reference of the Committee were 'to consider and report what general arrangements might be made by the government for the preservation, maintenance and use of houses of outstanding historic or architectural interest which might otherwise not be preserved, including, where desirable, the preservation of a house and its contents as a unity'.

The conclusions to which the Gowers Committee might come, and the recommendations which it might make, were clearly of the first importance to the Trust. After long discussion and the preparation of documents by the Trust's Historic Buildings Committee, written and oral evidence was submitted to the Gowers Committee in 1949. The written evidence included an impressive and tragic list of houses demolished since 1945 and made a number of recommendations.

The Gowers Committee presented its report in 1950, and a Bill was in due course laid before Parliament. The Bill omitted to include tax relief for the owners of historic buildings, advocated by the Gowers Committee, but it incorporated two of the Committee's recommendations which were of the first importance and which have arrested the losses and demolitions which were so lamentable a feature of the previous decade. The Bill enabled the Minister of Public Buildings and Works (since the summer of 1966 the Minister of Housing and Local Government), and the appropriate ministers in Wales and Scotland, on the recommendation of Historic Buildings Councils to be set up for England, Wales, and Scotland, to make grants for the repair and maintenance of houses of outstanding architectural or historic importance, and of their contents, and also to acquire such houses or their contents, when in danger, and transfer them into the keeping of the Trust and certain other bodies.

In September 1951 an extraordinary meeting of the Executive Committee considered the draft of the Historic Buildings and Ancient Monuments Bill and made recommendations. A year later a special sub-committee was set up to examine a further draft of the Bill. As the result of representations made by the Trust, certain modifications to the Bill were agreed by the Minister. Later in Parliament the government accepted a major amendment to enable endowments to be provided for houses given to the Trust. The amendment was accepted with reluctance. Though in Ulster the power to create endowments (under the Ulster Land Fund Act) has proved invaluable, it has never been used in England. Indeed the Treasury has remained so opposed to the conception that it has been unwilling even to allow the indirect creation of an endowment by means of the purchase, under the terms of the Act, of the works of art in a great house where the owner has declared his intention of passing on the purchase price to the Trust by way of endowment.

The Bill was a good one, as was the Gowers Report from which it derived, and it became law as the Historic Buildings and Ancient Monuments Act in 1953. In legislation of a character unprecedented in this country it was not possible to anticipate every eventuality. In time it became clear that there had been one serious omission. The Act could offer no help to great gardens unless attached to an historic country house. There was thus no relief for gardens such as the Trust's Gardens Scheme had been devised to help, and which included many of the foremost examples of a horticultural tradition which is the envy of Europe. The Trust was well placed to judge the effects of this legislative oversight and in 1961 represented to the Chancellor and the Minister of Works that an amendment to the Historic Buildings and Ancient Monuments Act was required. The representation was well received, and the Trust has since been informed that, when the legislative programme permits, consideration will be given to helping gardens by way of grant.

Under the Historic Buildings and Ancient Monuments Act the Trust qualified on precisely the same terms as any owner of an historic building for repair and maintenance grants. None the less the Trust has profited from larger single grants than any private owner, and has received particularly generous and sympathetic treatment in its applications to the Historic Buildings Council for England. It is no exaggeration to say that help under the Act, in the form both of repair and maintenance grants, has alone made possible not only the effective structural preservation of many of the Trust's earlier acquisitions, but has enabled it to take over threatened houses which it would otherwise have had to refuse. The first grants received under the Act were for Treasurer's House in York and Dunsland in Devon, the former a property acquired many years earlier, the latter a remote and romantic house with fine late seventeenth-century plasterwork which in 1954 could not have been saved without a subvention. The first grants for the repair of chattels followed a year later and included the cost of restoring the picture collections which intimately illustrate the history of taste at Stourhead and Uppark. In the course of thirteen years the Trust has received, on the recommendation of the Historic Buildings Council for England, repair and maintenance grants totalling £1,007,748.[4]

Use has also been made by the government of powers under the Act which enable houses and their contents to be bought and conveyed to the Trust. Dyrham Park in Gloucestershire, which incorporates one of William Talman's finest architectural conceptions and is a repository of the taste of the late seventeenth-century, was so acquired in 1956, as were in 1958 many of the contents of Beningbrough Hall near York, associated with the Chesterfield family.

The procedure by which the Trust and other owners of historic buildings obtain grants under the Act has proved efficient and expeditious. A grant application is submitted to the relevant Historic Buildings Council, with supporting documents (a brief statement as to the historic and architectural importance of the building, photographs, and an architect's report on the repairs that are necessary and their cost). A Ministry architect, and sometimes also a Ministry inspector, visits the house and makes a report to the Historic Buildings Council. The Council, if it thinks the application well grounded, then submits a grant recommendation to the Minister. It is rare that such recommendations are not approved. In according a grant the Minister makes specific stipulations to ensure that the work is carried out in conformity with proper architectural standards and is subject to inspection by the Ministry's architects. Reasonable public access, usually one day a week, is a condition usually attached to any grant under the Act.

COOPERATION WITH GOVERNMENT AGENCIES

The government's postwar concern for the protection of the countryside led to the establishment of two agencies with which the Trust was drawn into close contact, the National Parks Commission and the Nature Conservancy.

As early as 1904 the Trust in its annual report had advocated the creation of a national park in the heart of the Lake District and had referred to the successful pattern established in America at Yellowstone and Banff, and Canon Rawnsley, its honorary secretary, in a letter to *The Times* in 1919 had urged that the Lake District should be made a 'national reserve'. Unfortunately in 1931 the Addison Committee's proposals for national parks in Britain, coinciding with the economic depression, had been shelved. In the forties the initiatives that led to the long-awaited appointment of the Hobhouse Committee to consider the setting up of national parks were welcomed by the Trust. Evidence was submitted to the Committee and when, two years after the publication of the Hobhouse Report, the National Parks and Access to the Country-side Bill was presented to Parliament in 1949, the Trust expressed its regret that the Bill was not based more closely on the recommendations contained in the Report and, after proposing amendments to the Minister of Town and Country Planning, received satisfactory con-cessions in regard to its inalienable property. As the owners of much land in the National Parks, and as a body concerned with access to the countryside, the Trust since the passing of the Act has given every support to the National Parks Commission and has been able usefully to cooperate, particularly in the Lake District and Snowdonia.

The establishment of the Nature Conservancy in 1949 was also directly relevant to the work of the Trust. The preservation of flora and fauna has always been the special interest of many Trust members. A panel of experts advises the Trust on such matters. Wicken Fen was secured as early as 1899, Blakeney Point before the First World War, Scolt Head in 1923, and the Farne Islands two years later. In the Nature Conservancy the Trust acquired an ally to whom it could not only look for specialist advice in the management of its nature reserves, but to whose keeping it seemed wise in the best interests of nature conservation to commit the care of certain properties. 1952 saw the lease of Scolt Head and other reserves to the Conservancy. The latter now manages seven properties on behalf of the Trust (see Chapter 10).

With rights over large areas of common land, of which there are in all a million and a half acres, the Trust was concerned at the deterioration of commons during and after the war, and welcomed the setting up of a Royal Commission in 1955 to study the problem of their conservation and future use. The Trust gave evidence to the Commission and is in general agreement with its recommendations as embodied in the Commons Registration Act of 1967. The registration of commons and common rights, and the ultimate establishment of statutory committees to administer schemes for commons, directly affects much land in which the Trust is interested.

THE ANCIENT MONUMENTS DEPARTMENT AND THE
FORESTRY COMMISSION

Something must be said of the Trust's relations after the Second War with the Ancient Monuments Department of the Ministry of Public Building and Works and the Forestry Commission. The Trust owns some 180 sites or buildings in England and Wales scheduled as Ancient Monuments and they range from a famous Roman villa such as Chedworth to obscure tumuli. The care of the latter is not always easy. When situated on arable land, tenant farmers are apt to regard them as a nuisance. To ensure the better protection of these monuments, for which the Trust is responsible to the Ancient Monuments Department, a standard clause is incorporated in its tenancy agreements drawing attention to the existence of tumuli and similar remains and forbidding ploughing over them.

In pursuit of a policy initiated before the war, the Trust in 1952 placed the Roman fort at Segontium in the guardianship of the Ministry, whose Ancient Monuments Department has unique experience in the care of such sites. Close cooperation with the Ministry has developed at Avebury, the most important site of its kind in Europe, where as tenancies fall in or the Trust acquires further property within the pre-historic circle the land is placed under Ministry guardianship. At Stonehenge, where the Trust owns much of the adjoining land, a care-fully concerted scheme has been agreed with the Ministry for the better preservation of the monument, free of cars and wire fences (see Chapter 9). In Northumberland, where at one time there was considerable divergence of view between the Ancient Monuments Department and the Trust as to the treatment of the Roman Wall, agreement has been reached on a policy for the impressive stretches of wall in Trust owner-ship.

The Forestry Commission when acquiring land for afforestation naturally looks to wild upland areas where the soil is unsuited to agri-culture. It is thus frequently the Trust's neighbour in Wales and the north of England. In the years following the establishment of the Commission in 1919 relations were less than cordial. The Trust was among the most determined critics of the rectangular planting of spruce, carried out with little regard to the character and shape of the adjacent countryside, and was quick to welcome a later change of policy which indicated a more sensitive approach to landscape. In 1932 and again in 1948 meetings were held with the Commission to exchange views and discover how far cooperation was possible. The meetings in 1948 revealed a useful measure of common ground. In 1952 prolonged negotiation—the Trust with 30,000 acres of woodland was by then one of the large foresters in the country—led to agreement with the Commission on a special form of dedication for the Trust's woods. The Commission recognised the Trust's special responsibilities and its duty to give particular regard to amenity and the planting of traditional hardwoods. In dedicating woodlands to the Forestry Commission the Trust was therefore exempted from the obligation to carry out forestry operations which, in its opinion, were inconsistent with the purposes of the Trust or detrimental either to the amenity of its woods or to adjoining land in its ownership. The safeguards incorporated in this agreement enabled the Trust to enter into deeds of dedication for woodlands which seemed suited to such treatment and to obtain valuable grants. By 1966 woods, totalling 14,000 acres, were being managed in this way with the help of the Forestry Commission.[5]

THE TRUST AND LOCAL AUTHORITIES

The Town and Country Planning Act of 1947, with its contribution to the rational preservation of buildings and the countryside, was of the first importance to the Trust, whose special status was mentioned in the Act. In spite of deficiencies the Act marked a great step forward, and many of its purposes, such as the protection of 'green belts' round towns, had long been advocated by the Trust and had been the concern of Octavia Hill before the beginning of the century. The operation of the Act notably furthered the causes in which the Trust was interested, in so far as it protected the countryside and tended to prevent the alteration or demolition of historic buildings listed under the machinery set up by the Act. On the other hand, as time has decisively shown, it did not make the work of the Trust any less necessary. Indeed since 1947, with the mounting pressure on open land and a growing temptation to exploit the site value of historic buildings, the inalienable status which the Trust alone can confer on property has become of increased importance.

Since the local authorities were the bodies entrusted with planning under the Act, the Trust was brought into a new and closer relationship with many of them. Contacts developed, and were maintained, between planning officers and the Trust's regional staff. They produced not only a useful exchange of ideas and information but they made local authorities aware of what the Trust had done and was trying to do. This was to have important consequences and to result in a greatly increased use of the powers conferred on local authorities by the National Trust Act of 1937.

This Act empowered local authorities to give, subject to the consent of the appropriate minister, land and buildings to the Trust, or to contribute to the acquisition and maintenance of Trust property. The Act was a recognition of the fact that, for people living in the district, access to the Trust's buildings, and in particular to its open spaces, added something to their pleasure. It also recognised that the Trust was often doing work of value to the community which must otherwise have been tackled by the local authority at the ratepayers' expense.

Though by 1938 the Trust was receiving help from the Great Yarmouth Corporation, who assumed the charge of an interesting old house on the quay, and from local authorities for the acquisition of parts of the Manifold valley, response to the Act of 1937 was initially slow. Local authorities were invited to look in a novel direction. By 1950 the idea of creative partnership had become more familiar. No less than forty local authorities, thirty-four of them concerned to protect open spaces, were committed in one way or another to the support of Trust properties in their areas. An appeal in 1953 to thirty county councils resulted in grants by fifteen towards the maintenance and extension of Trust work in their counties. In 1966 local authorities were making contributions to the upkeep of fifty properties; forty-two others were leased to, or managed by, local authorities; and forty-five authorities were making a subvention to the funds of the Trust to further its general work in their areas. The 200 acres of heath and moorland at Kinver Edge in Staffordshire on the fringe of a densely populated district are the financial responsibility of twenty-one different authorities. Among the landmarks in this fruitful cooperation are the gift of Brean Down, a dramatic and ecologically important promontory on the Somerset coast, by the Axbridge Rural District Council in 1951 as their contribution to the Festival of Britain; the gift of Holmwood Common in Surrey by three local authorities in 1956; and the annual contributions, or the management agreements and leases, which enabled the Trust to accept and preserve Clumber Park, acquired following a public appeal that raised £75,000, (1946: several authorities); Lyme Park, an imposing Palladian house (1947: Stockport Corporation); Buckland Abbey with its Drake associations (1948: Plymouth Corporation); Sheffield Park, one of the great landscape gardens of Sussex (1954: several authorities); Shugborough, with its eighteenth-century temples (1966: Staffordshire County Council); and not least Sudbury Hall, perhaps the finest mid-seventeenth-century house in the Midlands (1967: Derbyshire County Council).

The increasing cooperation of local authorities has unquestionably been one of the most valuable developments of the postwar period. It has enabled the Trust to do more and save more than would otherwise have been possible. It has also established local links and stimulated local enthusiasms. Where open spaces are concerned, partnership has almost always been successful. Arrangements have sometimes been less happy where local authorities, generously and at considerable expense it must be added, have taken over by lease or management agreement the control of a great country house and its contents. Experience seems to show that a local authority, however enlightened, is rarely able to maintain the semblance of life in a country house from which the owners have departed or to preserve the cultural and historical flavour of the past which is as elusive as quicksilver. Consideration moreover for what ratepayers would wish to find in house or garden, even when inappropriate, inevitably influences management decisions.

Where local authorities contribute substantially to the maintenance of country houses, the ideal arrangement, and that most likely to satisfy the Trust's obligation to future generations, is a joint management agreement, whereby responsibility for day to day administration lies, subject to control by a joint committee, with the staff of the Trust. The use of the Trust's administrative machinery not only proves cheaper for the ratepayers, but ensures that the Trust has discretion in matters which fall within its special competence, such as the arrangement and decoration of rooms open to the public, the planting and layout of gardens, and the many small but important decisions on which the continuing character of a house depends. Such an agreement has recently been concluded at Sudbury Hall, thanks to the understanding of the Derbyshire County Council. A joint committee has been set up, representing the three parties with a stake in the future of the hall: the County Council, the Historic Buildings Council for England, and the Trust. It is hoped that this committee may serve as a model when in future the Trust and local authorities act in concert to save a great house.

BATTLES

It is characteristic of the postwar years that while central and local government show increasing concern for the preservation of open spaces many of their undertakings are calculated to destroy them. Different policies are coincidentally pursued and Jekyll remains unaware of Hyde's existence. The same government which provides money from the Land Fund to save moor and coast erects microwave towers of extreme inelegance with little thought to the effect that their siting will have on the landscape, carries overhead cables up remote dales, and permits roads to be carved in inappropriate places. The local authorities which generously contribute to the maintenance of the Trust's open spaces promote schemes which will irreparably damage them.

It is thus as inevitable as it is ironic that the Trust in recent years has had to fight an increasing number of battles, sometimes victorious and sometimes not, to protect its properties. The projects of government departments and agencies, and of local authorities, must be carefully watched, since they are not always made public before irrevocable decisions are taken. They have repeatedly called for the intervention of the Executive Committee. More is said about resistance to developments damaging to Trust property in Chapter 10, but mention must be made here of overhead wires and water extraction.

The Trust was protesting to the authorities about wirescape in the Lake District before the turn of the century. It was a premonition of things to come. Fortunately overhead wires, one of the least attractive features of the twentieth century, and now so familiar in most villages that people have ceased to notice them, are perhaps only a temporary evil. With modern trenching tools the grounding of telephone and low tension wires is becoming the cheaper course, since it eliminates the high cost of subsequent maintenance. The Post Office has taken a lead and the grounding of telephone wires since 1959 at Avebury, Langdale, and on other Trust properties, such as coastal promontories in Cornwall, is a happy augury for the future. By contrast, and in spite of constant research, the grounding of high-power cables is not yet a general economic possibility. Battles to secure their better routeing have taken place up and down the country.

The Trust, while appreciating the vast amounts of water now required by industry, has a primary duty to safeguard the amenity of the land it conserves. Nothing is more damaging to the beauty of lakes and rivers than the extraction of water with a consequent lowering of natural levels and the creation of an artificial shoreline or river edge. The Trust has felt obliged actively to oppose several local authority water projects, such as those embodied in 1957 in the Liverpool Corporation's Conway Water Bill and in the Manchester Corporation's Bill in 1962. The threat to the Conway, which would have affected a stretch of one of the most beautiful rivers in Wales, was successfully averted, and (thanks to the late Lord Birkett's skilful advocacy in the House of Lords) the Manchester Corporation's Bill was after a long struggle so amended as to render it innocuous, sparing the shores of Ullswater. The Corporation renewed its attack on the waters of the Lake District in 1966. A second Bill passed in that year, in spite of the strenuous opposition of the Trust and other societies, fortunately made concessions to amenity and the ultimate effects on the appearance of Lake Windermere, though regrettable, will not be disastrous.

Clevedon Court, Somerset. The chapel with reticulated tracery windows is XIV century. Transferred through the Treasury 1961
(*below*) Great Coxwell Tithe Barn, Berkshire. Bequeathed in 1956. Re-roofed in 1962 with a grant under the Historic Buildings and Ancient Monuments Act

Ivinghoe Windmill, Buckinghamshire. One of the oldest surviving post mills. Given in 1937

Houghton Mill, Huntingdonshire. Given in 1939, and let to the Youth Hostels Association

Chapter 8

The Continuing Purpose

I

In 1965 Lord Crawford retired after having directed the Trust for twenty years. He was succeeded by Lord Antrim. Though it is still premature to treat recent developments in detail, mention must be made of three important issues that immediately confronted the new chairman.

THE FARNE ISLANDS' SEALS

Probably no issue has more unhappily divided that section of the Trust's membership interested in nature conservancy than the control of the grey seals of the Farne Islands. The islands were acquired by the Trust in 1925. Thanks to protective legislation passed seven years later, the grey seal stock, though harassed during the war when surveillance was difficult, had risen to over eight hundred by 1945. The increase on the Farnes of the grey seal—and also of the eider duck—was a source of satisfaction to members; but by 1960 with continuing protection the seal population had reached some 3,500 and was giving concern to fishing interests. It was expected by 1970 to reach 7,000. The grey seal, it was alleged, was a menace. There were complaints of broken nets and loss of catch. Though evidence of damage related almost entirely to salmon—in Parliament the salmon loss attributable to seals between Orkney and the Farnes was estimated in 1966 at between £50,000 and £100,000 a year—it was also maintained that the increasing infestation of cod by a parasite, of which seals are the only known host, was partly due to the growing population of the Farnes. It was impossible accurately to gauge the damage done, but there seemed presumptive evidence of guilt.

On this evidence, and with the grey seals increasing at a rate of over 6 per cent a year, the Ministry of Agriculture felt bound to intervene. In 1963 they asked permission to carry out an experimental cull of the Farnes over a five year period in order to reduce the breeding potential by 25 per cent. The request put the Trust in a difficult position. The grey seals were a source of immense interest to visitors—some 9,000 visit the Farnes every summer—and the thriving colony was an achievement in conservation. On the other hand, Parliament, if confronted with a

6

blank refusal, could take compulsory powers. The Trust resorted to compromise. If a cull was inevitable, it seemed better that it should take place by consent and under Trust observation. Permission was accordingly given for an experimental cull for three years only.

The three annual culls—the first took place in 1963—were carried out in the presence of R.S.P.C.A. inspectors, who made a complaint in respect of one incident. The press, with less knowledge, observed less restraint. Sensational reporting, particularly in 1963, led to wide outcry. Many members were understandably indignant. At the same time the premises on which the cull was based were questioned by responsible authorities. It was suggested that the evidence for damage to fisheries was inconclusive and that there was reason to expect a stabilisation of the seal population due to overcrowding and other causes. The matter was raised, and elicited the expression of strong feeling, at the Annual General Meetings in 1964 and 1965. It came to a head in 1966. In that year the Minister of Agriculture asked for the Trust's agreement to further culls beginning in 1967. The Executive Committee, after careful consideration of the evidence, decided that the case for culling was not proved and gave an assurance to members in the autumn of 1966 that permission for a further cull would not be given without their sanction at an Annual General Meeting. At the same time it was suggested to the Ministry that closer scientific investigation of the grey seal problem was necessary. A conference, on which the Trust and other interested bodies are represented, has since been convened by the Natural Environmental Research Council to study the problem. The Trust on its own account has also set up a Scientific Committee to study the changing ecology of the Farnes as it relates not only to the grey seals but to other forms of plant and animal life.

AN ATTACK

By 1966 the direction of Enterprise Neptune, the national appeal to save the coast (see Chapter 6) was giving, and indeed had long given, concern on many grounds. The Appeal Director, appointed in the summer of 1963 had found it difficult to work in harmony with the Executive Committee or to gain the confidence of his colleagues on the staff. In the spring of 1966 the Executive Committee began also to be seriously worried at the rising cost of the appeal. By the autumn of the same year Enterprise Neptune had raised, exclusive of a Government grant of £250,000 and a grant from the Pilgrim Trust of £50,000, both of which were secured on the personal initiative of Lord Crawford,

£516,428 for an outlay of £111,512. Costs in fact were running at 21·6 per cent and more than one pound in every five was being spent on the expenses of the campaign.

The high costs of Enterprise Neptune were in part attributable to the fact that it had been established as a semi-independent organisation outside the framework of the Trust. In October 1966 the Executive decided, partly on grounds of economy, that it should be integrated into the machinery of the Trust as from March 1967, and that the services of the Director should be terminated at that date. This parting had already been long delayed. The Director's dismissal had been urged as early as June 1964, and time had only served to emphasise that the Trust and the Director were mutually incompatible. The latter was at once informed by the chairman of the Committee's decisions and of the generous financial terms on which he was to leave.

In Plymouth ten days later, at a public meeting to which the press had been invited, the Director launched a violent attack on the Trust, while still in its employ. In the circumstances the Executive Committee saw no alternative to his immediate dismissal. Events in Plymouth it became clear were the first salvo in a sustained campaign to discredit the Trust and in particular the Executive Committee responsible for the Director's dismissal. The campaign was facilitated by provisions in the National Trust Act of 1907, which stipulated that an Extraordinary General Meeting must be called on the requisition of thirty members and a poll on the requisition of twenty members. These provisions, reasonable enough in 1907 when there were some 550 members, were ludicrously out of date in 1966 when membership stood at nearly 170,000. The ex-director was to make effective use of them. At the Annual General Meeting at Cheltenham in November, he and a group of supporters proceeded to requisition an Extraordinary General Meeting. This, attended by some 4,500 members, was held in London in February. Though all motions hostile to the Executive of the Trust were decisively defeated, the requisitionists were unwilling to accept the clear verdict of the members present and, again having recourse to the Act of 1907, demanded and obtained a poll on the following motion:

That this meeting recommends the Council of the National Trust that not later than four weeks from the date of this resolution the Council shall appoint a special purpose committee to consider all aspects of the constitution policy finance and administration of the National Trust and recommends that this Committee consists of an independent Chairman nominated by the President of the Law Society and 8 members of the National Trust 4 to be appointed by the Council of the Trust and 4 to be appointed by those members who have requisitioned this Extraordinary General Meeting.

Since it never harms an organisation to scrutinise its methods and policies, this carefully chosen motion appeared innocuous. The fact that it was both an implicit condemnation of the Council and Executive, and inspired by an ex-employee, was only clear to those who knew the full story or had seen the violence and prejudice with which the motion was pressed at the Extraordinary General Meeting. Despite this the Council did not think it proper to recommend when sending out the polling papers that members should reject the motion. Even so, when the result of the poll was announced in May it was learnt that they had done so by a majority of over two to one. The Extraordinary General Meeting and the poll cost the general funds of the Trust some £6,400. Moreover the ex-director's criticisms of policy and administration, which received wide press publicity, undoubtedly did the Trust at the time much harm. They are answered explicitly or by implication in Chapters 6 and 7 and in the later sections of this book.

Though less than a third of the members voted in the poll, the figures none the less revealed that almost 10 per cent would welcome a review of the Trust's policies and administration. The Council were not opposed to such a review, provided it were carried out by an expert committee which understood and welcomed the Trust's fundamental purposes. Indeed they considered that after seventy years' activity there was much to recommend a review. Accordingly in July 1967 an Advisory Committee was set up, consisting of Sir Henry Benson (Chairman), Sir William Hayter and Mr L. J. Clark (members of the Council nominated respectively by the British Museum and the Youth Hotels Association), and Mr Patrick Gibson (an elected member of the Council). The Committee is considering the management, organisation, and responsibilities of the Trust, and the amendment of the National Trust Acts. It held its first meeting in September 1967 and will report to the Council in 1968.

DECENTRALISATION

A need for greater decentralisation had become evident in the mid-fifties (see Chapter 6). A decade later it was urgent. The Executive Committee recognised that the Trust had attained a size, and a stage in its history, when decentralisation was essential if sensitive contact was to be maintained with local support and local problems. Administration of so large an organisation from London, however effective it might otherwise be, was bound to lack a sure touch in dealing with regional issues. No one was better qualified than Lord Antrim to promote a change. As chairman for twenty years of the Northern Ireland Committee, where considerations of distance and a different legislative background had led to a wide degree of autonomy, he knew both the advantages and problems of regionalism.

A sub-committee reporting on decentralisation in 1958 had rejected the idea of regional committees. It did so on the grounds that people adequately qualified and able to devote sufficient time to the work would be difficult to find. The efficiency of regional committees in Ulster and the Lake District, though admittedly areas of a special nature, led in 1964 to reconsideration of this solution. On reflection it had much to commend it. Provided suitable people could be found to serve, regional committees would supply valuable local knowledge and contacts, and would give effective expression to the local support on which the Trust has always relied. Moreover such committees would minimise the dual control which for twenty years had characterised the Trust's organisation. The Historic Buildings and Estates Committees would in the long run become largely technical and advisory, and both representatives and agents would in the first instance be responsible to their Regional Committees. It was envisaged that in most areas the representatives would become the secretaries to these committees.

Following discussions in 1964, it was decided gradually to extend regional control. This control was to be subject to the reservation to the Executive Committee of decisions on certain specific matters (see Chapter 17). In the last four years new Committees have been established for Northumberland and Durham, for Devon and Cornwall, for East Anglia, and for the Severn Valley (Gloucestershire, Worcestershire, and Herefordshire).[1] This development represents probably the most constructive and radical change in policy since the war.

2

Though the continuing purpose is constant, it is possible to foresee further changes over the next few years, particularly in the sphere of public relations and in cooperation with government. Circumstances have always modified the Trust's methods, and the degree of emphasis accorded to different aspects of its work.

In the future the Trust is likely to come under increasing pressure from those who put access before conservation and those who see the Trust primarily in terms of tourism. Their criticisms will sometimes have the support of the press and always of the powerful interests which regard inalienable land as an intolerable bar to development. If the Trust is to remain true to its purposes, it must resolutely withstand this pressure. There can be no question of sacrificing the achievement of seventy years for short-term objectives.

On the other hand there is much that the Trust can do, and must do, to meet criticism. In the first place it must ensure the maximum access to properties consistent with its objectives. This has always been policy, but new ways and means for its realisation must be devised. With access in mind, the Trust will also do well to prefer, as does the National Trust for Scotland, money or investments to agricultural land as endowment for its properties. The fact that agricultural land can never be thrown open to the public without restriction is not easily explained. In the second place, since conservation both removes land from development and often necessarily means control or limitation of access, the Trust must be scrupulous to protect only country and buildings that are outstandingly beautiful or important. The Trust must be able to justify on grounds of the highest amenity every property it acquires. When any extension of Trust ownership provokes opposition in certain quarters, it becomes the more important to confer inalienability only on the best, on land or buildings which are without argument of national significance.

In the third place, and certainly not least, the Trust must make its aims and methods better known. Its achievements are considerable; knowledge of them is restricted. Born before the age of publicity, the Trust has usually been content to do rather than to explain. The resulting ignorance of its purposes provides a fertile field for misconception. As an organisation which spends annually one and three-quarter million pounds, whose work brings it in touch with a widening public, its financial provision for public relations and publicity is inadequate. Created late in the day, a starved publicity department has done its best under difficult conditions. The special nature of the Trust, its aims which seem remote, and its responsibility to the future, are not to be explained in a few words. Yet explanation must be attempted, on a massive scale and with the necessary funds. Though criticism is often irrelevant it must be answered, and the true answer lies in knowledge of the Trust's work.

Publicity of a different sort must also in the years ahead play a vital role in relation to access. Many Trust properties are overcrowded, while others remain almost unvisited. Judicious publicity can do much to spread the load. Only by stimulating visits to certain places, and thus

74

reducing pressure at others, can the best use be made of the Trust's varied properties.

Cooperation with government and local authorities is a feature of the Trust's history. Planning legislation, which is perhaps more comprehensive here than in any other country, bulwarks the Trust's purposes. In a sense its work is a special extension of planning applied to land and buildings of national importance. The 'Countryside in 1970' conferences were in the Trust's view the most imaginative development in recent years and the resulting establishment of Countryside Committees, on many of which the Trust is to be represented, should do much to ensure a wiser use of land. In the coming decade it must be hoped, and can perhaps be expected, that links with the planning authorities will be tightened, and that progressively more use will be made of the Trust as agent and ally in conservation. The problem is so large, and the forces of destruction so active, that in isolation the Trust's achievement must always be limited. Increased cooperation with government and local authorities can alone realise the Trust's full potential.

As G. M. Trevelyan wrote many years ago 'the importance of the Trust is a measure of the constant diminution of all that is lovely and solitary in Britain'. This is still true. Technology and the very instruments devised for our well-being accelerate the destruction of our habitat. The bulldozer turns savagely upon its masters. Without harmonious contact between men and buildings, between men and landscape, people are adrift. In an era of remote decisions made on maps and carried out by mammoth firms, the forces of conservation, though they grow, marshal too slowly. In a context of irreparable loss, the achievements of the Trust and other preservation societies are pitifully inadequate. Determined and costly government action alone can save more than a fragment of the setting which the founders of the Trust, and those who furthered its work, have seen as essential to civilised life.

Part Two

The Trust at Work

Chapter 9

The Countryside:
Changing Threats, Organisation, and Access

I

The airman and the soaring buzzard are always in sight of Trust land.
Somewhere in their horizon stands an oak-leaf symbol: beside a gate
leading to a beech wood; where a lane climbs to a chalk down or a track
leads to the moors; on the edge of the last stretch of Fen; where people
land on islands, like Brownsea and the Farnes; in Lakeland and Derbyshire dales; beneath Devon Tors, the Brecons, and the Carneddau; on
headlands, retreating in fainter perspective down the Cornish coast.
At such and numberless other sites this symbol is an invitation to pleasure
that is received in different ways by different people. Most frequently
the invitation is to quiet and to creative escape from the pressures of the
modern world.

On over a thousand properties, the symbol distinguishes a small cross-
section of beautiful and unspoilt land, something of the best of mountain
and marsh, of moor and forest, of pasture, down, and coast. Yet in the
context of shoddy acres where little now can be salvaged, the Trust's
achievement is limited. It must be seen against a national failure and a
general deterioration of the countryside.

None the less the larger failure, making ironic comment on the
fragment saved, can only emphasise its importance. With every year
each acre in Trust protection assumes greater significance. The significance is not only a material one. As G. M. Trevelyan wisely put it,
'Without vision the people perish, and without natural beauty the
English people will perish in the spiritual sense'. It is the Trust's first duty
jealously to guard the spiritual resources of its lands, their quiet, remoteness, and all that contributes to their beauty. They are more than lungs or
playgrounds. Therein consists the first significance of the widely
scattered symbols.

GENEROSITY OF DONORS

Though from time to time land comes to the Trust as a totally unexpected
devise, a gift (it is to be hoped) from heaven, much of the finer country

in its possession has been secured by foresight and negotiation. The Trust's agents and representatives usually have a fair idea of the finest country in the areas for which they are responsible, and they know which stretches are threatened and which are relatively safe. Their ears are to the ground, a posture as taxing as it is inelegant. Friendly relations with landowners, large and small, are essential, for the Trust's staff can achieve little without the cooperation of donors. The amount of land that can be bought from special funds or as the result of public appeal is limited. Fortunately the generosity of donors is not. Many donors, it should be remarked, are not rich. Gifts of land are made to the Trust at personal sacrifice because people know and love a stretch of country. The money that bought part of the dramatic Aberglaslyn pass in Caernarvonshire came in a thousand pound notes, the savings of a retired cotton-mill worker. The form of the gift was unusual; the spirit which inspired it was not. The number of anoymous gifts, often modest only in their anonymity, is remarkable. Entries in the Trust's *List of Properties* such as that which stands against 130 acres of Pencarrow Head, stated simply to be the gift of 'a lover of Cornwall', go far to explain the Trust's achievement. To the private gifts on which the Trust has so much depended have been added, since1946, the gifts of land received from the government after their acceptance by the Revenue in satisfaction of death duties. Open spaces acquired in this way include extensive stretches of moorland in Yorkshire, Derbyshire, and important areas in the Lakes and Snowdonia.

THE FRUITS OF EXPERIENCE

With the passage of time there have been modifications in the Trust's attitude to the conservation of the countryside. Even twenty years ago it could be said 'the National Trust may be reckoned fairly omnivorous. It does not despise the day of small things. It can, and does, accept and care for with equal alacrity a half-acre field and an estate of ten square miles.' This is no longer true. The Trust now insists that the land it acquires, whatever its particular character, shall be outstanding of its sort. Moreover it has discovered that small disjunct parcels of land can rarely be effectively protected. There is no purpose in holding a field that may end up as an enclave in a housing estate or as a no-man's-land between caravan camps. A few small properties gratefully accepted in early days, pretty enough bits of country which once were in agreeable surroundings, have now, owing to adjacent development that the Trust was powerless to prevent, lost all attraction. Forlorn in a situation that was unforeseen, they serve no purpose but to attract vandals and litter. Thus it has become Trust policy as far as possible only to acquire land of sufficient area to form in itself a satisfactory landscape unit, in other words areas large enough to retain their significance even if the adjacent countryside is lost to development.

The Trust is also less prompt than it once was to accept land on the periphery of densely populated areas. In such places valuable green patches, whether large or small, must at all costs be salvaged but the intensity and nature of the use to which they will, and should be, put gives them necessarily something of the character of municipal parks. The Trust thus finds that they are often best cared for by the local authority. Where the Trust owns such properties, as at Clumber, Kinver Edge, Kyson Hill and Morven Park, the local authorities usually either manage them on behalf of the Trust or are closely associated with their management.

Interest has perhaps also shifted from the home counties where there are now few considerable stretches of country to be saved. In its early years the Trust was preponderantly a landowner in Surrey and Kent, and it is a chastening thought to imagine the fate of areas like Box Hill, Hindhead, and Toy's Hill had the Trust not existed. Today, with the motorcar and the motorway, new threats are developing to remote areas that once were relatively secure. In these areas the Trust can now make its most valuable contribution. It is perhaps too late to achieve much in the increasing stretches of the semi-country where man and nature are often both seen at their least attractive.

THE DANGER POINTS

The Trust's protecting arm is all too short. Much of the best country must take its rough economic chance. But experience has taught the Trust where danger and relative security lie. Danger, and if possible the Trust's saving intervention, most commonly follow on the break-up of extensive estates. Where great landlords are secure, there is less danger to the landscape pattern. From end to end of England where-ever you meet seemly villages and a countryside that speaks of under-standing and affection, the chances are that you will be on a large estate. Where such estates exist, and as long as they can survive, the Trust has a limited contribution to make. There are rights of way and often a long private tradition that allows public access to places of outstanding natural beauty. The landscape is in good hands, and it would be both unnecessary and presumptuous for the Trust to advocate change. The pattern of the

Trust's holdings thus tends to reflect the character of land tenure in different parts of the country. In the North and East Ridings, where an almost eighteenth-century paternalism jealously protects the country-side, its role is limited. By contrast where there are few large and many small landowners, as for instance in Surrey, the Lake District, and Cornwall, the danger of unsuitable development and a consequent transformation of the landscape are constantly present. It is understand-able that such areas have witnessed the Trust's greatest activity. The adjoining counties of Devon and Dorset provide an object lesson. The coastline of the former is mainly owned in small parcels and every convenient access to the sea is subject to pressure. In Dorset by contrast much of the coast and hinterland are in traditional ownership, the danger is less, and the areas in which the Trust can usefully intervene are fewer. In the latter county it has thus been able, very successfully, to concentrate on the area between Lyme Regis and Bridport where ownership is fragmented. Much of the endangered and outstandingly beautiful coast that stretches for seven miles east of Charmouth has been acquired recently by the Trust.

In the areas of greatest danger, because of their evident insecurity, the Trust finds the readiest local support. Those who live there seem to realise that in the context of the twentieth-century there is no other body to which they can turn with confidence, and that if the solitude of headlands, the character of upland dales, of heath and marsh, or the elegance of noble parkland, are to survive, the Trust must assume responsibilities which in the past were often exercised by imaginative landlords.

CORNWALL

The altering nature of the threat to landscape within the boundaries of a single county, and also the decisive role played by local support, are illustrated by the story of the Trust's activity in Cornwall. The advent of the Great Western Railway in 1859 first brought visitors. They came to stay either in rooms, the terraced boarding-houses of Falmouth, Penzance, and Newquay (sometimes attractive enough), or in the mammoth hotels which at this period rose on the headlands, finding favour with the late Victorians who often preferred a good view of the sea to contact with the water. Forlorn as abandoned fortresses, these great hotels survive about Newquay, on the Lizard peninsular, and elsewhere. The most formidable is perhaps King Arthur's Castle at Tintagel, foursquare, four-storied, visible for many miles, an embattled pile in 'Great Western' taste. From 1860-1910 the headlands were the chief danger points.

It was the aura of legend with which Tennyson and others invested Tintagel, an aura that neither scholarship nor the atlantic gales have been able to disperse, which led to a first acquisition by the Trust. A plan to develop Barras Nose, a fine open cliff beyond the vast Tintagel hotel, and marching with the outworks of the true Tintagel Castle built by Richard Earl of Cornwall in the thirteenth century, provoked strong reaction. The devotees of Arthurian legend turned to the newly formed Trust and the headland was bought by public subscription in 1897.

Barras Nose was an isolated acquisition. It took twenty years and a new threat to alert Cornish opinion. Meanwhile massive hotels continued to be dumped on the headlands, and where there was easy access to the ancient fishing villages—often medieval settlements behind safe cove anchorages—the Edwardian terraces climbed steadily up the hillsides. Yet it was not until after the First World War, as at Port Isaac and St Ives, that building began to spill indiscriminately over the surrounding countryside, and it is surprising how little was damaged. In 1919 much of the best of the Cornish coast was still untouched. It was not to remain so for long.

The roads now brought an invasion more dangerous than the railways. The motorcar, ironically almost coeval with the Trust, began after the war to penetrate the deep winding lanes and splutter to remote coves hitherto inviolate. Down rough tracks, in the dust of the bull-nosed Morris and the 30/98 Vauxhall, came the developer. Land values rose. A minority of Cornishmen realised that something must be done if their coast was not to be fringed with shacks and bungalows. Recalling Tintagel, they turned to the Trust. Soon the first substantial stretches of coast came by way of gift. Though 145 acres of the Dodman Point, that resolute headland dominating much of the south coast, came as early as 1919 (nearly fifty years later the last fields which adjoin the Iron Age fort on the promontory were bought to complete the Trust's ownership of the whole headland), it was in the late twenties and early thirties, no doubt reflecting a growing consciousness of growing danger, that real progress was made with acquisitions such as Glebe Cliff, an addition to the Tintagel property; Pendarves Point; Nare Head; part of Kynance Cove and the Lizard; Treen Cliff, given by the Vyvyan family in whose ownership it had been for eight centuries; and Mayon and Trevescan Cliff, the gift of Ferguson's mysterious Gang (see Chapter 5). In the years immediately before the Second

World War there followed Rosemullion Head; Pentire Point, one of the noblest headlands of the North Cornish coast; Godrevy, a property including five cliffs and headlands, most of the remote Godrevy peninsular, and cavernous inlets, the haunt of the atlantic seal; and Lansallos Cliff (in 1965 the acquisition of Barton Farm in the hinterland rounded off a scheme to which many gifts have contributed and which now ensures the conservation of nearly a thousand acres of wonderful cliff and coastal farmland). Some of these properties such as Pentire and Lansallos were acquired by public subscription. The progress made was the more remarkable as the Trust at this period possessed no formal organisation in Cornwall.

It was not until 1953 that a Cornish agent was appointed and not until 1959 that there were both an agent and a regional representative. Since 1957 the staff has been able to rely on the help of the Cornish Coast Advisory Committee, its twelve members each having a particular knowledge of different parts of the coast. It was this Committee which established the wise principle, later adopted nationally when Enterprise Neptune was launched, that available funds should be directed to buying substantial stretches of unspoilt coast rather than to piecemeal acquisition. Finally in 1965, in accordance with a new policy of decentralisation (see Chapter 8) a regional committee was set up for Devon and Cornwall, coordinating the work of the staff, the Coastal Advisory Committee, and local committees of long standing at Fowey, Mullion, Tintagel and Polperro. Since the establishment of a Cornish office in 1953 the Trust's holding has more than quadrupled. As in the Lake District and elsewhere, the activity of dedicated staff, latterly guided by a powerful regional committee, has rallied local support.

In the 1950s both staff and support were needed. The railway hotels, stranded on their headlands, had been followed by the scattered building development created for the early motorist. After 1945 with paid holidays came the era of the caravan, of the new car owner who dispensed with hotel or boarding house. His demand for somewhere to park his caravan was legitimate and it was right that it should be met. It was disastrous that it was not met more intelligently. Lack of foresight led to the establishment of permanent caravan camps, those lugubrious and often insanitary agglomerations where the 'caras' with chocked wheels stand hock-deep in weeds. Instead of being carefully sited well away from the coast, camps were situated on cliff tops or allowed to block the access to coves and beaches. There was at first no insistence on the proper planting of trees to provide screens, and little understanding of the problems of landscaping. It was fortunate that the

Nyman's Sussex. Bequest 1954

Sheffield Park Gardens, Sussex. Bought in 1954

The Dining Room, Saltram, Devon. Plasterwork, carpet, and furniture designed by Robert Adam. Transferred through the Treasury in 1957

The Cartoon Gallery, Knole, Kent. Given in 1946

Trust with staff and local support was able in a limited measure to do something to mitigate the new menace. Camps, where the Trust has been able to acquire land, have been removed from inappropriate sites, but the proper solution to the problem, the provision of cheap and well-designed chalet-bungalows, unfortunately far exceeded the resources of a private organisation. It is only fair to say that the Trust has lately received the valuable support of the Planning Authority. As the results of earlier decisions became all too apparent, policy has been reviewed. In Cornwall, as often elsewhere, what the Trust can achieve must in large measure depend on the cooperation of the local authorities. It is being given with increasing understanding.

Though the threat to the Cornish coast has changed—railways, cars, caravans—the strong concern of Cornishmen, which is the most effective means to combat it, has not. Nowhere, except in the Lake District, has local generosity and local feeling played so important a role. The first great benefactor, the donor of the Dodman, preserves his anonymity nearly fifty years later. The names of other Cornish donors, such as Sir Courtney Vyvyan, Donald Thomas, Lord St. Levan, T. P. Fulford, Sir John Carew Pole, J. C. Williams, are gratefully recorded. But the man to whom the Cornish coast and the Trust in Cornwall owe most is Treve Holman. An engineer, like his father and grandfather, responsible for the running of an industrial concern that would have fully occupied most men, he found time to fight for Cornwall persistently and with good effect. Secretary and later chairman of the Cornish branch of the Council for the Preservation of Rural England—the senior county branch of this organisation—he for years made the conservation of the coast his first concern. When news of ill-judged development reached him, a council of war was held at his country house near Truro, a plan concerted, and the developing enemy either shamed by conscience or thwarted by well-timed intervention. Enlisting the help of Cornishmen no less dedicated, such as Bishop Hunkin of Truro and Sir Arthur Quiller-Couch, he roused local opinion and gave direction to the movement which brought to the Trust before the launching of Enterprise Neptune sixty miles of coast.

THE LAKE DISTRICT

The changing dangers that menace landscape and the debt that the Trust owes to the concern of local men can be as well illustrated in the Lake District, where some 90,000 acres, one-sixth of the National Park, are now owned or controlled. Here also the first danger came with the railways and it affected principally, indeed almost exclusively, the lakesides, which were developed with large hotels and with villas, many in a vaguely Italianate style. The villas were built by prosperous businessmen, a class that was commuting from Manchester to Windermere before the end of the nineteenth century. It followed that the Trust's energies were concentrated on the lake shores. Brandelhow (1902) and Manesty (1908) on Derwentwater, and Aira Force and Gowbarrow Fell (1906) on Ullswater, were among the first acquisitions and typical of the period. That more was achieved in early years in the Lakes than in Cornwall was due to Canon Rawnsley, who lived at Keswick and acted as the Trust's tireless representative in the area.

Concern for the upper reaches of the dales dates from 1929, and coincides with the gift of farms at the head both of Great Langdale and the Duddon valley. It is difficult to believe that these acquisitions did not reflect, as did those at a similar date in Cornwall, an appreciation of the new danger which motorcars and consequential development presented to areas which had previously seemed safe. The next thirty-five years witnessed the Trust's efforts to obtain control of the daleheads, such as those of Wasdale, Borrowdale, Duddon, and Eskdale, which were seen to be extremely vulnerable. The success of these efforts—here again there is a parallel with Cornwall—owed much to the appointment in 1937 of a local agent/representative, Bruce Thompson, with an area office, and the establishment of an active Lake District Committee in 1942.

The postwar problems raised by caravans in the Lake District have been more happily solved than in Cornwall, largely owing to the early appreciation by the Planning Authority of the complex issues involved. In reaching a solution the Trust has played a useful part. At the same time steadily increasing access to the Lake District, particularly in the last decade, has prompted a further change of emphasis in the policy of conservation. Though even ten years ago concern was predominantly for the daleheads, today when these areas attract a volume of traffic that cannot be easily absorbed in spite of Trust ownership the emphasis is shifting to control of the lower stretches of the dales and of additional fell and lake shore. This for two reasons: first, to draw off the public from overcrowded areas, and secondly to provide the solitude which a minority come to find. These aims might appear to be incompatible. They are not. At Fell Foot (1948–53), at the south-east corner of Windermere, there are carefully-sited tent and caravan camps, a café, and sailing and canoeing clubs. By contrast at The Side (1949), there are nearly 900 acres of perfect solitude on the south of Ennerdale. As pressure grows, this policy for the dispersion of visitors from the more notable and popular areas to others where they can find, as taste dictates, recreation or quiet will assume increasing importance.

In the Lakes the Trust's work has been carried forward on a strong tide of local patriotism. Its supporters in this area have not been the usual tenacious minority fighting desperate actions, but a force with a long record of battle honours advancing confidently to new positions. Widespread dedication to the cause of the Lakes dates from the time of the Romantic Poets and finds expression not only in the Trust but in such valuable organisations as the Friends of the Lake District founded in 1934. Where so many have made a contribution it is difficult to mention individuals, but it would be impossible to omit the name of Canon Rawnsley whose association with Borrowdale has contributed to the acquisition of over fifty properties in the valley, of G. M. Trevelyan, of Beatrix Potter, and not least of Sir Samuel Scott, the first and active chairman of the Lake District Committee. Such names exemplify in striking fashion how success is almost always the outcome of a joint operation in which local support and the machinery of the Trust play complementary roles.

2

The Estates Committee is charged with the management of the Trust's land. It is an expert body and its members currently include the Director of the Natural History Museum, the recent Director of the Nature Conservancy, and the President of the Youth Hostels Association. Lord De La Warr, the present Chairman, who succeeded G. M. Trevelyan in 1949, has been Parliamentary Secretary for Agriculture, and Chairman of the Agricultural Research Council[1]. The Committee also has its specialist advisers on such matters as ecology, physiography, and housing.

Set up in 1899, the Committee's terms of reference were:

1. To deal with all matters arising in connection with the properties of the Trust;
2. To expend on repairs and maintenance of the properties of the Trust sums not exceeding the revenue derived from those properties.

Though, with the creation of the Historic Buildings Committee in 1945, historic buildings and their surroundings were removed from its direct purview, the management and finance of estates and open spaces, subject to the overriding control of the Executive Committee, remain as in 1899 the Estates Committee's primary responsibilities. The complexity and importance of these responsibilities are illustrated in the following pages.[2]

The policies initiated by the Estates Committee are carried out by the area staff. England and Wales are at present divided into fifteen areas.[3] These vary in size and may comprise a single county, as in Cornwall with its many properties, or larger regions such as Wessex, and East Anglia. Each area office is in the charge of an area agent, often helped by one, and sometimes by two, assistant agents.[4] On the efficiency of these men, who are qualified land agents, the successful management of the properties ultimately depends. They have a tradition of loyalty to the Trust and are dedicated to its cause.

In implementing management policy agents work closely with the Chief Agent in London, with the Trust's regional committees (or where these do not yet exist with the regional representatives), and not least with local committees. The latter, of which there are eighty-three, date for the most part from early days when the Trust had no area staff and when it was set policy 'almost always', as the Estates Committee stated in 1913, to establish a voluntary local committee to assume the care of important new acquisitions. The concern of local committees is usually confined to single properties and their members are recruited among residents in the area. The powers of local committees vary, some enjoying managerial responsibility, while others are advisory. The more active local committees carry a burden of work which would otherwise fall on the area agents. The latter often act as secretaries to local committees, and attend local committee meetings. The Estates Committee from time to time organises a conference of local committees to discuss policy on current issues and publishes a handbook on the management of Trust property for their guidance.

Area agents in addition to secretarial staff sometimes employ a head forester and a clerk of works with a small building team. The labour force varies widely from one area to another and is chiefly dependent on two factors: first, the number of properties where wardens are required to supervise public access; secondly, the amount of woodland. The Trust employs several hundred wardens and many of them give their services free. On the Longshaw Estate in Derybshire, to take a single example, there is a rota of forty voluntary wardens. Though the Trust does not farm, it manages woods that vary in size from spinneys to forests. Thus an agent whose area includes extensive woodlands may employ a number of foresters. On the Ashridge, Blickling, Clumber, and Holnicote estates there are seven woodmen; at Brockhampton and

Ickworth six. Wherever the Trust owns gardens the area agent is responsible, after consultation with the representative or Gardens Adviser, for the appointment of gardeners. There are six at Hidcote and Nymans, eight at Blickling, and twenty at Bodnant (see Chap. 13).

The varied tasks which the Trust's area machinery is designed to carry out may be considered under three separate heads: access, conservation, and the management of land to produce revenue. The first is concerned with the Trust's duty to the public, the second with its duty to the future, and the third with the simple necessity to derive from its farms and woods sufficient income both to maintain its estates as a good landlord should and to contribute to the expenses of the Trust's general administration. Conservation and land management are considered in Chapters 10 and 11.

3

The Trust owns some 360,000 acres, much of it farmland. There cannot be unrestricted access to tenanted farms, to young plantations and woods where forestry operations are in progress, or to nature reserves where the preservation of rare fauna and flora is paramount. There is none the less access to over 200,000 acres, which include some of the most beautiful vales, downs, moors, heaths, and coastland in the country. Access to open spaces is almost always free to those on foot, though at some twenty properties charges are made for car-parking.[5]

Two things follow from public access: the obligation first for supervision and secondly for facilities so that people derive the maximum pleasure from their visits. Both can be costly and they impose a severe financial strain on properties where there is little or no revenue.

Every year many millions enjoy the Trust's open spaces. This widespread access is one of the chief purposes of the Trust. None the less its very volume creates serious problems which first began to preoccupy the Executive Committee in 1946. A careful tally on a bank holiday weekend at Clumber Park in 1955 showed an estimated 50,000 visitors. By 1964 the estimate had risen to 106,000. In the following year at Hatfield Forest there were 28,300 cars, and at Runnymede 80,000. Litter was a concern as early as 1924, and six years later two hundred sacks of it were collected on Box Hill after a Whitsun weekend.[6] With the dumping of refuse and derelict cars on Trust property, litter begins to assume a quality of nightmare. No less worrying is the persistent hooliganism at many properties, particularly those near industrial centres such as Allen Banks in Northumberland. Even innocent visitors tend to damage trees, break fences and start fires. Uncontrolled dogs worry sheep, and deer are poisoned by the refuse of pleasant picnics.[7] On certain open spaces there is interference with the commoners' grazing rights.

Ability to control abuses derives from the bye-laws. First promulgated in 1909 they are from time to time revised and resubmitted to the Home Office for approval. Though recourse is rarely had to proceedings under the bye-laws, they provide the sanction which enables the Trust to prohibit the destruction of trees and fences, the lighting of fires, and other things likely to cause damage or to annoy visitors.

A grave damage, and one which bye-laws are powerless to prevent, is the long-term effect of an excessive number of visitors on plant and animal ecology. If more than a given number of people in a given year pass over a dale or mountain path, regeneration becomes impossible and erosion follows. The bald and widening tracks scarring Dovedale that convert to morass in bad weather, and certain favourite cross-country routes in the Lakes, are sad indications of this. At Kinver Edge in Staffordshire, and Kynance Cove in Cornwall, which are much visisted, the sward over large areas has been completely destroyed and erosion has set in. Consequently it has proved necessary to close and fence parts of the land in order to restore the natural ground cover. Sand dunes create a similar problem and have proved extremely vulnerable to constant access.

The problems posed by the welcome but alarming increase in the number of visitors can be tackled in two ways. The first is a corresponding increase in the number of wardens. The Trust accepts this as an expensive necessity. They now constitute a growing army, recruited to help, advise, and control the public. Many wardens are countrymen, sometimes naturalists or retired foresters, and their knowledge contributes directly to the pleasure of visitors. Happily people are often ready to serve as part-time wardens in a voluntary capacity. Reference has been made to the wardens at Longshaw. At Brownsea Island, where the fire danger is acute, no less than fifty people in the summer give unpaid service as watchers and wardens.

The second course open to the Trust, and one to which its publicity must be progressively directed, is to achieve a wider dispersal. The putative airman and buzzard, whose comprehensive vision has been thought of as ranging over Trust land, look down indifferently on properties that seem to stir like anthills or that preserve an almost Saxon solitude. The Trust's aim must be to spread the load, alleviating the pressure where it grows intolerable and dispersing it to spaces that may still be called 'open'. There is little danger in this. Solitude will always remain for those who wish to find it.

Apart from closure, which is contrary to Trust policy and which can only be justified for limited periods in desperate cases, there is a third course which the Trust may in extremity be forced to adopt at certain properties if numbers continue to increase as they have in the last decade. It is the control of access by rationing. The brake could be applied either by charging an admission fee, or, as has proved necessary at one country house, by limiting the numbers admitted on a given day. The Trust hopes that such measures can be avoided. They would only be necessary at peak periods. It is well to recall that most wardens have a well-earned rest for six months, that dense visitor traffic is usually as temporary as the holiday season, and that many of the airman's most restless anthills enjoy a long winter quiet.

A PLANNED WELCOME

At one time it was enough that the Trust's open spaces should exist. A limited number of people were happy to find them. Nature and the visitor met; this was sufficient. The latter expected, and needed, no special services. In the last twenty years numbers and the motorcar have altered this simple confrontation. As a result the Trust has recognised a responsibility to provide a variety of services which in the changed circumstances of the times will promote creative contact between the countryside and the visitor. In providing these services the Trust must always think not only of the public, but of the future. It follows that every service, whether it is a car park, a camping site, or a lavatory, must be so planned and situated that the landscape can absorb it and suffer no damage. It also follows that there are properties, usually of small extent, where such facilities have not been, and can never be, provided. Their provision would be ruin to the very land whose character the Trust is charged to preserve.

Within the limitations imposed on the Trust by its primary purpose, much in recent years has been done, and at a greatly accelerating pace, to make its lands more accessible and more acceptable to visitors. The work, once again, is costly and owes a growing debt to the local authorities who frequently exercise their statutory powers to make grants for car parks, lavatories and other services, or provide them at their own expense.

The first requisite is that people should be able to find the land which is thrown open to them. The Trust *Atlas*, and the precise directions with grid reference given in the *List of Properties*, reach a limited public. Informative signposting is therefore essential. It receives careful attention and a report on signposting is submitted annually to the Executive. No less important are approaches to properties and the routes across them. New roads of access have recently been made, but they are not always within the means of the Trust nor do they always accord with the belief that the countryside is best seen on foot. By contrast new paths, particularly in areas such as Cornwall, the Lake District and Northern Ireland are regularly opened. This often entails delicate negotiation with farm tenants, and with private owners whose land breaks the continuity of a Trust estate. In association with paths in the Lake District some twenty new stiles are put up every year. These are equally welcome to walkers and to the farm tenants whose freestone walls and fences are spared destruction. The Estates Committee ensures that the design of stiles is in conformity with local tradition.

CARS, CAMPS AND CARAVANS

Nothing is less attractive in the country than a scatter of cars. They must be shepherded into car parks. There are now some 180 on Trust land. They cannot be pretty things, but they can, and must, be well sited and if possible well screened. The Trust has repeatedly proved that on carefully chosen sites they can be relatively innocuous. Anticipating where car parks will ultimately be wanted, the Trust starts planting the necessary screen of trees some years ahead. In the Lake District mountain ash seem to provide the most suitable cover. As a matter of policy car parks are set well back from the places that people come to visit. To walk a quarter or even half a mile is a small price to pay for the preservation of the natural character of a dalehead, waterfall, lake or beach.

The Executive Committee first considered requests for camping sixty years ago, and immediately after the First World War it was decided that no *general* permission could be given to camp on Trust land open to the public. This is still the position, though in fact the hiker with his tent and his rucksack is encouraged almost everywhere and is free of the vast high-level areas which the Trust owns in the Lake District and Snowdonia. Formal camp sites, and this applies equally to the caravan sites for which a need has arisen in the last twenty years, pose more complicated problems. Siting again is a vital consideration. Camps must be so placed and screened that the confidence of those who gave lands to the Trust for preservation as open spaces is not betrayed. Arrangements, which always cost money, must be made for sanitation, refuse, and control. Seventy-three camp and caravan sites have now been established, often with the help of local authorities and other bodies such as the Caravan Club of Great Britain, the Camping Club, and the Boy Scouts' Association. A case has even occurred where ill-sited caravans have been welcomed from adjoining land to Trust property where they could be screened and placed inoffensively. Most progress has been made in the Lake District, where the Trust's belief that careful siting can make camps and caravans acceptable has sometimes led to the adoption of a more liberal policy than the Planning Authority thought justified. New camp sites in Great Langdale and Wasdale have been particularly successful, putting an end to indiscriminate camping in the daleheads. In 1966 Langdale accommodated some 20,000 campers and produced a net revenue of £1,000. It proved conclusively that in proper conditions the concentration of campers and caravans is a positive contribution to the preservation of the landscape.

Campers and caravaners affect the Trust's tenants. Many working farmers find them an intolerable nuisance. Others welcome them as a source of income. Where a tenant holds a farm under an agreement with a previous landowner, the Trust often has no control over tents and caravans, but something can be done to close obnoxious sites by rent concessions and persuasion. Often tenants can be induced to shift camps to better screened and less prominent fields.

ADVENTURE AND RELAXATION

Many open spaces provide ideal mountaineering and adventure training. Wild country could not be put to better use. In the heart of Snowdonia permission has been given to build mountaineering huts (plans and materials are approved by the Trust), and in Derbyshire and Yorkshire where the adjoining Hope Woodlands and Derwent Estates cover 22,500 acres, mainly moorland, over twenty-nine different bodies use the area for adventure training. Provision for another sort of adventure—sailing—is made at seventy-four properties inland or on the coast. Last year a new and much-needed jetty was built at Brownsea Island. The more contemplative find fishing on sixty different inland waters. Where appropriate there are sports grounds (18) and children's playgrounds (15). In 1966 £25,000 was spent on such facilities.

The story of recent events at Stonehenge illustrates the Trust's concern for improved services and how they can be combined with intelligent conservation. As early as 1900 the Trust was preoccupied about the future of this great Neolithic monument. Eventually the circle and a small protective area came into the keeping of the Ministry of Works, while the Trust acquired most of the surrounding downland. This division of responsibility made control difficult. Ticket kiosks and wire fences began to mar the site. Following an unacceptable request from the Ministry to build a restaurant on Trust land, consultation took place between the two bodies and in 1961 the Trust proposed a scheme for the better presentation of Stonehenge. It received the generous support of the Ministry on whom most of the cost will fall. The scheme, which involves the lease of Trust land to the Ministry, the diversion of a track in front of Stonehenge (which was used for indiscriminate car-parking), and the creation of an underpass below the main road, will enable fences to be swept away and all the existing huts to be placed underground. At the same time facilities for the public—a sales counter and a snack bar—will be improved. Most important of all, the traveller from the west will see Stonehenge in uncluttered splendour much as it appeared in earlier times.

Mention must be made of the Trust's holiday cottages. Reduction of labour with the mechanisation of farming, and the amalgamation of tenancies on hill farms where grazing is poor, has led to cottages falling vacant that are not needed for local housing. Many people prefer a fortnight's holiday in a remote cottage to the bustle, restrictions, and expense of lodgings at a seaside resort. For them the Trust furnishes and lets its redundant cottages. There are now fifty-five and the number increases each year. They are usually booked many months ahead and clearly fulfil a want. They also produce a useful revenue.

Chapter 10

The Countryside: Conservation

I

Landscape is continually changing. The character of the English countryside which we tend to regard as immemorial is for the most part recently acquired. In the Lake District the harmonious accord between the works of man and nature is hardly older than the eighteenth century. Even the stone walling that provides so satisfactory a counterpoint to the flowing line of dale and fell dates from the enclosures of that period. Though the pattern of the Lake District, the seemly scale on which its beauty so largely depends, is pre-eminently worth keeping, it does not follow that less successful patterns must necessarily be sacrosanct and that a countryside is perfect because it is familiar. The approach to landscape must be empiric and, since decisions depend largely on aesthetic judgments, few rules can be laid down. Hence much of the difficulty of the Trust's primary task of conservation.

PARKLAND AND CONTROL OF LANDSCAPE

Since landscape is not static, it follows that conservation must be positive. To maintain the character of fen or valley, of wood or parkland, calls for creative action. The Trust is continually *making* landscape. Parks are not the least of its creative problems. The timber on which the imaginative landscape layouts of the eighteenth century so much depend is reaching its term. In recent generations there has been little thought for the future.[1] If our parks, among the most beautiful features of the countryside and without parallel in Europe, are to exist in another hundred years they must be replanted and the job must be done with as much intelligence and vision as was shown two centuries ago. In 1961 a comprehensive scheme was launched to meet this challenge. A planting plan is being drawn up for every park. After approval in London most of these plans are now being carried out, phased over five, ten, and even twenty year periods. They will ensure the survival of parkscape. The replanting of decaying and gat-toothed avenues presents a comparable problem. With imagination much else can be done to restore

95

the harmonious relationship of a great house and its landscape. By the removal of fences and the reinstatement of ha-has, the unity of a lost composition can be rediscovered, as was recently demonstrated at Saltram and Lanhydrock. Policy also maintains parks as grassland. A number of parks have been acquired with tenancies that permit ploughing; whenever possible they are returned to pasture. It is understandable that the private owner should sometimes split and plough his park to obtain a greater return. The Trust has other obligations.

In the maintenance of existing woodlands the need for creative conservation is generally recognised. It is no less necessary where the shape of a valley or the background to a vista seem to call for the added weight and colour of trees. This may mean new planting or, as is now happening at Blake's Wood in Essex and at Hembury on the southern flank of Dartmoor, the gradual conversion of coppice into high forest by a process of thinning. The tendency of woodland to change, sometimes for reasons that are not fully understood, has economic implications for the private owner. For the Trust different issues are involved. At Holne Woods in Devon the old timber cover is mysteriously and spontaneously changing from oak to beech. The change is being studied by the Nature Conservancy, but its effect on the surrounding landscape, its significance as part of a visual pattern, prompt aesthetic considerations to which the Trust must give thought.

Visual problems posed by the conservation of ancient open-timbered forests, such as Hatfield with its chases, are particularly difficult. Hedgerow trees present another problem. They are perhaps the most characteristic feature of the English countryside, and in counties such as Berkshire the hedgerow elms are the most significant element in the landscape composition. Mechanical hedge-trimming prevents the emergence of replacements as the old trees disappear. Positive measures are necessary, and the area agent's eye must attempt the felicitously haphazard *pointillisme* of nature. The adverse changes affecting commons have for years been a matter of national concern (see Chapter 7). When few commoners exercise their rights, and fewer still own sheep, the ungrazed commons degenerate into scrub. The thorn thickets grow impenetrable and the pleasant swards are lost. Only labour maintains the traditional character both of commons and of most other lands for which the Trust is responsible. In England natural plant succession will usually produce in the end woodland of one type or another. The vegetation of the Trust's Surrey heaths with their heather cover would transform to sombre pinewoods if the seedlings were not checked.

The need for creative conservation is nowhere better illustrated than in the fens. At Wicken and Burwell the Trust owns almost all that is left of the once extensive fens of the Great Level. There is nothing in England like this area with its unusual plant, insect, and bird life. The invasion of scrub began in the nineteenth century, and when sedge after the last war ceased to be economically profitable, and large areas were no longer cut, buckthorn spread rapidly. It threatened to destroy the area visually and ecologically. As the result of action by the Local Committee the invasion has been stemmed, the invader is being laboriously eradicated, and true fen vegetation restored.[2]

NATURE RESERVES

At a number of properties such as Wicken Fen the conservation of plant, animal, and insect life, takes precedence over the aesthetics of landscape, though they are interconnected. Much Trust land offers a refuge for rare species and was given that they might be protected. It is policy to record and conserve those species already present, and to establish others by providing a suitable environment.

On one of the Lake District properties twenty different mammals have been recorded. Some of the coastal areas, such as Scolt Head, Blakeney, and Whiteford Burrows are famous for their ducks and waders. Among the rarer birds which have bred recently on Trust land are kites, choughs, corncrakes, and Dartford warblers. On several of its Surrey commons the Trust undertakes the clearance of scrub in order to produce a habitat for the woodlark. This bird of limited and local range has repaid the attention by nesting in areas specially cleared for the purpose.

The Trust's open spaces are the home of botanical rarities. They include a number of orchids, chalk-loving species on the downs, and small plants that inhabit remote rock-faces. The Martagon lily is to be found on Trust land almost within the London suburbs. North Wales properties harbour *serotina Lloydii* and curious Alpine survivals from the Ice Age. On East Anglian estates can be found belladonna, bog parsnip, marsh fern, marsh pea, bladderwort, and water violets, and in the Midlands that rarity *ledum groenlandicum*, whose seed was perhaps brought by birds on migration. A single property in the north yields Jacob's ladder, baneberry, bog rosemary, cloudberry, bird's eye primula, and an unusual whitebeam.

Properties where rare animals, birds, or plants exist create a conflict of interest and with it problems of access. Some places by reason of their unique ecological character and the existence of very local or rare species must be treated primarily as nature reserves. Human beings in large numbers would be destructive of the essential work of conservation. Certain areas must be established as sanctuaries to which only naturalists have access. To others the public can be safely admitted outside the breeding season. This is an unfortunate deprivation, but it must be remembered that from closed nature reserves, where rare species are able to establish themselves, distribution to other areas will often follow. Nature reserves have benefited those who were never able to visit them.

The protection and active encouragement of flora and fauna are specialised skills. The Trust is fortunately able to obtain expert help. Seven properties, including Scolt Head, are managed by the Nature Conservancy and fourteen by naturalist societies; others, such as Malham in Yorkshire, by the Field Studies Council. Yet others, such as Blakeney Point and Wicken Fen, are managed by expert local committees. Such arrangements enable areas primarily of interest for their natural history to be maintained as open air laboratories where surveys can be carried out, field courses conducted, and hides set up. At the same time knowledgeable management can judge the maximum public access that is safe, while ensuring that it is properly supervised. Only the presence of expert wardens makes it possible for places such as Blakeney Point (a breeding ground for three species of tern, oystercatchers, ringed plover, redshank, and rarer birds) to be open during the breeding season.

Over thirty-five years ago the menace of the grey squirrel first claimed the attention of the Estates Committee and problems of a similar nature, such as the destruction caused by the rapidly increasing number of roe deer, continue to do so. At the present moment the control of the oystercatcher population at Whiteford Burrows in Glamorganshire, where the birds are said to be damaging the local cockle industry, poses a delicate issue in conservation. This is an aspect of the Trust's activity which closely concerns many members. There are those who regarded the excavation of a new mere at Wicken Fen in 1955, at the cost of several thousand pounds, to provide a much-needed habitat for wildfowl, of greater importance than the contemporary acquisition of palladian splendour at Clandon Park, and who look on the achievement in the Farne Islands, where the grey seal population quadrupled in fifteen years, and the eider duck now nests in vast numbers, as one of the Trust's greatest triumphs. The fact that the control of the grey seals led to profound controversy between 1963 and 1966, and to much feeling among members of the Trust, is perhaps a useful reminder of the complexity of nature conservation and the strong feelings that it arouses.

Creative in a pedestrian but no less useful fashion are the extensive works of improvement which the Trust carries out as a matter of routine, though an expensive routine, when properties come into its ownership. Typical operations are the demolition of hutments and gun positions on coastal headlands, and the removal of a clutter of sheds at Coxwell to reveal the splendour of a thirteenth-century tithe barn. At Attingham forty acres of airstrip have been broken up and returned to agricultural use; 80,000 tons of rubble were removed. In Cornwall over 100,000 tons have been lifted, the detritus of the War Department.

THE HUMAN ELEMENT

Where ownership brings the Trust into contact with people, and where the aesthetics of landscape link closely with human and social factors, creative conservation is particularly complicated. The Trust, like most landlords today, appreciates the value of the amalgamation of small farms to create more economic units, yet it also recognises a special responsibility for the maintenance of rural communities. The two are not always compatible. In the mountainous areas of North Wales where groups of scattered farms form small homogeneous societies centred round the local chapel, and sustain a tradition of verse, song and drama, the indiscriminate amalgamation of tenant holdings would reduce the population until its numbers were insufficient to form a satisfactory community. The traditional framework would break up, the life would become lonely, and the drift to the towns would accelerate. Eventually the hills would become ranched areas and the pattern of a self-reliant rural society, providing much of its own recreation, would distintegrate.[3]

Dolaucothi in South Wales is one of a number of estates which present a similar social challenge. The farms are small and most of the tenants are old. Only a management sympathetic to local problems, and prepared to sacrifice a maximum economic return in the interest of human values, is likely to induce a younger generation to carry on. In the absence of young men attached to the land as their fathers were, such estates will become depopulated *latifundia*. Even nearer London the same challenges exist. In recent years Stourton on the Stourhead estate has lost its parson, its policeman, and its school. Its future seems to be that of a beautiful cadaver, the dead though elegant preface to the most famous of eighteenth-century landscapes.

At Styal, in Cheshire, the Trust is attempting the ambitious revival of a moribund village. Built in the late eighteenth century to house the labour for a cotton mill, the village is a rare example of early industrial planning. Its eighty cottages are for the most part still occupied by the descendants of the millworkers. Modernisation and amalgamation will in due course reduce the number of cottages to sixty. Meanwhile the large vegetable gardens which were provided with the cottages 150 years ago lie derelict. The cottagers prefer to buy their vegetables. A landscape architect has been called in and a new plan drawn up for the village. While respecting the valuable features of the eighteenth-century scheme, it involves the provision of garages, the reduction of the gardens, and the removal or realignment of fences, hedges, and paths. It will give a new coherence to Styal and it is hoped, in conjunction with cottage modernisation, a new vitality.

In flourishing villages, such as Lacock and West Wycombe, where there is a housing shortage, the Trust has a different social contribution to make. Such villages, architecturally distinguished and enjoying the guarantee of Trust protection, attract outsiders. There are half-a-dozen applicants of means for every vacant cottage. If money were the sole criterion such cottages could be let handsomely to weekenders and retired businessmen: a profitable course that would destroy the village community as effectively as has happened in many parts of the Cotswolds. The Trust thinks it right to give preference to the families who have long lived in such villages, thus conserving their spirit and tradition.

Lacock may be taken to exemplify the Trust's policy in such a village. In 1944 ninety-one cottages in this village, one of the most beautiful in England and with a strong sense of community, were acquired by gift with Lacock Abbey. Nearly £42,000 was spent between 1961 and 1965, mainly on modernisation, while rents received in the same period amounted to only £17,500. The area agent has applications from 120 'outsiders' many of whom would be prepared in return for leases to bear the costs of modernisation themselves. He has felt justified in accepting only four. It can be argued that the reconciliation of a financial predicament and a duty towards the villagers might admit of a slightly higher percentage. The Trust has preferred to err on the side of social discretion.

BUILDING AND STREET FURNITURE

Cottages must be modernised. This can most effectively be done by the amalgamation of two cottages when there is vacant possession of both,

The Red Drawing Room, Waddesdon Manor, Buckinghamshire. The State
Rooms contain the superb Rothschild collection. Bequeathed in 1957

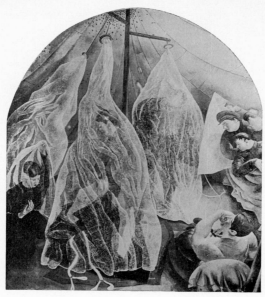

Tent in Macedonia by Stanley Spencer. Mural at Sandham Memorial Chapel
Given in 1947

Murals by Lanscroon on the Staircase at Powis Castle. Given in 1952

but whatever the method creative conservation must ensure that appropriate materials are used and that additions and alterations accord with, for instance, the character of a village street. One of the growing problems is the provision of garages, but it is remarkable how often these can be innocuously contrived at the back of cottages and with access to a subsidiary road rather than to the main street. New farm buildings pose related problems of siting, design, and materials. In some places there will be no alternative to a traditional building. In others a modern design well sited will be acceptable provided elementary solecisms—such as the use of exposed brickwork and red-tiled roofs in a stone and slate area, or recourse to green paint out of doors—are avoided. In some situations the Trust sees no objection to the modern Dutch barn with asbestos roof. The relation of new buildings to old, in a word grouping and the shape of the farm, is often more important in the landscape setting than the materials used.

The growing scarcity of certain traditional building materials makes the work of repairing and re-roofing buildings of an earlier period progressively more difficult. When demolitions are carried out, the Trust consequently steps in to buy old tiles or stone slates for later use. There is also a shortage of craftsmen for certain types of work, such as thatching, though the Rural Industries Bureau does much to promote special skills. The Trust, owning a large number of thatched buildings, including one or two fine barns, is concerned to preserve thatch when it is slowly disappearing on most private estates.

Reference has been made to Lacock in the context of tenancies. It also provides an illustration of how, by action and persuasion, the Trust is able to improve the detail of its villages by attention to such things as television aerials, wirescape, notices, and street furniture. With the help of a grant from the Chase Charity a communal television aerial, inconspicuously sited, has been installed to serve the whole village. It gives better reception than did the forest of private aerials which the Trust has removed. At the same time with the cooperation of the Post Office and the Electricity Board the four main streets have been largely freed from wirescape. Thanks to the helpful attitude of the local council it has been possible to avoid lamp standards of unsuitable scale and to light the village with lanterns of traditional type. Ownership of most of the shops and cottages has enabled the Trust to insist on decent fascia boards and simple lettering on notices. Such improvement can be carried out without in any way allowing villages to develop an old-world flavour. The County Council in 1964 made an important contribution at Lacock by providing a bypass.

NEGATIVE CONSERVATION

Though much of the Trust's activity is positive and ensures that good things happen to the countryside in desirable ways, negative conservation is an inevitable aspect of its work. As it tends to get into the press, it is the aspect of which the public is most often aware. Battles, protests, and public enquiries, reach the headlines: much else does not. It is learnt in the papers that the Trust has turned down a proposal for an ill-sited caravan camp, has shifted a car park inland from a beach, has in the face of protest demolished an ice cream kiosk and shacks for the sale of souvenirs (as was recently the case in Cornwall and at the Giant's Causeway). The wider reference, the policy that lies behind such action, and the fact that it is undertaken in the long-term interest of the public is not always apparent.

Planning legislation for all its imperfections, and due to the cooperation of many planning authorities, has greatly reduced the physical threat to Trust land. Fewer battles are now fought. On the other hand the engagements tend to be more serious and the enemy more powerful since threats to the countryside come usually from government departments. The Trust is not always victorious, but the case for amenity well presented, and presented in good time, often triumphs or produces an acceptable compromise.

In Britain, owing to timely legislation, advertising is not the menace that it is on many parts of the Continent. The major threats come from building development, electricity projects, extraction of water from lakes and rivers, road widening schemes, and telecommunications. The vast towers, links in a nationwide microwave system, which are due to go up all over the country and which must be sited on high land, are a new and worrying development. At present none is projected on Trust property, and the Post Office by agreement consult the Trust as to the likely effect on amenity of the possible sites in each area. The co-operative attitude of the Post Office over the grounding of telephone wires has already been mentioned.

Inalienability (see Chapter 16) offers effective protection against building development on Trust land, as there cannot be compulsory acquisition without the will of parliament. It is on land adjacent to Trust property that the danger of building development exists and can sometimes be serious. An ill-sited petrol station or a broiler house placed just off Trust land can effectively spoil a stretch of country whose preservation is otherwise assured. Fortunately in such cases the Trust is usually consulted by the planning authority. But this is not always so, and from time to time neighbouring development must be resisted with the same determination as if it were on Trust land. Unhappily it cannot be resisted with the same assurance of success. Great Coxwell tithe barn, possibly the finest medieval barn in the country, was repaired at a cost of £14,000 in 1962. Within three years, in spite of the Trust's representations at two public enquiries, speculative building was permitted on neighbouring land across the road. Comparable cases have occurred elsewhere from time to time.

ELECTRICITY

The distribution of electricity is a necessary service that is particularly important to the Trust with its remote farms and cottages. It is the method of distribution which is sometimes at fault. There are areas of such scenic importance that supply routes must be carefully sited, and over strategic stretches wires must be underground. Before the First World War the Trust was protesting at wirescape in the Lake District and it is not surprising that in such an area some of the major battles have been fought, often, it must be confessed, with a chivalrous opponent. In 1948 the Ministry of Fuel and Power invoked the Trust's help in siting poles in Great Langdale. It was therefore disappointing nearly a decade later to discover that the electrification of Little Langdale and the area southwards to the head of Coniston water was being planned without consultation and that a request to the Electricity Board for information as to the proposed route was refused. When the scheme was eventually submitted it was highly unsatisfactory and the Trust had no choice but to oppose it. Better proposals were put forward and secured the support of the Minister of Fuel and Power. In spite of the fact that much of the line was underground, the revised scheme, as suggested by the Trust, proved cheaper to construct and more profitable to the Electricity Board. On another occasion inacceptable proposals for Borrowdale again led to energetic intervention and a satisfactory compromise was found. An agreement has now been reached for early consultation with the Electricity Board in the Lake District before proposals affecting Trust land receive planning approval. As a result new lines have been negotiated with little difficulty in the area of High Close and Loughrigg Tarn, in the Duddon valley, in Eskdale, and in Ennerdale. The story in the Lakes finds a parallel in other remote areas, though the Trust elsewhere has not always been able to achieve the same degree of co-operation with the Electricity Board.

High-tension cables, which can at present rarely be satisfactorily grounded, present a more intractable problem, but one which does not often occur in the context of remote and unspoilt country. There is little that the Trust can do about pylons but oppose ill-conceived routes and suggest more acceptable alternatives. It sometimes happens that a line planned to pass over Trust property is likely to be less damaging to the landscape pattern than if diverted elsewhere. In such cases the Trust does not oppose. Though in the Malvern Hills in 1951, where covenanted land was affected, it notably failed (owing to a legal technicality) to modify an unhappy scheme, on the whole its representations receive consideration. In 1958 a line was rerouted that would have passed in full view of Hardwick Hall. Five years later the Trust achieved the diversion of a line in the Dedham Vale, and in 1965 of lines affecting Benthall Hall in Shropshire and Lanhydrock in Cornwall.

MINING AND WATER EXTRACTION

In 1965 a proposal for opencast mining was defeated near Benthall Hall. Fortunately opencast has thus far affected only land adjacent to Trust property, and only at one or two places, such as Upton House and Hardwick Hall. In spite of the high standard of reinstatement now achieved, the damage done to the natural character of landscape is often irreparable. From deep mining the Trust has suffered more directly and repeated representations have been made to the Coal Board. Owing to mining subsidence, Penshaw Monument, an imposing Doric temple near Sunderland, has been closed to the public for several years, the level of the lake at Nostell Priory for a time dropped disastrously, and historic houses such as Moseley Old Hall have received damage. It is limited consolation that a pillar of coal has been left to support certain important Trust buildings and that compensation for subsidence is paid.

Since water is one of the most genial elements in any landscape, it is not surprising that the Trust owns many miles of lakeshore and riverside. The excessive extraction of water, usually for industry and often as the result of short-sighted plans hastily conceived, has by the unnatural lowering of water levels a disastrous effect on amenity. Where Trust property is affected there is clear duty to oppose it. Extraction is most dangerous in areas such as North Wales and the Lakes, and it is there that the Trust's fight to preserve the water level has received most publicity. Reference has been made (Chapter 7) to the schemes of the Liverpool and Manchester Corporations. The effect of water extraction can be almost equally unfortunate elsewhere, and proposals which would have affected Flatford Mill and the famous stretch of the Stour familiar from

Constable's paintings have been thrice successfully opposed in recent years by the Trust and other bodies.

Though the immediate result is less apparent, excessive water extraction also affects the character of the countryside by lowering the water table. In certain areas in the Midlands, such as the Trust's Clumber estate, where a generation ago the saturation point was some thirty feet below the surface, it has now sunk to twice that level. In such circumstances it is not only the wish for a quick financial return that prompts owners to plant surface-feeding trees, such as Scots and Corsican pine. The lowered water level is inevitably and adversely changing the face of the woods and the landscape.

ROADS

Reference is made in Chapter 16 to the problem created for the Trust by the construction of new motorways and carriageways which encroach on inalienable land. Broadly but hesitantly the Trust has taken the view, where the proposed route is the best possible and no reasonable alternative exists, that alienation is an evil to which, in the public interest, it must sometimes submit. By contrast, where a new route is clearly ill sited or would do irreparable damage to land of national importance the Trust recognises an obligation to fight. It has already expressed its determined opposition to bypass schemes that would disastrously affect Headley Heath, the Blickling estate, and the parks at Knole and Petworth. It will probably have to do so elsewhere. In such cases, if the need arises, it is ready to take the defence of its inalienable land to Parliament.

The Trust often regards the widening of country roads in remote districts, and they are those in which its properties are most often situated, as a more serious issue than motorways which tend to pass through populous areas. Road widening in remote districts is utterly destructive of the landscape scale. In the Lakes, Snowdonia, or a Devon valley, where everything is so nearly in perfect proportion, the widening of a road from fifteen to forty feet creates irreparable disharmony and introduces an alien note which alters the subtle balance of the landscape. The damage is done in the interests of a traffic which lasts from July to September. For most of the year the widened roads are empty, while it is now generally recognised, by all except those responsible, that such widening solves no traffic problems. Wider roads in such areas merely bring more cars. The landscape suffers but the road blockages grow more frequent.

Both the ill-effects of road widening in a remote valley and its futility are illustrated by Nantgwynant, where the Trust property of Hafod

Lwyfog lies in perhaps the loveliest valley that nature created or man enjoyed. A small road lately led between dry-stone walls to Pen-y-Gwryd, hesitated above the Nantgwynant valley, and plunged downward to emerge after many convolutions on the shores of an enchanting lake. The tarmac version of an immemorial route, it fitted the scale of narrow pastures and small farms. It was not an alien intrusion, and it did not scar the landscape. The hurrying motorist avoided it and pressed on by highways to Bangor or Caernarvon. Coaches feared to negotiate it. True, in places it was awkward to pass other cars, and it was always necessary to drive slowly. The scenery was the more appreciated. A road widening scheme has sliced off corners, gouged out the hillsides, and set a car park on a promontory. The road has become an intrusion. And to no purpose. For months it is little used, and in high summer it attracts so much casual traffic that frustrated drivers crawl through Nantgwynant in a queue and in the aura of petrol fumes. The valley will not be the same again. As was stated in the Annual Report for 1903, when the Trust opposed the Aberglaslyn railway farther down the same valley: 'It is futile to take large numbers of people to see a country whose attraction is its picturesqueness, if, in doing so, you destroy the very beauty they come to enjoy.'

The Trust has no choice but always to oppose such 'improvements' where the ownership of inalienable land gives it a responsibility and a right to intervene. Cautionary tales, such as that told at Nantgwynant, must not be repeated at the expense of other remote roads and lanes in Snowdonia, Cornwall, and the Lakes. With the opening of the M6 motorway the situation in the Lake District gives particular concern. In this area where man and nature have achieved so delicate and satisfactory a balance, there are projects not only for the widening of major roads, which may well be necessary, but for little roads that lead nowhere. Typical of this extravagance is a proposal for a carriageway up Langdale which will have *three lanes* as far as Skelwith Bridge. In an area where all the country is of outstanding beauty, and moreover in a National Park, this argues a degree of insensibility which passes comprehension. It also highlights a curious weakness in planning legislation. While planning permission is required for trivial alterations to a listed cottage, the Planning Authority has no right even of consultation in regard to Ministry of Transport schemes which can completely and for ever change the character of the landscape.

Only a farseeing plan can avert the grave threat to the Lake District. If the necessary money can be raised—it may well cost £25,000—the Trust, as the largest landowner in the area, hopes with the support of the National Parks Commission and the local Planning Board, to produce such a plan. It will be a comprehensive survey of traffic problems in the Lake District seen in relation to the special landscape qualities of the area. An eminent authority has agreed to undertake the survey on behalf of the Trust. His terms of reference, as suggested by the Trust's Regional Committee, are:

(a) To survey the Lake District and the surrounding area to assess the impact of increasing leisure and traffic upon the intrinsic character of the Lake District, distinguishing between those forms of recreation for which the district is by its nature fitted, and those which would be better pursued outside an area of great beauty, much of which still possesses the rare qualities of remoteness and quiet.

(b) To prepare a plan for roads, traffic control and transport which would allow the greatest possible enjoyment of the essential qualities of the Lake District without destroying them.

(c) To suggest ways of creating new focal areas for holidays in the country which surrounds it, especially the Pennines, the Cumberland coast, and the north shore of Morecambe Bay.

(d) To take account of long-term trends and indicate priorities, distinguishing between measures or controls which are permanently necessary and those which would only be needed at peak holiday periods.

(e) To study the feasibility of a West Coast main road to improve communications to the West Cumberland coast, both from the south and from the north, thus limiting the amount of traffic traversing the Lake District.

Such a survey would not only make an essential contribution to the conservation of the Lake District, but would establish principles applicable to road widening and traffic elsewhere in the deep countryside.

COVENANTED LAND

Covenanted land of its nature (see Chapter 16) involves negative conservation. Covenants give the Trust control over such things as building development or the felling of timber. The exercise of this control is often difficult. Moreover covenants cannot protect land from compulsory acquisition by local authorities. The problems posed by the maintenance of covenants are most acute in areas such as the Upper Thames valley, where the Trust some twenty-five years ago acquired covenants over an estate of 3,900 acres, including two villages. Pressure for development was then less intense. In the intervening period increasing resort to the Thames has created problems of car parking and caravans; there is a demand by weekenders for additions to simple cottages; and altered farming methods call for new farm buildings. All such changes must be approved by the Trust which, without the status of a landowner, has none the less a responsibility for the character of the area. Though strategically and scenically of the first importance, a part of the estate has not been designated as an area of Outstanding Natural Beauty, and the Trust cannot always rely on the support of the planning authority. Yet the problem of conservation, as so often elsewhere, is one of planning, of the reconciliation of new requirements with an existing landscape pattern. This reconciliation the Trust has constantly to attempt on all its covenanted land. In vetoing development it invariably does so in what it believes to be the long-term interests of the countryside.

Chapter 11

The Trust as Landlord

The Trust must make its estates self-supporting. To achieve this end its properties, whether the large agricultural holdings that provide an endowment for a great house or the scattered fields whose grazing covers the cost of maintaining a strip of coast, must yield an economic rent.

Each of the sixteen administrative areas is given a yearly financial target which the agents must try to attain. Their task is not easy. Properties were rarely acquired primarily as investments. Preserved for the quality of their landscape, they may be hill farms with excessive rainfall or salty pastures bordering the sea. Much is unproductive moorland. The Trust also owns an inordinate number of artificial lakes. These waters, which lend charm to many of its parks, are subject to the stringent provisions of the Reservoirs Act of 1930, and since many date from the eighteenth century they need attention. Dredging and the maintenance of dams are an abnormal and recurring expense.[1]

Farms given to the Trust are frequently remote and inconveniently situated; a stretch of beautiful country does not necessarily form a viable agricultural unit. Administration is complicated and holdings are often so scattered that it is uneconomic to employ direct labour. No agricultural company intent on a substantial return would look at most of the Trust's properties. Their spread and diversity create other problems. One agent must employ a Welsh-speaking staff; another must deal with the complexities of Ulster land tenure; a third must pass with equal competence from the repair of a palladian temple to the supervision of half-a-dozen public houses. At Charlecote the agent must ensure the survival of a flock of Jacob sheep, and at Boscastle in Cornwall of a rare example of the strip cultivation of the Middle Ages. Over 180 scheduled monuments are situated on Trust land.

Unlike the ordinary landowner, the Trust must reconcile access and farming. While recognising that the country is the workshop of the farmer, it must wherever possible and reasonable admit the public. Most types of access adversely affect tenants. The land they rent sustains the wear, tear, and damage. Disturbance to stock often makes it impossible to graze rough pasture beside paths; visitors even complain if they have to cross fields where cattle are pastured. If tenants are to have fair treatment, access may mean a reduction in farm rents. On the reletting of farms summer grazing has sometimes to be excluded, particularly on the coast. The tenant can only graze the land in winter and the Trust must accept a lesser return. Compensating income can sometimes be obtained, at properties with many visitors, from car park charges which bring in a net annual income of about £11,000, and from collecting boxes.

The Trust, as explained in the previous chapter, is also at a disadvantage in the maintenance of its farms and cottages. It cannot necessarily use, as another landlord might choose to do, the cheapest materials. Regardless of cost, it has a duty to maintain the character of good buildings, to see that thatch is replaced, and stone used when other materials would be inappropriate. Often post and rail fencing will be called for rather than something cheaper. Economic considerations can never be paramount, for the Trust holds most of its land for reasons of amenity.

WOODS

This is particularly true where its woods are concerned. Many are of great beauty. The lakeside woods of Cumberland, the woods of Hembury and Holne that overhang the Dart, of Watersmeet and Trelissick, all offering the magic combination of trees and water, the high wind-exposed stands of Haresfield in the Cotswolds, the beeches of Slindon, their trunks tall and smooth as the piers of a cathedral, the ancient oaks at Ickworth, the giant and yet more venerable Spanish chestnuts at Croft Castle, and the strange pollards at Toys Hill and Willoughby Cleeve—from these and numberless other Trust woods the surrounding countryside acquires much of its character. Certain properties, notably Gatton Park and Leith Hill Place in Surrey, Drovers in Sussex, and High Close and Allen Banks in the North, were accepted almost solely on account of the beauty of their woodlands. Such timber cannot be treated simply in terms of economic forestry.

Most of the Trust's woods were planted before 1850. With the agricultural depression in the second half of the nineteenth century little new afforestation was carried out. It follows that much timber is reaching its term and that if woods are to be preserved for future generations there must be a sustained programme of replanting. This is costly since the Trust's amenity policy rarely permits the clear felling of large areas. When natural regeneration cannot be successfully achieved, woods must be maintained by the felling of small areas and careful interplanting. Rejuvenation by selection felling must not destroy the shape of woods or the tapestry of colour and texture. The Trust must also for obvious reasons concentrate on native hardwoods. Though some income can be derived from spruces used as 'nurses', the broad-leaved trees will not yield a timber crop for a century and a half. The long-term policy is to create, by careful planting, woodlands which will hold timber of all ages, so that in time they can be cropped annually without damage to the landscape, and the forester, like the farmer, take a seasonal return from his labour. It is a policy, calling for great and continuing outlay, whose fruits are only realisable in terms of decades.

Conifers have long been a cause of dispute. When plantings first appeared in the Lake District in the late eighteenth century, Wordsworth contemptuously referred to them as 'vegetable manufactories'. Yet a larch plantation in early spring can be a thing of beauty, and a bold clump of Scots pine can add just the right note in a wild landscape. The Lake District valleys now owe much to some of the conifers planted for amenity in the nineteenth-century. Though the Trust's first concern as forester is the propagation of hardwoods, it does not reject the conifer. While recognising that conifers tend to be too uniform in colour and that their balding tops age ungracefully, it believes they can be planted—and plants them—in the right setting and with careful regard to contours and the avoidance of straight lines. The insensitive block plantations of commercial forestry that have done much to give the conifer a bad name are another matter.

The maximum possible access is given to woodlands. In this respect they do not present the same problems as farmland. Provided the public do not destroy wild life or young plantations, access does little damage. Woods seem to enjoy a multiple use. Places like Ashridge, Blackdown, Clumber Park, and Leigh Woods above the Avon Gorge, serve numberless people and thrive on it. The Trust's chief preoccupation arising from public access is fire, the forester's perpetual nightmare. At properties such as Brownsea and Holnicote there are teams of fire-watchers on duty throughout the summer.

The Trust owns nearly 40,000 acres of tree or scrub-covered land. Of this a large part is wild mountain slopes and gorges. The timber is often dwarf oak, such as characterises the steep-sided combes that run down to the Devon seaboard, beautiful but valueless. Extraction and planting are equally impracticable, and such woods must be left largely to nature and the process of regeneration. By contrast about 18,500 acres of the total are under active management.[2] They are controlled by the area agents with the help of a full time Forestry Adviser,[3] and a staff of 115 foresters and woodmen. Though a few minor woodland properties are dealt with by contract labour, the force employed by the Trust is well below that regarded as normal for forestry operations (one man per hundred acres). Owing to mechanisation and other economies the staff is also smaller, relative to the size of the woodlands managed, than it was ten or fifteen years ago. Of the 18,500 acres of managed woodland nearly 14,000 acres, which include most of the larger woods, enjoy the benefit of the special deed of dedication agreed with the Forestry Commission in 1952 (see Chapter 7). For the care and planting of these woods statutory grants are received. Owing to the understanding attitude of the Commission, these grants make it possible to reconcile timber production with amenity at reduced cost to the Trust. The Commission has proved increasingly sympathetic to the Trust's aims, and it is rare that the latter has to forego grants in order that old trees of exceptional beauty but no economic value may be retained.

A scheme for the progressive replanting of the Trust's woods began soon after the last war. On an average some two hundred acres have been replanted yearly. Until the mid-fifties operations showed an average annual profit of about £12,000. This was due to the felling of over-mature timber and to high market prices. In the following decade prices were halved and wages more than doubled. Since 1957 the Trust's woodlands have shown a deficit. In 1965, with 170 acres replanted, it amounted to nearly £31,000 on an expenditure of over £99,000. This is perhaps not a high price to pay in relation to the pleasure that the Trust's woods give all the year round to hundreds of thousands of people. The deficit is not attributable only to the price of timber, but to the special cost of amenity forestry and the charges resulting from public access (wardens, maintenance of paths, fences and stiles, collection of litter, car parking, and so on). Together these are estimated to account for between twenty and twenty-five per cent of the total labour costs of the Trust's forestry operations. These additional costs derive from a permanent obligation, and until such distant time as the new plantings become progressively ripe for felling the financial position can improve only with a rise in the price of timber.

RENTS

The Trust's income as landowner derives chiefly from farm rents; in 1966, 146,239 acres were leased for agriculture at a rental of £345,282. This land may be roughly divided into three types: lowland farms, hill farms, and land let without farm buildings, usually for grazing or horticulture. The return from these types of land was as follows:

	1966 Acreage	1966 Rent per acre	1956 Rent per acre (approx.)
Lowland farms	65,746	84s 1d	39s 2d
Hill farms	68,144	13s 1d	8s 5d
Land without buildings	12,349	39s 5d	—

Rents on lowland farms have more than doubled in a decade, and the present figure approaches the national average for lowland farms which in 1966 was 89s 6d. The return on hill farms over the same period represents an increase of some 55 per cent. Given the character of much of the Trust's land and the special conditions that apply, these increases have not been achieved without difficulty. They were in many cases the direct result of the policy of farm improvement referred to below.[4]

Sporting rights, let over nearly 20,000 acres, produce a substantial income. An East Anglian pheasant shoot, and coarse fishing on a lake in the Midlands, each bring in £2,500 a year. Though shooting is often let subject to public access and thus does not yield overall a high rent per acre, such contributions usefully supplement the finances of many Trust properties. Policy with regard to shooting, fishing, and hunting is unequivocal. Except on nature reserves, and in certain special circumstances, the Trust permits them when they were permitted under private ownership. Unless a donor has expressed a wish to the contrary, the Trust thus observes local custom.

Some thirty years ago there was a move among a minority of members to prohibit hunting and shooting on Trust land. A motion to this effect was overwhelmingly defeated at the Annual General Meeting in 1934. Even if the Trust were minded to do so, it would be impossible to prevent hunting and shooting on all its property. In areas such as the Lake District, where the fox has been hunted for centuries, much of the Trust's land is unenclosed and without clearly marked boundaries. On a number of properties the shooting rights have been reserved by the donors, and on most land the Ground Game Acts give tenants the right to take ground game.

FARM AND COTTAGE IMPROVEMENTS

Though the Trust's estates provide a valuable and increasing revenue, they have called since the war for large capital investment. In 1945 the arrears of farm and cottage improvements were formidable. Estates, often of great beauty, had come to the Trust with under-equipped farms and primitive cottages. In a changing agricultural economy, they were soon hopelessly out of date. The increase and even the maintenance of the rent roll, no less than social and humane considerations, made extensive modernisation imperative (see Chapter 6).

An improvement programme launched soon after the war has cost in all some £1,700,000. In recent years expenditure has been running at about £195,000 exclusive of government grants, and in 1967 an allocation of £205,000 was provided. Though a proportion of this expenditure has been met each year from special funds, the greater part has fallen on the free reserves of the Trust which are mainly derived from legacies and donations. Thus of the £205,000 provided in 1967, some £180,000 came from the Trust's limited reserves.

As a result of this sustained expenditure, farms are now reasonably equipped by the standards prevailing in different parts of the country. Arrears, in some cases the arrears of decades, have largely been made good. This does not mean an end to the programme of farm improvements. They are a continuing responsibility that is never discharged. It does however imply that improvements can proceed at a more normal tempo and that the farm programme should in the future make less taxing demands on the Trust's free funds.

The modernisation of cottages has proved a slower and also a more thankless task, since it does not always produce comparable rent increases. It is complicated by the fact that improvements must often wait on vacant possession, as many long-established tenants do not want changes or are unwilling to pay for them. The Trust finds that old people often prefer not to be disturbed. In other cases it is impractical to undertake modernisation until adjoining cottages are vacant and can be amalgamated. Moreover it is a process that seems unending, as more old cottages pass into Trust ownership every year. Though the programme of cottage modernisation also began soon after the war, and some 150 cottages are dealt with annually, there are still nearly 900 lacking baths, while rather over 100 are without running water.

Most cottage rents are low—in Ulster and South Wales they average under thirty shillings a week—and improvements cannot be met from income. They must thus, like farm improvements, be financed from capital. The cost per unit rises steadily. So does the standard required. In 1963, after taking into account government grants, full modernisation cost on an average £600; the figure is now about £1,000. Of the 900 cottages with improvements still outstanding a third can be financed from special resources, but some 600 will fall on the general funds of the Trust and if prices do not rise will cost £600,000. In recent years some £70,000 has been allocated annually from general funds for cottage improvements; in 1967 this allocation rose to £130,000, more than half the total provision for improvements (£205,000). Even if this rate of expenditure is maintained the modernisation of the Trust's existing cottages will not be completed until 1972 at the earliest.

Enough has been said to indicate the great drain over more than twenty years on the Trust's free funds arising from the obligation to bring farms and cottages to a standard which was not envisaged when most of them were accepted during and immediately after the last war. Modernisation has been the chief problem facing the Estates Committee and the major financial preoccupation of the Trust. A time is perhaps almost in sight when the burden will be eased. A greater proportion of free reserves can then be devoted to other purposes.

Chapter 12

Historic Buildings

The Trust's buildings are accepted by the Executive on the recommendation of the Historic Buildings Committee. The latter is a sub-committee with specialised knowledge of architecture and works of art. Its chairman since 1956 is Lord Rosse, who is also chairman of the Georgian Group and of the Standing Commission on Museums and Galleries. An Historic Buildings secretary, and regional secretaries or representatives—there are at present five—are responsible to the committee and ultimately to the Executive for the presentation and arrangement of the Trust's buildings. They can count on the help of a number of honorary representatives who act in a voluntary capacity and have special knowledge of the counties in which they live. These officials must work closely with the area agents who deal with estate management problems as they affect buildings.

The Historic Buildings Committee was constituted in 1936.[1] It owes much to the late Lord Esher who from its inception was chairman for twenty years, and to James Lees-Milne who served as its first secretary and subsequently as architectural adviser. Their partnership laid the lines and established the principles on which policy rests. Between them, they were responsible for elaborating and implementing the Country House Scheme (see below).

Given the desirability of preserving good buildings, the question arises where to begin or, more pertinently, where to end. Not all can be saved nor would this be desirable. Though in early days the Trust sometimes accepted buildings not of the first class, it now applies a more rigorous standard, recognizing that preservation must be confined to buildings outstanding in their type. In assessing architectural importance, the Trust attempts to put off the spectacles of contemporary fashion. Acceptability is a matter of quality and not of period. Whether the fate of a seventeenth-century manor, a Georgian country house, or a Victorian villa is in question the Trust asks, 'Is this building important in its class?' In borderline cases, it is agreed that situation may tip the scales. It is perhaps illogical to apply the same standard to Wales or to Ulster,

Vey Navigation, Surrey. Repairing Triggs Lock, 1966

Telford's Suspension Bridge at Conway (1826). Acquired by gift from the Conway Corporation and partly endowed by public appeal in 1966

Benz 1900 at Tatton Park, Cheshire, after restoration in 1962 by apprentices at the Rolls Royce factory

L.N.W.R. Coal Tank being coaxed into the stables at Penrhyn, Caernarvonshire, 1964

where good buildings are relatively few, as to Yorkshire or Wiltshire where they still abound.

The influence of fashion is not always easy to avoid. In 1935 when the Trust had been in existence forty years, its buildings were almost exclusively medieval or of the Tudor period. In matters of architecture its founders shared the enlightened ideas of their time, the ideas of Morris and Ruskin. They prized all that survived from a heroic Middle Ages. Ruskin, who profoundly influenced Octavia Hill, referred in his finest denunciatory vein to 'the foul tide of the Renaissance'. No wonder that the young Trust looked coldly on such imports as palladian architecture.

Today the majority of the Trust's buildings date from the second half of the seventeenth-century or from the Georgian period. This marked change of emphasis reflects, among other things, the change in taste which began somewhere about 1914 and which can be associated with the publication of Geoffrey Scott's *Architecture of Humanism*. Classical and renaissance building became acceptable to, and then preferred by, a widening public. It can be argued that the pendulum of taste has swung too far and that there is now a tendency to overvalue un-distinguished buildings which derive their inspiration from Italy. As may be inferred from its *List of Properties*, the Trust tries to remain catholic and objective in its judgments.

Buildings acquired by the Trust in early years tended to be small and unfurnished. They were rarely inhabited or habitable. Typical acqui-sitions were the Alfriston Clergy House, the Old Post Office at Tintagel, Buckingham Chantry Chapel, and Joiner's Hall at Salisbury. Barrington Court in Somerset was the only large house acquired before 1930 and the terms of its transfer, providing for a long lease to a tenant, were unusual. In the thirties only one other mansion, Montacute, also in Somerset, came to the Trust. Few buildings acquired before the Second World War posed serious problems of upkeep or called for large endowments.

Few were country houses. This was understandable. Before 1940 such houses rarely needed protection. Set in their landscaped parks, the Elizabethan manors, the seemly redbrick façades of the Restoration, the porticoed palladian mansions, and the cool neo-Greek houses of the Regency, seemed with their obelisks and shell grottoes, their gazebos and garden temples, subject only to the mellowing influence of time. Like the families which lived in them, and had sometimes built them, they appeared as permanent a part of the countryside as the surrounding woods and pastures.

THREAT TO COUNTRY HOUSES

The Second World War brought a change in the economic structure of society that altered their position almost overnight. An increase in wages that was overdue, a sharp increase in taxation, the impact of higher death duties which often seemed to fall with ironic weight when owners died on active service, imperilled their future. Mansions which had survived the cannonades of the Civil War, the financial panic of the South Sea Bubble, the changes of the Industrial Revolution, and even the accession of profligate or incompetent heirs, were gravely threatened. Maintenance was neglected; dry rot and the insidious beetle set about their work. As owners grew hard-up, mortgages were called in and banks foreclosed. Fine houses were sold for their marble chimneypieces and the lead on their roofs. Timber merchants in a week mercilessly denuded parks which had taken two centuries to mature. The shadow of the demolition contractor fell across the countryside.

A national asset, unique and irreplaceable, was wasting. Octavia Hill had said half a century earlier, 'New occasions teach new duties'. The Trust rose to the occasion that now presented itself. So did government. With the support of all political parties, the measures were enacted that are referred to in Chapters 5 and 7. This legislation was an example of the native genius for compromise. Government, having by severe taxation produced conditions in which numbers of important country houses could not survive, but realising the aesthetic and historic loss that this must entail, sensibly provided mechanisms to offset some of the effects of taxation and to secure the preservation of a minority of the buildings threatened. In so far as the Trust is concerned, it remains to consider in detail how this preservation was achieved.

THE COUNTRY HOUSE SCHEME

The Trust's Country House Scheme, as it was initially called, took shape two years before the outbreak of war and owed much to the foresight and public spirit of the Marquess of Lothian (see Chapter 5). It was in connection with Blickling Hall and his Norfolk estate, devised on his death in 1940—it was the first important agricultural property to be acquired—that the Trust gave detailed study to the problem of preserving a large country house and estate, evolving the formula that since has secured the future of other great houses.

Before examining the Country House Scheme, reference must be made to two considerations which influence policy. First, the Trust has no wish to acquire country houses which are not in danger. Though there are certain buildings of unique importance whose future should in all circumstances be exempt from the vagaries of time and chance, the Trust believes that the best owner of a country house is generally the private owner. No organisation, however flexible or sensitive, can extend the same affectionate care to a house and its contents as the family who may have lived there for generations or a newer master who may have restored it and furnished it over a lifetime with taste and knowledge. The Trust regards its ownership as a solution only for special circumstances. It is a lifebelt which the owner may grasp when problems of money and management become insuperable. It follows that, though the lifebelt exists, it is rarely proffered. The Trust avoids making an unsolicited approach and would usually think it improper to do so. Buildings, and in particular country houses, thus differ from coastland and unspoilt country, for which a positive approach some- times seems justified. The countryside, in spite of planning legislation, is often in more obvious danger from development.

The second consideration which weighs with the Trust is a wish to see its houses lived in. They need the breath of life. Built for a family and the life a family creates, they know no better use. Moreover the best curator of a house is normally the donor who knows and cherishes it.[2] From time to time circumstances arise in which the Trust must take over a house in which neither the donor nor his descendants, nor even a tenant, can be persuaded to live. It does so in the interests of the house (or sometimes of its contents), but it does so with hesitation. It has no wish to create museums in the countryside, and is not particularly equipped to run them. Only in exceptional instances, as at Waddesdon Manor, where a great family collection is of outstanding quality, does the creation of a museum seem justified. The Trust, it can be said, is always more ready to accept a house if the owner and his descendants are pre- pared to live there. It will thus serve its natural function with little change. A degree of public access, on which the Trust insists, is com- patible. Many famous country houses have admitted the curious visitor since the seventeenth-century.

In its simplest terms the Country House Scheme enables an owner to transfer to the Trust the freehold of a house of outstanding architectural or historic interest, together with a capital sum, or rent-producing land, sufficient to provide an endowment for upkeep. Owing to special legislation both property and endowment are exempt from death duties, and for tax purposes are not aggregated with the rest of the donor's estate. The income that the Trust, as a charity, derives from the endowment is tax free. With this gross income the Trust is able to maintain the fabric of the house, the contents of the state rooms (pictures, furniture, tapestries, and so on), the gardens, and the estate. As part of the bargain the Trust can arrange for the donor, and his heirs or assigns, to continue living in the house, either as tenants on a long lease at a nominal rent or under the terms of a memorandum of wishes. The latter is not legally enforceable but the Trust's good name depends on its faithful observance. Most donors prefer a memorandum of wishes to a long tenancy at a nominal rent, since such a tenancy represents a financial asset and is subject to death duties.

The public benefits in two ways: by the permanent preservation of a building of national importance, and by the arrangements made for visitors to see the principal rooms and the gardens at reasonable times and at a reasonable charge. By a single operation, the Country House Scheme enables houses to be preserved—but as homes rather than museums, maintaining the family connection which lends many of them special significance and interest—and at the same time opened with their gardens for the enjoyment of the public.

A family connection can be maintained even when a property is accepted by the Treasury under the Finance Acts in lieu of death duties and transferred to the Trust, provided—and the proviso is mandatory on the Trust—that the family makes a substantial contribution by way of endowment or by the gift of the contents of the house. The principle always to be observed, and it is cardinal to the Country House Scheme, is that the right to live in a house maintained with tax-free funds must be bought, either by the gift of property or money, or both.

Under the Country House Scheme the Trust's relationship to the donor or his heirs presents a psychological problem. It can only be solved if the relationship is one of confidence. The establishment of confidence is the first task confronting the staff when a property is taken over. A donor accustomed to exercising unfettered control finds himself overnight obliged to consult the Trust on many issues, and to adjust himself to living in a family house which he no longer owns. The Trust's role is to make this situation acceptable, not only by a readiness to meet the donor's reasonable wishes but by creating a partnership in which the donor and the Trust work for a common end, the wellbeing of the house. It is remarkable how often such a partnership is established and how fruitful it can be.

HOW THE SCHEME WORKS

Since an owner transferring a house to the Trust must usually both give and endow it, the question is often asked, 'How can the Country

House Scheme offer help to owners or commend itself as a possible and sometimes attractive expedient?' Exemption from death duties is not the whole answer. The operation of the scheme as it affects both a donor and the Trust can best be clarified by reference to a hypothetical case.

Suppose that Squire Headlong offers Headlong Hall, a mansion familiar to readers of Peacock, with the intention that he and his heirs shall continue to live there. In addition to the eighteenth-century family seat he offers its major contents, including the fine series of portraits by Reynolds and Gainsborough, the gardens, the park landscaped by Repton, and the estate of 1,200 acres. The offer is first considered by the Historic Buildings Committee. If they judge the house to be of national importance, they will recommend its acceptance subject to finance, a recommendation that the Executive Committee is likely to endorse. A second stage follows with the preparation of a full financial report on the property. The regional secretary or representative, and the area agent, visit Headlong Hall. There are discussions with Squire Headlong. These may be complex, as every property presents new and different problems. Consideration must be given to the likely cost of repairing and maintaining the fabric (an architect's report will be needed), of cleaning, heating, and showing the state rooms, and of maintaining the gardens. The contents of the hall, a collection that has accumulated over three centuries, must be considered by the Trust's adviser on paintings and other experts. Squire Headlong's agent will have to clarify matters relating to the estate, and discuss with the Trust's agent agricultural rents, farm improvements, and questions as diverse as tithe, land drainage, and forestry. A visit to the Headlong woods by the Trust's forestry adviser may be necessary. Finally the Trust will have to settle the days and times of public access, which in spite of the Squire's reputation for keeping open house may not be easily agreed. The staff will also have to estimate the likely receipts from admission fees when Headlong Hall is open. These will depend as much on its situation as on the intrinsic interest of the house, and the number of visitors is often difficult to predict. By the time sufficient information has been compiled, and much is always required, Squire Headlong may well tire of answering questions.

The report on Headlong Hall (submitted to the General Purposes Committee) will be detailed and comprehensive, and will forecast the cost of maintaining the hall and estate in the foreseeable future. On the credit side it will enter the anticipated revenue, which will include such items as farm rents, garden produce, venison from the deer park, timber, wayleaves, and visitors' fees. On the debit side will fall maintenance and improvement of farm buildings and cottages, wages of gardeners and foresters, upkeep of the structure of the hall, redecoration of the show rooms and repair of their contents, the costs of showing to the public, a proportion of the rates, heating and lighting, and lastly tithe, insurance, and management. The report does not include, nor could it, any outgoings of a personal nature, such as the wages of the Squire's household servants, or his living expenses. These cannot be met out of the tax-free income which will be required to maintain Headlong Hall.

The Trust's figures sometimes show an estimated surplus and no question of further endowment arises. Unfortunately the Headlong Hall estate includes a number of scattered hill farms and is poor agricultural land. The financial report anticipates an annual deficit of £2,500 a year. The Trust, without funds of its own to meet the deficiency, has no choice but to ask Square Headling to supplement a proffered gift that is already generous with a capital endowment. At 5 per cent the sum required to produce £2,500 a year is £50,000. This is a substantial figure, yet if the Squire is a rich man it may be to his advantage to ensure the preservation of Headlong Hall by such an endowment. The top £50,000 of his capital is no doubt subject to heavy surtax. It earns a negligible net income. In the hands of the Trust it attracts no tax and the full yield is available for the upkeep of the hall, its contents, and the estate. Both the property and the endowment will be exempt from estate duty, whether given in the Squire's lifetime or left on his death as a devise. There is thus a chance that the Country House Scheme will commend itself to Squire Headlong. In saving the Hall, he can both benefit the public, and secure material advantages.

Though simpler, the procedure is no different if Mr X wishes to make over his little manor in Wiltshire, whose unique architectural features have been illustrated in *Country Life*. In such a case the estimated annual deficit might be nearer £500 than £2,500, and the endowment required correspondingly less. However as there are usually people ready to buy and cherish such a house, the Trust, where less danger threatens, will be less ready to intervene.

In the Trust's financial report, there will always be imponderables. Thus there must always be risk. When the Trust assumes responsibility for a property it does so in perpetuity. It is part of the bargain, and rightly so, that when the Trust has stated its financial requirements it cannot normally go back and ask for more. Any deficit that subsequently arises will thus fall on its free reserves.

WHERE THE SCHEME FAILS

It is pertinent to ask what happens when Squire Headlong is not a rich man and is unable to provide the required endowment. Owners of houses of architectural importance are not necessarily well off. In such cases the Trust can exceptionally find an endowment by appealing to other charitable bodies, or to its members and the public. But the money to be raised from such sources is limited and appeals to generosity must be infrequent and made only on the strongest grounds. It follows that houses are offered which the Trust is unable to save. Their subsequent fate may involve demolition or dereliction. These are cases for which the Country House Scheme unfortunately can provide no solution.

On the other hand few country houses of the first importance have been demolished or become derelict in the last fifteen years. Possibly more were lost between the world wars. Much credit for this must go to the Historic Buildings Council whose valuable work is referred to in Chapter 7. Government grants for repair have often made the difference which has enabled owners to carry on. Owners have also adapted to changed circumstances. Houses that were built for a multitude of servants are run almost without help. Stoking has been replaced by oil-fired central heating, The vast kitchen, two hundred yards from the dining room, has been abandoned, and a small electrically equipped kitchen takes its place in the old servery. Machines do the work of men. The economy of the country house has also been supported by a rising stock market. Capital gains have replaced failing roofs and eradicated dry rot. But markets cannot always rise, and the effects of the new Capital Gains and Selective Employment taxes are likely to be serious. There is little cause for long-term optimism and no reason to believe that this architectural front, so surprisingly defended in recent years, will hold if economic circumstances worsen. Also another generation, the new owners on whom the survival of these houses primarily depends, may grow tired of making sacrifices for brick and stone. Many people live in large cold houses in straitened circumstances who could, if they chose, live warmly and comfortably in smaller ones. No one connected with the Trust can question the discomfort to which people submit in order to save an important house which they and their forbears have known and loved. A large country house in the second half of the twentieth century is not necessarily an asset. The future of such houses often depends on the dedication of their owners. The time may come when the price paid seems excessive. The nation will then be the loser.

TEMPLES, FOLLIES AND SHRINES

The acquisition of houses such as Headlong Hall has been dealt with at some length, because since 1940 this has been an important extension of the Trust's work. This does not imply that the preservation of buildings other than country houses receives less attention that it did, or that the Trust has ceased to be concerned with their fate. It is the smaller buildings which have outlived their purpose—windmills and watermills, chapels that are deconsecrated, classical temples abandoned by their devotees, pleasaunces from which the rococo shepherdesses have fled—that are often most threatened. The Trust is active in their preservation. Important recent acquisitions include an enchanting little temple on Windermere, Gibside Chapel by Paine in County Durham, the Priest's House at Easton-on-the-Hill, and Paxton's Tower in Carmarthenshire. Such buildings could hardly have survived but for the Trust's intervention.

The same may be said of the many old cottages on the Trust's estates, charming but unpractical, for which tenants often can be found only after modernisation. Cottage preservation becomes a major undertaking where a whole village is concerned, and the charge of maintaining and modernising villages such as Lacock, West Wycombe, and Blaise Hamlet is considerable. Such villages are among the happiest examples of Trust ownership. It ensures homogeneous treatment of the buildings and enables the Trust, while conserving their architectural character, rigorously to exclude both fake antiquarianism and the vulgar conversions that have overtaken many villages houses.

The Trust also preserves houses which may be architecturally insignificant in themselves but which derive their importance from their association with great men. Chartwell, Winston Churchill's home for over forty years, and Moseley Old Hall which played a dramatic role in the escape of Charles II after the battle of Worcester, are typical examples. Many of the Trust's houses associated with famous people or events differ from these in that they are also of architectural distinction. They thus qualify for preservation on two counts. Buildings such as Compton Castle (Humphrey Gilbert), Lacock Abbey (Fox Talbot) and Bateman's (Kipling), are outstanding in their own right.

The case for acquiring a house on grounds of association is stronger when the association extends to the contents. The fascination of Chartwell, 24 Cheyne Row (Carlyle), Hughenden (Disraeli), Smallhythe Place (Ellen Terry), Clouds Hill (T. E. Lawrence), and Shaw's Corner (Shaw), lies precisely in the fact that the contents reflect the personalities of their owners, and that the rooms have often remained unaltered. The position is different, and preservation more questionable, when the Trust is offered an empty shrine. Wordsworth was born in a house at Cockermouth and left it as a child. When it came unfurnished to the Trust it had little to tell the poet. There seems small case for regarding the birthplace of a great man as in itself sufficient warrant for preservation.

The Trust also holds a number of houses exclusively for the works of art they contain. This is a relatively new development, as the acquisition of chattels did not become a statutory purpose of the Trust until 1937. The Trust is hesitant to accept buildings for this reason unless the contents are of exceptional significance. They may be so either as the accumulation of a family over the centuries, reflecting the history of taste, or as an outstanding collection, reflecting the judgment of a single connoisseur. A house in which family accumulations are found tends also to be a building of historic or architectural importance, and thus qualifies for preservation by the Trust for more than one reason. Such a house and its collection form a single entity.

PREHISTORIC AND ROMAN SITES

The Trust is equally concerned to preserve remains of the prehistoric and Roman past. Since men in the Iron and Bronze Ages tended to build their camps and fortifications, and to inter their dead, on the chalk downlands, many of the more important prehistoric sites are situated in splendid country. Remains such as Cissbury Ring in Sussex, Figsbury Rings in Wiltshire, and the great sanctuary at Avebury, combine in striking fashion the Trust's two major concerns: the preservation of 'buildings' and unspoilt landscape. Some of the Trust's Roman remains such as Chedworth in Gloucestershire, perhaps the best preserved villa in England, and stretches of Hadrian's incomparable wall, are also wonderfully situated.

As the owner of ancient sites, the Trust receives requests for permission to excavate. When the sites concerned are scheduled under the Ancient Monuments Acts, requests are referred to the Ministry, which usually authorises the Trust to grant the necessary permission if the proposed programme of excavation is well conceived. In other cases, requests are referred to the Trust's honorary archaeological advisers or to the Trust's archaeological correspondent. The Trust specifies where finds from excavations on its land shall be deposited, and this, in accordance with the present policy of the Council for British Archaeology, is usually in the county museum. The extent of digging on

Trust land may be gauged from the fact that in 1965 and 1966 excavation was carried out at Glastonbury Tor, Chedworth Villa, Croft Ambrey, Midsummer Hill, Mam Tor, Hope Woodlands, Hatfield Forest and the Rumps. A handbook of the Trust's prehistoric sites was published in 1967.

The care of ancient sites calls for specialised knowledge. This the Ancient Monuments Department of the Ministry of Public Building and Works pre-eminently possesses, and the Trust has placed in the care of the Ministry, under deed of guardianship, nine properties which include Avebury, Housesteads Fort on Hadrian's Wall, Hailes Abbey, and the Roman remains at Letocetum. The maintenance of the military architecture of the Middle Ages also often demands an expertise and an outlay which the Ministry is better able to provide. Though at the most romantic of English castles, Bodiam in Sussex, and at Tattershall in Lincolnshire, both meticulously restored by Lord Curzon, the Trust can meet the charges of maintenance, there are other castles such as Cilgerran and Skenfrith which it has been grateful to transfer into the guardianship of the Ministry. Dunstanburgh was already in the Ministry's care when it came to the Trust as part of a long stretch of unspoilt Northumberland coast.

INDUSTRIAL MONUMENTS

Preservation of the best buildings in their kind, whatever that kind may be, has led the Trust in recent years to welcome the offer of outstanding industrial monuments (see Chapter 6). Taste moves slowly, and it is probably right that it should, for time alone creates perspective. Even so the appreciation of our industrial buildings has been long delayed. Taste and interest have strangely lagged. Two hundred years have elapsed since some of these industrial monuments were built. Europe, that often outbids us with its classical and modern architecture, has little comparable to offer. Britain, the first great industrial power, has in its early factories, warehouses, bridges, and canals, a unique inheritance. In its preservation the Trust has a useful role to play. Apart from a number of windmills and watermills, the Trust has been able to acquire half a dozen industrial monuments, of which the most important are the cotton mill and village at Styal, the latter a rare example of eighteenth-century industrial planning, some of the earliest Cornish beam engines, an old printing press at Strabane in Ulster, Telford's Conway Bridge, fifteen miles of the River Wey Navigation, and thirteen miles of the Stratford-on-Avon Canal. Related to the preservation of such monuments is the creation of an industrial locomotive museum at Penrhyn Castle, a carriage museum at Arlington Court, and a collection of early motor cars at Tatton Park.

The preservation of large industrial monuments has been found to present exceptional financial difficulties. The general public do not yet appreciate their significance—owing to the active propaganda of the Inland Waterways Association canals are a notable exception—and do not respond as to appeals for a house or garden. The busy owners are often unaware of the historic interest of these monuments, and even when they express concern for their future are rarely moved, as are the owners of houses and gardens, to contribute financially to their preservation. This is both unfortunate and ironic, for many of the most important industrial monuments are in the hands of business firms with ample means to conserve and endow them. The best that can be said is that, owing to the efforts of the Council for British Archaeology, a gradual appreciation of the importance of these monuments is becoming current among their owners and the public.

VARIETY OF THE TRUST'S BUILDINGS

The following list will convey some idea of the variety of buildings held by the Trust in 1966. It includes only buildings of special architectural or historic interest.[3]

1. Country houses lived in by the donor or his heirs or assigns — 43
2. Country houses let to tenants other than donors, including local authorities — 32
3. Country houses managed either by a resident Trust administrator (6) or by the regional staff (21) — 27
4. Houses associated with famous people not comprised in (1) to (3), i.e. not country houses — 13
5. Houses in towns not comprised in (4) and for the most part let to tenants — 19
6. Single cottages or groups of cottages held for their architectural merit — 16
7. Villages — 10
8. Small medieval buildings and bridges, market houses, gatehouses, dovecotes, chapels, classical temples and obelisks (not associated with country houses) — 45
9. Medieval castles and ecclesiastical foundations (ruined) — 9
10. Tithe barns — 5

ARCHITECTURAL AND DECORATIVE PROBLEMS

The charge of so many and such different buildings poses many problems. The first is their structural care. In addition to routine maintenance, the Historic Buildings Committee has, for some years, insisted on triennial or quinquennial architects' reports. The Trust does not employ its own architectural staff—the diversity of its problems, and the wide distribution of its buildings, make this impracticable—but relies on some twenty or thirty architects in private practice with a special knowledge of ancient buildings. When many graduates are barely able to distinguish the Doric from the Ionic order, this knowledge is becoming difficult to find in the provinces, where the Trust prefers, in the interests both of lower costs and closer supervision, to employ local men. In choosing architects the Trust is guided by the advice of the Society for the Protection of Ancient Buildings with whose views on maintenance and repair the Trust is in general sympathy. These views, deriving from those of William Morris, stress the importance of conservation rather than restoration, and enshrine the principle that notional restoration of fabric or ornament cannot be justified. Better a ruin than a fake. It follows that the Trust in adding to old buildings is concerned that new work shall be distinguishable. It is dated where any possibility of confusion could arise.

Given money and a good architect the structural maintenance of historic buildings is relatively straightforward. Other issues, such as the propriety of demolishing part of a building in order to restore an original design that later centuries saw fit to change, are more complicated. The alteration on aesthetic grounds of the always interesting but often unpleasing record of history calls for prudence. The Trust finds it justified only where later additions are clearly haphazard. At Ashdown in Berkshire, and at Springhill and Ardress House in Northern Ireland, the demolition of valueless accretions has revealed the architectural significance of the original designs.

Redecoration and furnishing raise equally controversial issues. In its decisions the Trust is governed by respect for the character and tradition of a house, and by the avoidance of any attempt to impose the canons of contemporary good taste. Nothing dates more quickly, or comes to look more out of place, than the mode of the moment. The elimination of the unfashionable is rarely wise, and thus the Trust usually makes a point of respecting the accretions of the late nineteenth and early twentieth centuries.

This does not imply that changes cannot be made on conclusive historical grounds. When Claydon House in Buckinghamshire came to the Trust, it seemed proper to strip the brown varnish, which probably dated from the days when Florence Nightingale stayed in the house, from the most exuberant rococo carving in the country and to attempt the reinstatement of an eighteenth-century colour-scheme. Where original colours have been preserved beneath successive layers of paint, such restoration need not be speculative. At Clandon Park near Guildford intelligent surmise predicted that the engaged columns in Leoni's Palladian hall might retain their eighteenth-century marbling under newer paint. So it proved, and now the original marbling once again emphasises the architectural character of the design. At Shugborough Park in Staffordshire judicious scraping revealed that in a moment of aberration even Samuel Wyatt's scagliola columns had been painted. They have now re-emerged. At Saltram House in Devon, to take another example, the fenestration in the saloon, one of Robert Adam's finest rooms, had been altered in the nineteenth-century by the insertion of a stained-glass panel over the central window. The panel was removed and carefully stored, and suitable glazing put back.

At Saltram a more difficult problem was posed by the discovery in an attic of a large roll of Chinese eighteenth-century wallpaper. For some reason it had never been used. Perhaps tastes changed soon after it was bought. Also in the house, but significantly not in the more important rooms, were a number of chinoiserie objects, painted mirrors and so on. After reflection it seemed sensible and permissible to carry out the apparent intention of an eighteenth-century owner, and to create a 'Chinese' bedroom. In making such changes the only guide is discretion. No rule applies in every case and the approach must be empirical. It might be added that the Trust enjoys one marked advantage: poverty. As many houses sadly witness, nothing is more destructive of character and atmosphere than too much money.

On the one hand the Trust in its country houses attempts to remain unswayed by contemporary taste; on the other it tries to avoid the approach of the art expert. While the Trust owes much to the national museums, whose help is often asked and always generously given, it is not its function to turn houses into museums. Its task is to show works of art, and objects which are less than works of art, in their natural setting and in the ambience of the past. The nature of this task can be illustrated by reference to the eighteenth-century habit of hanging walls from dado to ceiling with paintings ranged like postage stamps on the pages of a generous album. With the good and the bad indiscriminately mixed, pictures so hung, and set with their elaborate gilt frames on rich brocaded backgrounds, lend, and were meant to lend, a necessary warmth and animation to the formal rooms of the period. Perhaps no single feature of the country houses of the seventeenth- and eighteenth-centuries better expresses an atmosphere, and an attitude to art, now unfamiliar. Though judicious changes may be made in the 'stamp album' to bring paintings regarded as important into positions of greater prominence, the essential arrangement, so uncongenial to many experts, is precisely the sort of survival which it is the Trust's duty to preserve. Similarly the idiosyncrasy, so curious to our notions, of using tapestries as wallpaper and a background for paintings must be respected where it has the authority of long usage. We may rely on our museums for the imaginative presentation of great works of art, but the preservation of the interiors of our country houses as living organisms is no less important. It can be successfully achieved only by a scrupulous regard for objects and settings which do not always commend themselves to contemporary taste and expertise.

WORKS OF ART AND LIBRARIES

Conservation of the contents of the Trust's houses is a permanent preoccupation. The ills that beset pictures, furniture, and fabrics, are all too familiar, and even bronze, *aes perenne*, suffers its specific disease. There are now some twenty important picture collections in Trust houses, of which the outstanding are those at Upton, Waddesdon, Polesden Lacey, and Petworth. Their welfare since 1955 has been ensured by the appointment of a full-time adviser on paintings. He is also responsible for research into the history of the collections, for attributions, for maintaining a photographic record of the paintings, and for making information available to other scholars. The Trust receives numberless requests for loans to exhibitions. The adviser on paintings must in every case decide whether a particular picture can be subjected to the hazards and changes of temperature that travel involves. The glib assumption that paintings can be safely shunted round the continents is too current.

Hardly a week passes but in one house or another some work of art calls for attention. The expert advice of the Victoria and Albert Museum has long been invaluable. It would be difficult to exaggerate the debt which the Trust owes to the director and his associates not only for advice but for the generous way in which they enable the repair of works of art to be carried out in the Museum workshops. Without the interest of the keeper of the Textile Department the maintenance of the great collection of tapestries and needlework at Hardwick would present an almost insoluble problem. The Trust also receives generous help from other specialists.

Books are in the care of a library adviser, and thanks to a grant from the Pilgrim Trust a card catalogue of the works in the Trust's libraries published before 1700, has been completed. Copies are held by the British Museum and the National Trust of America. Libraries pose a special problem. Unlike most objects in a country house, books cannot normally be enjoyed by the visiting public, and they remain on their shelves unread. For this reason the Trust hesitates to assume the charge of rare books that would be better appreciated in a university library or in the ownership of a private collector. A scheme is under consideration which will enable graduate students at certain provincial universities to have access to libraries in Trust houses in the area. The policy for muniments has long been to deposit them for safe keeping in county record offices where they can be studied. An exception is made for the important Disraeli papers which are available to scholars at Hughenden Manor, the house in which he lived. Documents about a particular building or its contents, or the layout of its park and garden, are also retained in the house to which they relate. Whenever possible architects' letters, plans, and drawings, are framed and exhibited. Repton's 'Red Book' has greater significance at Attingham, where his proposals may be compared with the existing layout, than it would have elsewhere.

PUBLIC ACCESS

In preserving an historic house, the Trust has two obligations: to maintain the structure and contents, and to provide public access. Access is normally arranged and supervised by the Trust and not by the donor or tenant in residence. While the admission of visitors to a Roman villa, a ruined medieval castle, or any empty building, will normally show an appreciable profit, this is rarely the case with a furnished house. A warden will be required in each room and additional cleaners when the house closes. With the present cost of wages, outgoings often exceed admission fees, unless it is a 'popular' house which large numbers can be induced to visit. Fortunately the Trust's houses are, or should be, properly endowed. Thus while providing appropriate facilities for visitors, the Trust has no need to commercialise them by offering irrelevant attractions. Commercialisation would be a breach of faith with the donors (whether they live in the houses or not) who gave them to be preserved in dignified fashion and *as* country houses.

In 1966 the houses and gardens where an entrance fee is charged were visited by 122,000 Trust members and by over 2 million other people. The vast majority of the Trust's buildings are open three or more afternoons a week from April to September. Where there is public demand, many are also open in winter. However at a minority of houses there are fewer visitors than the Trust would wish. The position at these houses calls for explanation. First, some of them offer a specialised interest that appeals chiefly to scholars, or they are so remote from centres of population as to be difficult of access. Visitors in both cases will always be few and far between. To open such houses every day for the reception of stray arrivals would involve the Trust in a steady financial loss. By opening only on one or two days a week, and thus concentrating visitors on those days, the loss is minimised. Secondly, there are the houses where access, restricted under the terms of past agreements with donors, is less than the Trust would arrange if it had a free hand. The donors who generously give houses or collections to the Trust must also provide for their maintenance. The provision needed is often large. Thus the preservation of a house of importance is sometimes secured only after long and difficult negotiation. The Trust, as a charity exempt from taxation, has a responsibility to ensure the public reasonable access, but without some compromise on the number of opening days, especially during the lifetime of the donor, important houses would be lost to the nation. The limited nature of the opening arrangements is usually temporary; the preservation of the house is permanent. The Trust continually works to improve access arrangements and methods of showing, both at properties which are much visited and at those which appeal to a minority (see Chapter 6).

Arrangements for public access include the preparation of guidebooks which must deal with the architecture of the building, its history, and its contents in scholarly fashion. They vary in price from pamphlets selling at a few pence to authoritative catalogues to some of the larger houses and collections which cost several shillings.[4] Reliable guidebooks are essential, for it is policy whenever possible to avoid guided parties so that visitors may appreciate a house and its contents in quiet and at leisure. Each year more houses are shown in this way. It is also policy to show houses as far as possible in their natural state, as a guest might see them who had called on a summer afternoon. This means with a

Mr Leonard Davis, the Trust's Stourton Estate thatcher

Silk Houses, Stourton, Wiltshire. The cottages once housed silk-weavers. Rethatched 1967

Glencoyne Farm, Lake District. New sheep pens, 1965

The Trust as Forester. A fine stand of beech at Slindon, Sussex

minimum number of the notices, ropes, and posts, which effectively destroy their atmosphere. Unfortunately on grounds of security ropes and posts are often necessary, but the Trust is now experimenting with electronic equipment which may partially replace them and at the same time reduce the number of wardens and the costs of showing.

Ancillary to public access is the provision of unobtrusive car parks, and tea rooms situated perhaps in the stables or the old laundry. Not least there must be effective signposts. Though the Historic Buildings Committee has approved a standard colour for notices, and a Roman type, signposts on main roads cannot be put up without the permission of the Highway Authorities. Certain houses, where the Trust has been unable to obtain the necessary permission, remain for the time being inadequately signposted.

Chapter 13

Gardens

The Act of 1937 by empowering the Trust to augment the amenity of the land about its buildings formally recognised the fact—it had been evident for some time—that the Trust was a gardener. However, owning few country houses, it was still a gardener in a modest way. In 1937 the future of most great gardens seemed secure without the Trust's intervention. It was the economic circumstances arising from the Second World War that later endangered them, no less than the houses from which they depended. With increased taxation and higher wages, gardens famous throughout Europe—from Bridgeman's formal masterpieces to Gertrude Jekyll's brilliant conceptions of two centuries later, not to speak of more recent gardens such as Hidcote and Rowallane—were threatened. Yew hedges were uncut and shrubs unpruned, lawns turned to hayfields, and woodland walks grew impenetrable. Gardens were disappearing because their owners could no longer afford to maintain them. A nation of gardeners agreed that something must be done.

THE GARDENS SCHEME

In 1948 the Trust evolved a plan, analogous to the Country House Scheme, to save important gardens. After consultation with the Royal Horticultural Society, a joint Gardens Committee representative of both bodies was set up and an appeal for a Garden Fund, which would enable the Trust to hold and preserve gardens of outstanding importance, was launched in a letter to *The Times*. A broadcast followed by Victoria Sackville-West. Before the end of the year unexpected help came from the Queen's Institute of District Nursing. The Institute, deriving an income from admission fees to gardens all over the country which are open each summer on its behalf, generously agreed to donate a percentage of its takings to the new Garden Fund. This contribution, which in 1966 amounted to over £6,000 and tends yearly to increase, provides the fund's major source of recurring income. The capital of the Gardens Fund today stands at some £34,000.

134

The formal garden at Montacute came to the Trust as early as 1931, and by 1948 the Trust owned a number of good gardens, though in every case they had been acquired as an appendage to a country house and not on their own merits. The purpose of the new Gardens Committee and the fund it controlled was to enable the Trust to preserve a different type of garden: that important in itself by reason of its design or its plants and shrubs, whether or not situated in the curtilege of a great house. The Committee was composed in equal number of representatives of the Trust and the Royal Horticultural Society, with the addition of a member appointed by the Queen's Institute of District Nursing. The Chairman was to share the confidence both of the Executive Committee of the Trust and the Council of the Royal Horticultural Society. The terms of reference of the Committee were:

1. To recommend to the Trust gardens worthy of acceptance under the new scheme;
2. To recommend expenditure from the Gardens Fund on the maintenance of gardens so accepted;
3. To manage these gardens on behalf of the Trust.[1]

In 1949 these terms of reference were extended to enable the Committee to give its advice on Trust gardens other than those for which it was directly responsible. In view of the expert knowledge of the Committee—its present chairman is the director of the Royal Botanical Gardens at Kew, and his predecessors were presidents of the Royal Horticultural Society—the extension was logical and valuable. A gardens adviser was appointed in 1954. He reports to his committee on the gardens under their direct care and implements committee policy. He also regularly visits the Trust's other gardens and makes recommendations. The committee now directly controls seven gardens: Stourhead (1947), Hidcote (1948), Bodnant (1949), Nymans (1954), Sheffield Park (1954), Trengwainton (1961) and Sissinghurst (1967).[2] Other important gardens, closely associated with historic buildings, in regard to which the committee acts in an advisory capacity, are those of Blickling Hall, Cliveden, Hardwick Hall, Montacute, Packwood House, Polesden Lacey, Powis Castle, Tintinhull and Upton House.

PROBLEMS OF CONSERVATION

The perpetuation of certain types of garden, whether in the charge of the Gardens Committee or directly controlled by the Trust, presents a delicate problem. Given sufficient money, labour, and technical knowledge, a great formal garden may be easily maintained. Its character derives from its design, and this can be faithfully preserved. There is little excuse for serious error in dealing with the lineal simplicity, the yew hedges and formal canals, of a Westbury Court. The romantic landscapings of the eighteenth and early nineteenth-centuries present greater difficulties, but they are not insuperable. Such gardens are conceived in broad terms and almost invariably comprise four elements carefully related to the terrain: water, trees, sward, and temples. Lakes can be dredged and temples repointed. As the groups of trees which give emphasis to the composition, creating the vistas and the blocks of shadow, reach their term they can be replanted. The task calls for thought, but no one sensitive to the works of Brown or Repton finds it unduly difficult.

The personal and often highly poetic gardens of the late nineteenth and early twentieth-centuries pose a problem different in kind. They often owe their beauty rather to the sensibility of an individual than to the horticultural tradition of their time. They express in a special sense 'the touch of a vanished hand'. It is a touch expressed in a thousand sensitive details, in surprising *chiaroscuro*, in subtle contrasts of colour and form. At gardens such as Hidcote and Sissinghurst each errant spray seems to be intentional, reflecting the idiosyncrasy of the owner. This is not a touch that a society or a committee can easily reproduce. Hence the daunting problem of preserving the character of some of the Trust's youngest and finest gardens.

Probably uniformity of treatment is the greatest danger which confronts the Trust. Its gardens are wonderfully varied because they reflect not only differences of soil and climate but the personal tastes and enthusiasms of the men who conceived them from the seventeenth century onwards. The Trust sees among its most difficult tasks the preservation of this variety and individuality. It would be disastrous if its gardens—there is a close parallel here with the furnishing and management of its houses—ever came to bear the imprint of a National Trust taste or style. The Trust must ceaselessly combat a natural tendency for gardens under the same management to grow alike. As the gardens adviser has pointed out, it is a tendency that receives impulsion if head gardeners exchange, and so disseminate, their rare plants and shrubs, or if the adviser himself recommends the adoption of his favourite species regardless of the special character of the gardens under his care. The beauties of Bodnant are inappropriate to Stourhead, or those of Trelissick to Polesden Lacey. The Trust's aim is the conservation and development of the distinct *persona* of each garden. At Trengwainton it adds to the rhododendron species from one valley in China; at Sizergh

Castle it fosters the remarkable fern collection; at Sheffield Park it increases the autumn colour for which the place is renowned; and at Hidcote it adds to the collection of old-fashioned roses.

Where appropriate the Trust creates new gardens. At Hardwick Hall a herb garden has been made containing culinary and medicinal herbs in use when the house was built at the end of the sixteenth century. At Moseley Old Hall, where all trace of the original layout had disappeared, a seventeenth-century garden has been recreated such as Charles II might have found when he reached the house as a fugitive after the Battle of Worcester.

VISITORS

Gardens are among the most frequented of the Trust's properties. There are over 100,000 visitors a year at Stourhead, over 75,000 at Sheffield Park, and nearly 70,000 at Bodnant. Such an affluence poses problems. For gardens as for houses there is an optimum number of visitors. When that optimum is exceeded, as it is at Stourhead on certain days in spring and early summer, grass becomes worn, plants and shrubs are damaged, and litter mysteriously increases in geometrical progression. More important, the essential character of the garden is lost. Apart from its superb design, the charm of Stourhead is its sense of space and tranquillity. To destroy this is to destroy something of the garden itself and to fail in the task of preservation. The problem at Stourhead is not yet grave, and for most of the year the garden is not overcrowded. But in 1956 there were 48,500 visitors and in 1966 over 106,000. How many will there be in 1976? Already on a few Sundays in early summer there are over 4,000 visitors a day. This is more than any garden can stand for long periods. When serious overcrowding occurs, a remedy causing a minimum of inconvenience to visitors will not be easy to find. On the one hand it is hardly feasible to close a garden whenever it reaches saturation point, though this proved necessary at Chartwell in 1966; on the other, increased admission fees appear to have little limiting effect on numbers.

Stourhead also serves to illustrate another problem. Perhaps the finest of those eighteenth-century gardens to which reference has been made, Stourhead derives its effect from a combination of the four elements of water, trees, sward, and temples. The Trust's concern is to preserve this composition now and for the future. Yet the contemporary cry, here as elsewhere, is for colour and for the rhododendrons more appropriate to modern gardens. The Trust has no choice but to turn a deaf ear.

Fortunately at Stourhead, as often elsewhere, a satisfactory compromise can be achieved. Though the twentieth-century planting of rhododendrons round the lake, so alien to the original scheme, is being gradually reduced, colour deriving from fine rhododendron species is being introduced in the surrounding woods where it is innocuous. None the less such an easy accommodation to contemporary fashion in gardening is not always possible.

GARDENERS

The Trust employs some 150 gardeners. Like the owners of private gardens, it has increasing difficulty in finding skilled labour and in particular the dedicated and imaginative head-gardeners on whom so much depends. Gardens such as Bodnant, Blickling and Hidcote owe an immense debt to their head-gardeners. To enlist promising recruits to follow in their footsteps, the Trust in 1962 established an apprenticeship scheme for gardeners. It has got off to a slow start, but it is early to judge whether it can make a useful contribution to one of the major difficulties of maintaining a fine garden in the second half of the twentieth century.[3] The Trust also arranges conferences attended by its head-gardeners. These are popular and valuable, leading to a useful exchange of ideas. However this very exchange is not without its dangers and must be seen in relation to the duty, referred to above, jealously to safeguard the distinct and individual character of each garden.

Chapter 14

The Members and the Public

The Trust in early days welcomed members but made no serious effort to recruit them. There was perhaps an assumption that quality counted for more than quantity, a feeling that members should be deeply concerned for the countryside and dedicated to the purposes of the Trust. Such people, it could be argued, gravitated naturally to the organisation and found in it the expression of their cherished interests. In 1900 there were some 250 members. The thousand mark was not passed for nearly thirty years. Four figures were achieved by the establishment of a propaganda committee in 1928 and the attention drawn to the Trust by G. M. Trevelyan's pamphlet *Must England's Beauty Perish?* Yet much by this date had been accomplished. There were some 180 properties which included the Farne Islands, Scolt Head, Wicken Fen, Hatfield Forest, Box Hill, Ashridge, and large chunks of the Lake District. There were buildings such as Bodiam and Tattershall castles, Barrington Court, Chedworth Roman Villa, Housesteads Fort, and impressive stretches of the Roman Wall. It was a notable achievement for so small a society and it was largely due to the dedication of its members. Regarding themselves as the apostles of a new gospel, they not only belonged to the Trust but laboured on its behalf.

A positive policy to increase membership in the years after 1928 inspired misgiving in the President of the Trust, Princess Louise. How could members recruited by propaganda, many of whom joined for what they could get rather than what they could give, have the same knowledge and the same dedication? None the less there were cogent reasons for achieving an increased membership. The first, and the most important, was finance: more members meant more money. This is still the case. The Trust needs the subscriptions of a large membership. Less persuasive, but not without force, was the argument that members would lend strength to the Trust in its negotiations with national and local authorities; the argument sadly presupposes that ministers and councillors sometimes have regard less to the aims and achievements of a society than to the size of its membership.

By 1935 membership had reached 8,000. In the following decade—the war was in part responsible—there was little increase. In 1945 the figure stood at some 9,500. The big advance began soon after. Contributory factors were additional publicity and a changing economy. The latter brought holidays in the country within reach of a new type of visitor. The new visitors could see for themselves the dangers that a growing population presented to a small island and so learnt to value the work of the Trust. By 1950 membership had risen to 23,000, by 1955 to 56,000, by 1960 to 97,000, and by 1965 to 158,000. Membership now (1967) stands at some 175,000. If the rate of increase over the last decade is maintained, the Trust will have over half-a-million members by the end of the century. This would be financially desirable, but it could conceivably have its dangers. The tail has been known to wag the dog. The Trust did great things with less than a thousand members, and set high standards. Any lowering of these standards, any compromise in deference to a vast membership and the irrelevant pressures that such a membership might exert, would in the long run undermine its authority and hazard its future. The Trust's essential tasks cannot always be generally popular, though it is useful if they can be made to seem so. Time reveals their justification. Few of the campaigns that the Trust has undertaken immediately commanded wide support. Victories have been gained by a determined minority. It is only later that the fruits of victory—the unspoilt woods and moors, the undeveloped dales and headlands, the quiet country houses—are appreciated and taken for granted.

WHO ARE THE MEMBERS?

Who are the members of the Trust today? Membership has always cut across distinctions of class or money. If statistics were available they would indicate a high percentage of botanists and ornithologists, of those who like to walk, and of those who have a fondness for architecture and works of art. They would also indicate a percentage of dedicated cranks. Figures seem to reveal that, except in Trust strongholds like the Lake District where local enthusiasm happily furthers local interest, the most active support comes from suburbia, from modest people who since the last war have discovered in motorcars the pleasures and beauties of the coast and the countryside. The rate of recruitment is highest in May, when large numbers visit Trust gardens, and during the August holidays. It falls in the autumn to pick up again briefly in December, when people give Trust membership to their friends as a Christmas present. In February it reaches its nadir, and then rises slowly but steadily to its peak in late May. Once they have joined, people remain faithful to the Trust, and the average membership lasts between twenty-five and thirty years. The wastage through death, resignation, and default is astonishingly low, and over the last decade has averaged about $3\frac{1}{2}$ per cent per annum. An analysis giving an indication of how members were recruited in 1966 is attached as Appendix 4. The figures reveal the wide variety in the sources of recruitment, and the interesting fact that both press publicity and press advertisement made a negligible contribution. Advertisement it is only fair to add was little used owing to cost.

Ordinary membership in 1895 was 10s and the subscription stood at this figure until 1953. By that date it bore no sensible relation either to the costs of running the Trust or to the privileges its members enjoyed. The Council had drawn attention to this in 1946, pointing out that although membership was rising a decreasing number of members chose to pay more than the statutory minimum. Many had done so before the war. In 1939 the average subscription had brought in 19s; in 1946 the figure was 13s. Clearly an increase in subscription was justified and in 1953 it was raised to £1. Twelve years later, in 1965, to keep pace with rising costs, it was increased to £2. These increases only temporarily affected the rate of recruitment; indeed it is since 1953 that the growth of membership and the rise in subscription income have been most rapid. The Trust since 1937 has encouraged members to pay by deed of covenant, thus enabling income tax at the standard rate to be reclaimed on subscriptions. Some 17 per cent of members choose to do so.

The gross receipts from all membership subscriptions amounted in 1966 to some £216,000. Against this sum must be set the cost of servicing members and of the membership department. This amounted in the same year to about 7s per member. Since 1954 the membership department has been housed in the Blewcoat School at 23 Caxton Street, an attractive redbrick building with stone quoins built in 1709. It provides little more than a single pilastered hall, but with its contemporary panelling and crisply carved Corinthian capitals it makes an appropriate home for a branch of the Trust's work that brings it directly in touch with members. After 1960 rapid growth placed a severe strain both on the staff at the Blewcoat school and on the old method of registering and checking members. Accordingly early in 1967 computer methods were introduced to deal with membership records.

SPECIAL TYPES OF MEMBERSHIP

There are certain special types of membership. Family membership enables any Ordinary Member to introduce members of his family living at the same address at a reduced subscription of one pound. Corporate Membership, introduced in 1954, permits an organisation, such as a business firm, for an expenditure of £15 to obtain five transferable tickets for the use of its employees. A payment of £30 secures ten tickets, and so on *pro rata*. There are some 400 corporate members. A Junior Corporate Membership introduced in 1965 enables a school or youth group to become a member and to take parties of up to thirty students to visit Trust properties.

For nearly seventy years Life Membership cost £20. After a small increase (1964) to £25, it is now £50, a more realistic figure. Donors of £100 or more qualify for Honorary Membership. Benefactors are those who give £500 or more, or property of an equivalent value. There are some 8,000 Honorary and Life Members. They receive the Trust's silver medal designed in 1963 by Christopher Ironside. Struck by the Royal Mint, it carries on one side a portrait of Queen Elizabeth the Queen Mother, President of the Trust, and on the other the oak leaf symbol.

The original Articles of Association and the National Trust Act of 1907 provided for a category of Local Corresponding Members who paid no subscription but undertook to further the work of the Trust. There were usually between forty and seventy such members, acting somewhat as unofficial representatives in the counties. They ceased to be appointed after 1932. Other categories of membership have been tried and abandoned. Such were Associate Membership at half-a-crown and Junior Associate Membership at ten shillings introduced respectively in 1935 and 1958. The response to both was disappointing.

Members have the right to visit Trust properties without payment when they are open to the public. It is, curiously enough, a privilege of which they avail themselves sparingly. The average member uses his free pass to visit only one property a year. This implies that most people still join the Trust to give rather than to get. The right of free entry is also enjoyed by members of the National Trusts for Scotland, Jersey, the Isle of Man, Australia, and the United States. Members receive the Annual Report, a *News Letter* issued from time to time, and the *List of Properties*. The last, which currently runs to 125 pages and contains particulars of all the Trust's properties, is expensive to produce and a new edition appears every three years. It is kept up to date by the issue of annual supplements.[1]

When few houses, other than those owned by the Trust, were open to the public, privilege visits were arranged for members each summer. These ceased in 1956, but they have been succeeded by more ambitious tours. As long ago as 1939 the Historic Buildings Committee sponsored a tour to Belgian châteaux. Tours to France and Denmark followed in 1952, and to Sweden in 1954. More recently there have been tours to Denmark, Russia, Italy, and the United States, while coach tours of Ireland, and of the Lake District and other parts of England, are now an annual attraction. Following the example successfully set by the National Trust for Scotland, the Trust also organises cruises.

THE PUBLICITY COMMITTEE AND RECRUITMENT

As we have seen, the Trust for many years was little concerned with publicity. Occasionally a word in the right quarter produced an appreciative article in *The Times* or the *Spectator*, and a leaflet entitled *Aims and Work*, first published in the nineties, was periodically reprinted and brought up to date. Signs of change appear in the early twenties. Announcements about the work of the Trust in *The Times* became so frequent that the *Manchester Guardian* and *Yorkshire Post* complained in 1926 of the preferential treatment accorded to their rival. The Executive Committee agreed in future to release all announcements through the Press Association, but decided, perhaps with misplaced loyalty, to give *The Times* forty-eight hours prior warning of such announcements. Two years later, in 1928, came the decisive step mentioned in Chapter 4. A Propaganda Committee was set up 'to advise the Executive Committee on questions of propaganda and publicity'. This later became the Publicity Committee. It lapsed during the war, but was reconstituted in 1946 with wider terms of reference and more than advisory powers. Today it is composed of people associated with publicity in its various forms, with public relations, and with the Trust's lecture service. Though in 1931 the Committee acquired a publicity assistant, it was not until 1946 that a public relations officer was appointed and a publicity department set up. Consideration had previously been given more than once to the possibility of placing the Trust's external relations in the hands of a specialist firm. This alternative was rejected, probably wisely. Though the help provided by specialist firms has sometimes been valuable, the nature of the Trust is unusual and offers little parallel with that of other bodies; thus its publicity is perhaps best directed from within the framework of the organisation and by a staff which understands its special problems.

The publicity budget in 1928 was £500 a year, and in 1947, on the reconstitution of the Publicity Committee, was no more than £1,000. The amount allocated in 1966 was £17,000 (exclusive of the cost of running the Publicity Department). This is a disproportionately small sum for a concern spending over one and three-quarter millions a year.

The Publicity Department's first concern is to stimulate the recruitment of members and thus both to increase the Trust's income and widen the basis of its support. It does this by the dissemination of literature, and by features in the press and television, while in a dozen other ways membership of the Trust is made attractive and its advantages emphasised. As long ago as 1920 a course of lectures was delivered at University College and four years later the young B.B.C. put on a series of talks. In 1933 the Council announced that forty lectures had been given in the previous year and appealed for lecturers. De la Mare, Hugh Walpole, and Sir Harold Nicolson were among those who spoke for the Trust at this period. Today there is a panel of over a hundred volunteer lecturers; in their own time and for the sake of the cause, they speak up and down the country.

Many of the Trust's country houses were built in the great age of chamber music and since 1961 members and visitors have been able to enjoy performances of high standard. They are arranged by the National Trust Concerts Society, and they owe much of their success to the President, Mr Yehudi Menuhin. In the expansive days before the Second World War there was a biennial Trust dinner, and the Publicity Committee organised other gastronomic pleasures such as a dinner at which Winston Churchill was among the speakers, banquets in the halls of the City livery companies, and a fortieth anniversary dinner which the Prince of Wales attended. These feasts have now given place to more modest entertainment, and in particular to the spring meeting at the Festival Hall, where some 3,000 members gather each year to hear speakers on matters of concern to the Trust and to see films relating to its aims. All these activities attract members and raise money.

In 1948 the Trust for the first time took space at the Royal Show primarily 'to familiarise the agricultural community with the Trust's farming methods', but also to recruit new members from that community. This marked the inception of a policy which has led to regular representation at such functions as the Game Fair and the Chelsea Flower Show. Since 1958, when Christie's, the National Book League and the *Daily Mail*, all gave hospitality to works of art or books from the Trust's collections, exhibitions have been an almost annual occurrence. The Trust also mounts mobile exhibitions which tour the country by van.

Apart from the guidebooks which are the concern of the Historic

Buildings Department, the Publicity Committee supervises the production of literature. It is initially responsible for the Annual Report, the *List of Properties*, the *News Letter* (launched in 1954 to replace a quarterly bulletin that ceased publication in the war), general and regional publicity leaflets, advertisements both in the national press and in such valuable media as the *Law Gazette* (where solicitors learn that the Trust is among the deserving causes which they can recommend to testators), and also for editorial matter. A map of properties in Kent, a county where the Trust was particularly active in early days, was issued to members in 1914. In 1957, through the generosity of an anonymous benefactor, a book atlas of England and Wales showing the Trust's properties was printed. It was superseded in 1964 by a gazetteer, produced in conjunction with Messrs Bartholomew, showing not only Trust properties but other interesting buildings and landscape sites accessible to the public. The Trust has promoted books by Sir Compton Mackenzie, Clough Williams-Ellis, D. M. Matheson, and James Lees-Milne. It can claim credit for a design by Rex Whistler, an anti-litter cartoon by Fougasse, and posters in the Welsh language. In 1935 a first Trust film was exhibited at 122 cinemas, and the Trust in the last ten years has given facilities for the production of four documentary films, two sponsored by the National Benzole Company (*Beauty in Trust* and *The Vanishing Coast*), and two produced by the Rank Organization and Messrs Whitbread.

Following the establishment of the Publicity Committee in 1928, a photographic library of Trust properties was set up. It has been progressively enlarged and is now supplemented by an extensive collection of colour slides. In 1934 the first National Trust Christmas cards were produced, which have become a regular source of publicity and revenue. In the following year the Committee organised a competition for a National Trust symbol. One hundred and nine entries were received. The future Lord Harlech, the late Lord Crawford, Sir William Rothenstein, and Sir Kenneth Clark were among the judges. No entry was considered suitable and subsequently six prominent designers were invited to submit a drawing. That of Joseph Armitage, designer of the 'King's Beasts' at St George's Chapel at Windsor, was chosen. It incorporated the oak leaf symbol which has now become so familiar. A Trust tie and car badge have since been introduced. The publicity value of the sale of souvenirs is also recognised and a limited number are sold at Trust houses. Unfortunately most of the souvenirs now obtainable are of such lamentable design and quality as to be unacceptable. If specially commissioned they are usually too expensive to find a market.

PRESS AND TELEVISION

The Trust's experience, for what it is worth, indicates that where *membership* is concerned press advertisement does not produce results that justify the expenditure. Between 1959 and 1964 the Trust spent £8,690 on press and periodical advertisement for new members. The members directly attributable numbered 4,452. Results from television were even more disappointing. An outlay of £12,000 produced a mere 1,419 members. While television will draw crowds to see a particular house (see below), it apparently does not, as far as the Trust can judge, reach those sufficiently interested in the preservation of landscape and buildings to become members. The figures quoted may be compared with the results obtained by the distribution of the Trust's leaflets through such different media as the Historic Houses Guide and the Journal of the Royal Horticultural Society, and the results of special exhibitions mounted by the Trust. In the same period (1959–64) an outlay on leaflets of £10,613 brought 10,675 new members; exhibitions at a cost of £2,372 brought 2,967 members. In other words, for the specific purpose of enrolling members, the Trust's leaflets and exhibitions were pound for pound incomparably more effective than press advertising and television (see Appendix 4).

APPEALS

Hardly less important than the enrolment of new members are appeals for some specific work of preservation. Appeals for a stretch of coast or a threatened house have immediacy, and public response throughout the long history of the Trust has been remarkable. Hardly was the Trust under way when an appeal was launched for the repair of its second property, the fourteenth-century clergy house at Alfriston. It was an appeal of a sort to which members and the public over the years have grown accustomed but never insensible. Time and again a stretch of country or a building has been in danger; time and again it has been saved by money generously subscribed. In 1902 came the first appeal for the Lake District. The Brandelhow woods on Derwentwater were threatened. Canon Rawnsley thundered; public opinion was stirred; £7,000 was raised. It was then a considerable amount. One subscription arrived with the following note: 'I am a working man and cannot afford more than 2s but I once saw Derwentwater and I can never forget it.' Another subscriber sent a guinea with the words, 'I am blind and I am dying, but I remember my days on Derwentwater'. Much of the Trust's support has always come in small amounts and from those for whom a donation is a sacrifice. In 1906 a more ambitious appeal was launched for 750 acres of Gowbarrow on the shores of Ullswater; advertisements were inserted in *The Times* and the *Manchester Guardian*. £12,000 was raised. The first subscription received was a 3*d* piece. So the story of appeal and response has gone on. It is a comment on the generosity of the public.

In 1937 the Trust had seven public appeals on its hands and between the world wars properties were repeatedly saved in this way. Among notable appeals were those for Ashridge (1921) £45,000, Box Hill (1923) £7,000, land surrounding Stonehenge (1929) £9,000, Buttermere (1935) £14,000, Dovedale (1938) £13,900, and the Pembrokeshire Coast (1939) £15,000. In 1939, as in 1914, public appeals ceased for the duration of the war. Since 1945 the Trust has appealed to the public more sparingly, but for larger sums. There have been major appeals for Clumber Park (1945) £75,000, the Stratford-on-Avon Canal (1960) £22,000, and the Long Mynd (1965) for which £19,000 was found within six months. 1965 also saw the launching of Enterprise Neptune, a major appeal to raise £2 million for the acquisition and protection of unspoilt coastland (see Chapter 6). In recent years appeals for smaller sums have been addressed to members rather than the general public and have been circulated with the Annual Report. In this way money has been raised for buildings such as Maister's House in Hull, the Priest's House at Easton-on-the Hill, and Paine's elegant chapel at Gibside, and for woodlands and open spaces.

The Trust has only launched one major appeal for its general funds. This was the Jubilee Appeal of 1946, and its primary purpose was to enable the Trust to meet the liability for deferred repairs and farm improvements which had accumulated during the war. Dr Hugh Dalton, Chancellor of the Exchequer, whose name will always mean much to those concerned for the landscape and buildings of this country, offered from the Government pound for pound up to a maximum of £60,000. Ultimately the public found £62,806, and thus a total of £122,806 was realised.

Among the useful functions of publicity is to increase revenue from admission fees. When a house, accepted with an endowment that was thought to be adequate, begins for one reason or another to show a deficit, publicity can often bring in more paying visitors to redress the balance. Television in particular seems able to stimulate a flow of visitors overnight. In 1965 programmes on the regional station boosted the year's attendance at Nostell Priory by over 100 per cent. In 1966 television coverage at Saltram, produced results no less satisfactory and increased the number of visitors from 7,600 to 16,600.

LOCAL CENTRES

A review of recruitment and publicity is incomplete without reference to the Local Centres of the Trust. A shortlived centre was tentatively set up at Birmingham as early as 1899, and the formation of a Manchester Committee was discussed in 1907. Thirteen centres have now been established, the latest at Plymouth, dating from 1967. Others exist in London, Manchester, Birmingham, Coventry, Wolverhampton, Liverpool, Southend-on-Sea, Cambridge University, Cheltenham, Croydon, Leicester and North Wales.[2] These centres disseminate the Trust's message in the provinces. Their activity is primarily social. With lectures, evening meetings, and visits to houses, they provide entertainment and a sense of community for Trust members in a given area. At the same time they serve as observation posts, sending back timely information, here about a threatened stretch of countryside, there about a building which should be saved. They also fulfil a role as extensions of the Publicity Department, organising local appeals, mounting exhibitions, and not least providing the manpower to supervise publicity projects initiated at headquarters.

2

Over the years the annual reports of the Trust and the minutes of its Executive Committee record in sombre detail intensifying threats to the countryside and to historic buildings. They also indicate the marshalling of the forces of conservation. Reference has been made in Chapter 7 to the valuable contribution made by government and its agencies. The role of private organisations other than the Trust has also been important. Though 'private' each represents an active and enlightened section of the public, and the Trust's relation with these societies is appropriately dealt with here. The relation has been close. Propaganda rather than property-holding organisations, they have influenced opinion and promoted causes that contributed directly to the Trust's work.

In 1935 Nigel Bond, who had been secretary of the Trust, wrote that its first roots were to be found in the movement for the preservation of open spaces and that it might be said 'to have been the child of the Commons Preservation Society [1865], for it was among the members

Trimming Yew hedges at Blickling Hall, Norfolk. A week's work for two men

Box Hill, Surrey. The Litter Problem

The XVIII century Orangery at Saltram House, Devon. 1957

The Saltram Orangery after restoration, 1963

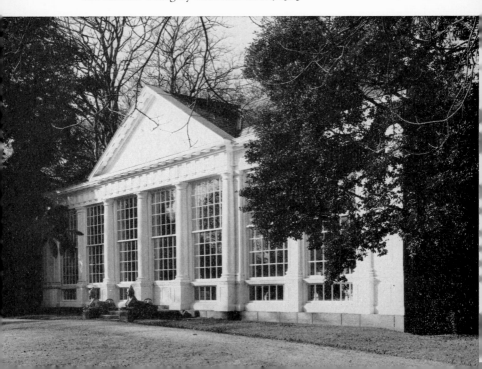

of that society that there was realised the need for such a body as the Trust.' Robert Hunter, it will be recalled, was for many years honorary solicitor to the Society; Octavia Hill was among its most active members. The Trust's debt to this parent is reflected both in the links maintained with the Society and with other private organisations concerned with the conservation of nature and open spaces. In 1896 the Commons Preservation Society and the Trust[3] circulated a memorandum to local authorities urging the suitability of establishing 'Victoria Open Spaces' as memorials of the Queen's diamond jubilee. Over a hundred were created. Forty years later the two bodies were still cooperating, and with the Council for the Preservation of Rural England discussed measures to preserve the coast. A result was the Pembrokeshire Coast Appeal launched in 1939. It was the first formal recognition of the need for Trust intervention on the coast.

In 1911 the Selborne Society consulted the Trust as to the possibility of the latter holding property for the creation of nature reserves and it was established that such reserves fell within the purposes of the Trust Act of 1907. In the following year the Society for the Promotion of Nature Reserves came into being and a cooperation began which has borne fruitful results. The Norfolk Naturalists' Trust, set up in 1927 and the forerunner of many county organisations of the same sort, had close connections from the start with the Trust's coastal properties in Norfolk. Today ten properties are leased as reserves to naturalists' trusts and four more are managed by such bodies on behalf of the Trust.

The creation of the Council for the Preservation of Rural England in 1926, of which the Trust is one of the forty-six constituent bodies (in addition there are roughly 200 affiliated bodies) had a direct influence on the organisation of the Trust itself. In 1934 a merger of the two societies was briefly considered and rejected, but measures were taken to avoid the overlapping which was becoming an embarrassment. The Trust Act of 1907 had provided for Local Corresponding Members (see above). With the creation of the Council for the Preservation of Rural England there seemed no longer need for such members and they gradually ceased to be appointed. Instead Trust representatives were elected to the local branches of the Council for the Preservation of Rural England as these were established. Fifteen such representatives were appointed in 1935, and by 1938 there were twenty-five, ensuring a close liaison between the Trust and the new organisation. Insensibly, and unfortunately, this practice later ceased, though the Trust still enjoys informal representation on the Council and on many of its branch committees.

In 1900 the Trust invited affiliation from archaeological and field societies, and the number of such affiliations at one time rose to eighty. A formal connection with these societies ceased in 1940. The Council for the Preservation of Rural England had been specifically created to coordinate the work of all bodies concerned with amenity, including the Trust, and affiliation to the Trust in addition to the Council for the Preservation of Rural England had become unnecessary. George V's silver jubilee in 1935 was the occasion of a joint appeal to local authorities by the Trust and the Council for the Preservation of Rural England. Recalling that launched in 1896 by the Trust and the Commons Preservation Society, the appeal urged that the best possible memorial would be to dedicate land for open spaces or playing fields. The idea provoked a national response, and found in one of its aspects vigorous expression in the achievements of the National Playing Fields Association.

Useful cooperation continues with the Council for the Preservation of Rural England. The Trust is represented on its Standing Committee on National Parks, and both bodies have fought and jointly contributed to expenses in the parliamentary battles of recent years, such as that fought over the Manchester Corporation's proposals to take water from the Lake District. The Executive Committee of the Trust, stressing the importance of joint action with the Council for the Preservation of Rural England, went so far as to minute in 1961 that no decisions on amenity matters likely to be of mutual interest should be taken without full consultation with the Council.

In the thirties the amicable relations of the two bodies were temporarily ruffled by the announcement that the Council for the Preservation of Rural England proposed to become incorporated for the purpose of holding land and buildings. To create a second holding body with an identical purpose would, the Trust thought, confuse public opinion. The matter was amicably resolved when the Council generously agreed not to seek powers to hold land inalienably and not to accept property which the Trust would be prepared to hold.

In a country where the appreciation of landscape is probably more widespread than anywhere in Europe, it is not surprising that the conservation of buildings has taken second place. The Commons Preservation Society antedated the Society for the Protection of Ancient Buildings (1877), the senior national body concerned with the preservation of historic buildings, by twelve years. Support for buildings was initially slow. Apart from the uninhabited buildings protected by the Ancient Monuments Acts, whose concern at one time inexplicably and abruptly terminated with the year 1714, there was no one to speak for the

English architectural tradition except the Society for the Protection of Ancient Buildings and the Trust. Further help came in 1924 with the creation of the Ancient Monuments Society, to be followed in 1937 by the Georgian Group, largely the child of its first chairman the late Lord Derwent, and in 1957 and 1958 by two new and active bodies, the Civic Trust and the Victorian Society. Lastly in 1963 came the Landmark Trust, whose concern is to preserve small buildings of merit and to put them whenever possible to practical use.

SOCIETY FOR THE PROTECTION OF ANCIENT BUILDINGS

Contacts with the Society for the Protection of Ancient Buildings have always been close. Its specialist committee concerned with windmills and watermills is consulted when the Trust assumes the charge of a mill, and it has frequently produced reports for the Trust on technical matters such as milling machinery. In 1945 an informal panel of architects with special understanding of the care of historic buildings was established on the advice of the Society to look after the Trust's houses, and additions to the panel are usually made after reference to the Society. The role of the latter in promoting the intelligent repair of old houses and in training architects in this special technique is invaluable. The Society's Lethaby (1931) and Bannister Fletcher (1953) scholarships, founded to provide training for young architects in the restoration of ancient buildings, its annual architectural courses organised since 1951, and its promotion of a Standing Conference on the Recruitment and Training of Architects, make today an important contribution to the maintenance of historic buildings. They are directly relevant to the work of the Trust. So too is the post-graduate course in the Conservation of Historical Monuments established, on the initiative of the Society for the Protection of Ancient Buildings, by the Institute of Archaeology of the University of London.

The association with the Society for the Protection of Ancient Buildings is a long one. The Report for 1896–97 referring to the Trust's first building, the clergy house at Alfriston, pointed out that it had been acquired 'with the cooperation and valuable help' of the Society. To such cooperation and help the Trust has since owed Montacute and the Bath Assembly Rooms, both acquired in 1931, not to speak of smaller buildings, such as West Pennard Court Barn which was repaired and given by the Society in 1938. The Society has also supervised the restoration of medieval buildings such as the Priest's House at Muchelney. In 1941 a closer cooperation was envisaged and the Trust took steps to become a trust corporation so that the Society, which was not incorporated and thus unable to acquire property, could hold buildings on lease from the Trust for periods of up to 300 years at a nominal rent. Ultimately, and for good reasons, this scheme was not put into operation.[4]

ACHIEVEMENT OF THE VOLUNTARY SOCIETIES AND CONTACTS ABROAD

The propaganda work of the amenity societies creates a climate of opinion favourable to the Trust, and has been directly responsible for gifts of land and buildings. It is also to these societies that the Trust, as a holding rather than a propaganda body, refers threats to buildings and open spaces which are not offered, and are never likely to be offered, to the Trust.

The impact of these societies, given their limited membership, is remarkable.[5] It is relevant that the Trust, before it had 700 supporters, secured the preservation of sixty-two properties. Looking back on its early days, the Trust may understandably view the achievements, one might almost say the disproportionate achievements, of the Georgian Group or the Victorian Society with a nostalgic envy. They indicate what can be done by a small and determined following. It seems that the effective role of an amenity society bears little relation to its members.

Through its honorary representatives abroad the Trust maintains useful links with foreign amenity societies. These links were strengthened by the formation of Europa Nostra. This international association of non-governmental bodies concerned with the preservation of historic buildings and their sites took shape in Paris in 1964 under the benevolent eye of the Council of Europe. Its annual assemblies provide a forum for the exchange of ideas, and the prestige that derives from its European character is brought to bear on national issues. Thus Europa Nostra has intervened to preserve the Venetian lagoons, the *Campagna* on either side of the Via Appia, the quarter of the *Halles* in Paris, and the coast of Malta. The Association has also made a study of the fiscal and legal provisions affecting the ownership and preservation of historic buildings throughout Europe.[6]

Chapter 15

The National Trust for Scotland

In 1899 a motion was passed in London advocating the creation of a branch of the National Trust in Scotland, and later Canon Rawnsley twice visited Edinburgh to promote a Scottish Trust. Nothing came of these initiatives. Action was taken when the Scots felt it was needed. In 1929 at a meeting of the Association for the Preservation of Rural Scotland a special Committee was set up to consider the formation of a National Trust for Scotland and two years later the Trust was established. Among those who played something of the role of the founding trinity in England must be mentioned Sir Iain Colquhoun (the first chairman), Arthur Russell (the first secretary and treasurer), the Duke of Atholl (the first president), and not least Sir John Stirling Maxwell.

In 1935 the Scottish Trust was incorporated by statute.[1] The National Trust for Scotland Confirmation Act was in general terms similar to the National Trust Act of 1907. However it wisely included among the purposes of the new body the preservation of chattels (in England this was not specifically provided for until the National Trust Act of 1937), and it differed in two other matters of consequence. First, the elected members of the Council were not all to present themselves annually to the suffrage of the General Meeting of the Trust, but one-fifth only were to retire by rotation each year; and secondly, the Trust had the power to increase or reduce the number of elected members of the Council, provided they were never fewer than the nominated members.[2]

Subsequent Trust legislation in Scotland has run parallel to that in England and has reflected concern with the same issues.[3] But in 1947 a Bill was promoted enabling the National Trust for Scotland to grant feus, which are analogous to leases in perpetuity, and also in certain circumstances to make exchanges affecting inalienable land (as for instance where it seemed desirable to straighten the boundary of a property).

ACHIEVEMENTS

An account of the history and work of the National Trust for Scotland cannot be given in a single chapter, and it would be presumptuous to attempt it. The Scottish achievement can be treated only in broad terms and with special emphasis on the differences between the two Trusts. Though the purposes and constitution of the two bodies are similar, Scotland has gone its own way. It is a way that reflects the special nature of local challenges and problems. The Scottish Trust also enjoys the enviable advantage of operating in a smaller community. Personal relationships and enthusiasms count for more; contacts are easier and more civilised. Aged observers are tempted to recall the Trust in England before the war.

Under the chairmanship of Lord Wemyss the Trust in the last twenty years has made rapid progress.[4] Membership in 1966 was 31,000, and in seven years had more than doubled despite an increase in the membership subscription from 10s to £1 in 1963. Income in 1966 amounted to £400,000, but there was a deficit on the year's operation of £20,000. This was met in part by legacies and donations (cf. National Trust, Chapter 18). The free general fund stood at £214,000, which in relation to the holding of the Scottish National Trust compares favourably with the general fund (£470,000) held by the Trust in London.

The Scottish Trust's eighty properties total some 70,000 acres, and are visited by a million people a year. Four properties have each over 80,000 visitors. The varied holdings include half a dozen imposing castles or country houses such as Crathes, Culzean, and Falkland Palace; many smaller buildings of interest, some of them associated with famous Scotsmen; fine gardens such as those at Inverewe and Brodick where tender species flourish in the mild climate of the Gulf Stream; and, as might be expected, superb mountain country—such as that of Glencoe, Kintail, Goat Fell, Torridon, and Ben Lawers with its rich flora—and remote islands such as Fair Isle and St Kilda. As in England some of the most important properties have been acquired through the Treasury in satisfaction of death duties. Brodick Castle with its contents came in this way, and numbers 5 to 7 Charlotte Square, Edinburgh. No. 5 is the Trust headquarters and the adjoining house is to be the official residence of the Secretary of State for Scotland. Through the Historic Buildings Council for Scotland grants are also received for the repair and maintenance of historic buildings. At present maintenance grants for four great houses total some £13,000 a year, of which Culzean receives £6,000.

In Scotland they have usually, and perhaps wisely, preferred to take endowments in cash rather than in land. The Trust thus holds neither large agricultural estates nor extensive woodlands. Its holding of 1,300 acres at Threave in Kirkcudbrightshire with four dairy farms is exceptional, and its woods cover barely 2,000 acres. As a result administration has developed on different lines. It has not been necessary to establish a system of area agents, and land agency is under the supervision of a single factor at the head office in Edinburgh. Administration in most areas is in the charge of representatives. Thus the problems created by a dual control do not arise. A representative can usually rely on the guidance of a member of the Executive Committee who knows his area. This arrangement, which establishes close personal links between the staff and the direction of the Trust, is one of the valuable features of the Scottish system.

A DIFFERENT CHALLENGE

Unrelenting pressure on open spaces, which in England makes the Trust's role primarily one of protection, hardly exists in Scotland. With a population of five million and a coastline longer than that of France, few of its beaches are threatened. In the Highlands large areas are underpopulated and their economy depends to some extent on attracting visitors. The issue is one of presentation rather than protection. People must be led, appropriately and wisely, into the country. The different context of the Trust's work in Scotland is illustrated by events at Balmacara in Wester Ross where inalienable land was recently provided for an airstrip in the hope that better transport would arrest a decline in the crofting population. In England the provision of land for an aerodrome on Trust property would cause astonishment. Policy on Fair Isle, where the Scottish Trust has contributed among other things to better landing facilities on which the life of the island much depends, illustrates a similar concern to maintain the local population and to create conditions in which a threatened community can survive.

Many of the characteristic activities of the National Trust for Scotland derive from the wish and the need to introduce people to the countryside. Since 1962 Information Centres have been created at considerable cost on the main routes to the Highlands, so that the holiday traveller may discover on the spot what is most worth seeing and learn something of the country he visits. A large centre at Bannockburn, to cost £110,000, with a museum, shop, and other services, will link with centres at Dunkeld, Killiecrankie, Culloden, Glencoe, and Glenfinnan Monument near Fort William. Other centres exist at Falkland Palace in Fife and at Inverewe Gardens in Wester Ross. At these centres the National Trust for Scotland stimulates and directs interest by the spoken word and with maps, posters, guidebooks and leaflets. Information is not confined to Trust properties, but attempts to cover everything worth visiting in the area. A special series of pamphlets evokes Scottish history and places the landscape setting in Glencoe, Culloden and elsewhere, in its historic context. The Trust is particularly qualified to offer an introduction to Scottish scenery. As the National Parks Act of 1949 does not in its main provisions apply across the Border and there are no national parks, the Trust in 1961 commissioned a landscape survey of the Highlands to identify and delimit the areas of the greatest landscape value.[5] It has long campaigned for an official body to protect the countryside, and its efforts seem about to bear fruit in the Countryside Commission for Scotland. The Trust's centres and the services they offer both promote the appreciation of the countryside and make a contribution to the tourist trade and to local economy. It is not surprising that the Scottish Tourist Board works closely with the Trust and nominates a member to its Council.

The Trust has other schemes which enable people, and not least Scots, to know Scotland and which open mind and imagination to the country's unrivalled landscape. Its cruises, which have been an outstanding success, were started in 1953 and are now an important and profitable feature of the Trust's summer activity. They were a logical development in a country where much of the most beautiful landscape, including Trust properties like St Kilda and Fair Isle, is only to be approached by boat. The lectures and the botanical and architectural expeditions associated with the cruises educate the public in the appreciation of the country and the purposes of the Trust. In the last fifteen years the *Dunera*, *Devonia* and *Meteor* have introduced tens of thousands to the West Coast and the Northern Isles.

An introduction to Scottish scenery is made no less effectively, and more cheaply, by the Trust's 'Meets'. Though often strenuous—ten to fifteen miles of wild country may be covered—they were attended in 1966 by over a thousand members. The number of 'Meets' and participants increases each year. A similar purpose is served by Nature Trails prepared in cooperation with the Nature Conservancy. The botanical trail on Ben Lawers, and the booklet that illustrates it, are models of their kind. Another example of Trust initiative that brings people to the countryside is the Adventure Camp. Such camps, started in 1963, were designed to introduce youth to the Trust's mountain properties and included voluntary service on some creative project. In the wonderful settings of Balmacara, Kintail, and Brodick, over 2,000 young people have been made welcome and have got to know the countryside and some of the countrymen who live there. Groups of volunteers have also carried out the restoration of the unique village on St Kilda and projects on Fair Isle.

THE 'LITTLE HOUSES'

The different background which accounts for the Trust's special approach to open spaces has also influenced policy in regard to buildings. In areas such as Fife there are attractive ancient burghs with a shrunken population where little houses of the seventeenth and eighteenth centuries lie empty and decaying for want of a tenant, a situation which would be inconceivable in the crowded South. From early days when it acquired property at Culross, one of the finest of the small and historic Fife burghs, the National Trust for Scotland has been preoccupied with the fate of these buildings. Owing to the vision of Lord Bute who in 1937 sponsored the National Trust's list of buildings of architectural or historic importance in Scotland (a decade before statutory listing under the Town and Country Planning Act of 1947), the variety and interest of the little houses in the small towns of Fife and elsewhere have long been recognised. Over the years a number have been acquired and declared inalienable. However, there are two drawbacks to a policy of ownership. Little inside such buildings warrants the admission of visitors, and the cost of acquiring a sufficient number to safeguard the architectural character of a burgh, or even part of a burgh, is prohibitive.

It seemed that a solution for the little houses of the burghs did not lie in Trust ownership. The real problem was one of repair and modernisation. If these could be carried out, suitable occupants could be found. This was the line of thought that lay behind the 'Little Houses Improvement Scheme', launched in 1960. The scheme enables the National Trust for Scotland to buy small houses in the burghs, restore them, modernise them while carefully retaining their character, and then sell them subject to restrictive covenants. This imaginative undertaking not only saves an increasing number of houses of intrinsic merit at the minimum cost, but has important social implications for the decayed economy of the burghs.

The scheme is financed by a revolving fund. Established with £10,000 from the reserves of the Scottish Trust, it has been supplemented by the Pilgrim Trust, by legacies and donations, and by an annual grant from the Fife County Council. With this financial instrument the Trust hopes in the next decade to improve properties to the value of over a quarter of a million pounds. Not the least satisfactory aspect of the Trust's initiative is the response from local authorities and individuals. The Little Houses Improvement Scheme has caught the public imagination and half-a-dozen amenity societies have been set up in Fife to carry out similar preservation. It is the Trust's policy wherever possible to promote intervention by other bodies or individuals rather than to confine its efforts to direct action.

Work is at present in progress or is due to start on a dozen houses in the burghs of Crail, Pittenweem, St Monance, Anstruther, and in Dysart which is part of the burgh of Kirkcaldy. A similar programme of modernisation, though not with a view to subsequent sale, is being carried out on inalienable properties at Culross, Falkland, and Dunkeld. At Dysart a picturesque but derelict group of houses on the shore are to be restored and modernised in cooperation with the Commissioners of Crown Estates and the Kirkcaldy Town Council. The former are the owners of the property and the Trust is to act as agent in the execution of a project which will cost not less than £50,000. This development is of unusual interest and points to the possibility of other public authorities making use of the Trust's special knowledge and experience in the restoration of old buildings.

GARDENS AND WORKS OF ART

It remains to speak of two other aspects of the work of the National Trust for Scotland which illustrate the provision of services for the public. The Trust has nine gardens administered by a Gardens Committee set up in 1950. But it is characteristic of the Scottish Trust that the activity of the Committee is not confined to this limited field. Acting as a coordinator for the various interests and organisations concerned with gardening in Scotland, it sees a duty to promote and foster gardening at all levels. Its status and its freedom from commercial interest enable it to fulfil this task. In 1965 a conference of gardening interests was convened, the first of its sort in Scotland, at which eleven organisations were represented. Five years earlier, to meet the increasing shortage of men with the knowledge and experience needed to make a competent head-gardener, a School of Practical Gardening was established at Threave in Kirkcudbrightshire. There young men can follow a two-year course which is unique in Britain and can expect to emerge equipped as highly trained gardeners.

In a different sphere, that of the conservation of works of art, the National Trust for Scotland has also made incursion into unexpected territory and created a public service. With the expansion of its work the restoration of tempera paintings began to pose a problem. Though derived from the Continent, this art form, characteristic of the Scottish Renaissance, was developed with such zest that by 1650 most important houses in eastern Scotland were decorated in this way. Many tempera paintings have survived, some of them in Trust houses, and their conservation presented a unique challenge. Nowhere else does work of this kind exist in such quantity. Until 1962 there was no art laboratory in Scotland competent to deal with them. In that year the Trust decided to establish a Restoration Centre. It remained to find a suitable home. In 1937, as a desperate salvage operation, Stenhouse, in the suburbs of Edinburgh, a little altered seventeenth-century building with rare original fittings, had been accepted by the Trust. For years it lay empty, lacking a use. A decision to lodge the Restoration Centre at Stenhouse ensured a future both for the building and for Scottish murals. With the help of grants from the Historic Buildings Council, the Gulbenkian Foundation, and an anonymous benefactor, a well-equipped centre was installed to deal—this is the significant point—not only with tempera paintings in the Trust's ownership but with others all over Scotland. Cooperation with the Ministry of Public Building and Works soon widened the field of the Centre's activities to include the restoration of sculpture and stone-carving. The complementary activities of the Trust and the Ministry have gone far, with the support of museums and galleries in Scotland, towards establishing at Stenhouse the nucleus of a national centre for art conservation.[6]

This brief review of the activity of the National Trust for Scotland has said little of its normal and essential work of preservation. This in character differs little from that of the Trust across the Border. Attention has purposely been drawn to those factors in Scotland which have presented a different challenge and to which a spirited response has been made. The National Trust for Scotland has not only achieved much in terms of preservation, but in default of other agencies has come to offer a range of services that would have surprised its founders but to which Scotland owes a growing debt.

Part 3

Law, Administration and Finance

Chapter 16

The Trust and the Law

In 1895 the Trust was registered as a charitable association under the Companies Acts, and minor amendments to its articles were passed by the Council in 1899 and 1901. Before the Trust was constituted, Sir Robert Hunter had spoken of the need for a special Act of Parliament or a Royal Charter, and as early as March 1895 the Executive Committee at its second meeting considered the possibility of special legislation. The matter was left with Sir Robert Hunter, and later in the year a legislative sub-committee was set up on which Lord Thring, Sir John Lubbock, James Bryce, General Pitt-Rivers, Miss Octavia Hill, and Canon Rawnsley were among those invited to serve. At the same time the secretary was instructed to discover through the Foreign Office how property holding trusts on the Continent stood in regard to the law.

Over a decade passed before these initiatives bore fruit. In 1906, when there were twenty-four properties and some 1,700 acres, the Executive Committee felt that the time had come for legislation. At the Annual General Meeting at Grosvenor House on 26 June it was resolved to promote a Bill to reconstitute the Trust. A more formal recognition of its privileges and responsibilities had become essential. In particular, powers were required for regulating public access to the increasing number of buildings in Trust ownership.

THE ACT OF 1907

Sir Robert Hunter prepared the necessary legislation. As solicitor to the Post Office he had drafted, without the aid of counsel, between forty and fifty successful Bills, and in 1900 he had drawn up Lord Balcarres's Ancient Monuments Protection Bill. No one knew better the Trust's requirements or was better equipped to formulate them. In June 1907 he was able to report to the Executive Committee that the Trust's Bill, virtually unaltered, had passed the House of Lords, and a first reading in the House of Commons. In August the National Trust Act 1907 became law, dissolving the Trust as a limited company under the Joint Stock Companies' Acts and reconstituting it as a statutory body.[1]

The costs of the Bill amounted to £651 of which over two-thirds were subscribed by supporters. Within three months the new powers conferred by the Act were invoked at Hindhead, where the Trust was able to prevent the local authorities digging for gravel on the common. The first annual meeting of the Trust as reconstituted by the Act was held in November 1907.[2]

Thanks to Sir Robert's drafting, the Act was so well conceived in terms of needs and purposes that no further legislation was promoted by the Trust for thirty years. The Act restated the objects of the Trust in words identical to those employed in the original Articles of Association, and in defining such matters as the role of the Annual General Meeting, and the function and powers of the Council and the Executive Committee, it substantially reproduced the original constitution.

Where the Act of 1907 enlarged significantly on the Articles of Association was in the power conferred, first, to declare property inalienable, and secondly, to create bye-laws for its regulation and protection. Inalienability is of vital importance to the Trust, and has been a key factor in its development. The concept is time-honoured, but its nature is not always understood. Inalienability is applicable to land and buildings, but not to chattels. If the former are declared inalienable they can never be sold, given away, or in any manner 'alienated'. The declaration confers ownership in perpetuity. It follows that inalienable land and buildings cannot be compulsorily acquired by government departments, local authorities, or any other agency, without special procedure in Parliament. The last alone can override the sanctity of inalienable property. While in no sense sterilising land, inalienability is thus an effective means to its conservation. It is also a powerful reassurance to donors who part with their property in order to safeguard its future.

Since 1907 the Council, acting through the Executive Committee, has been able to declare property inalienable that is 'proper to be held for the benefit of the nation'. This more explicitly is land of outstanding beauty or buildings of outstanding interest. Of the Trust's 360,000 acres, the great majority are protected in this way, and the special parliamentary procedure which alone could alienate them has not yet been invoked.

When the era of postwar planning arrived, the Trust recognised a responsibility not to declare inalienable land which formed part of approved development projects. Following a meeting in 1945 with officials of the Ministry of Town and Country Planning (now the Ministry of Housing and Local Government), it was agreed that the

Newtown Old Town Hall, Isle of Wight, 1933

Newtown Old Town Hall after restoration by Ferguson's Gang

The Treaty Room, Derrymore, 1952

The Treaty Room restored and furnished, 1957. The Act of Union is said to have been drafted in this room

Trust should submit to the Ministry its proposals for inalienability and that if these were given clearance the Ministry would offer the strongest possible backing should any attempt be made, from whatever source, to invoke special parliamentary procedure for compulsory acquisition. Since 1945 no land has been declared inalienable without the agreement of the Ministry, thus ensuring as far a possible that the protective measures taken by the Trust do not conflict with national planning.

By a device known as 'dedication' the Trust is able to make over small and inconsequential strips of inalienable land for such essential purposes as road widening, and the power to do so has often been exercised in the public interest. The development of a network of much-needed motorways poses a new problem, for they seem likely to affect stretches of inalienable land so considerable that the Trust will be unable to meet the problem by dedication. As it is the Trust's statutory duty to protect its inalienable land, there will be no legal alternative to formal opposition. Where however the route of a new motorway is the best possible in the circumstances, and where the damage to inalienable property is not serious, the Trust will not be obliged to press its objections to the point at which parliamentary procedure must be invoked. Doubtless in such cases objection will not be pressed home, and the Trust will be content with a formal protest.

Sections 29 and 30 of the Act of 1907 emphasise the Trust's obligations and duties in regard to common land. It might be thought curious that the Act, in view of the purposes and outlook of the Trust, should specify that common land must be preserved 'unenclosed and unbuilt on'; that enclosures and encroachments must be resisted by all lawful means; and that no charge shall be made for entry to common land. Such stipulations echo the long fight, conducted in the latter half of the nineteenth century, for rights of way and the integrity of common lands which culminated in the victory of 1874 that saved Epping Forest. In this fight Sir Robert Hunter played an outstanding role, and the threat to common land remained ever present to him. It was also belatedly of concern to the Board of Agriculture who wished to include a clause in the Act of 1907 enabling commoners to claim compensation from the Trust. This was the only point which led to serious difference of opinion in the drafting of the Bill. Sir Robert Hunter felt that commoners' rights were adequately protected by existing law and by safeguards in the proposed legislation. In the end Sir Robert's views prevailed and the Act of 1907 makes no reference to compensation.

Like other charities the Trust operates under the close but helpful scrutiny of the Charity Commissioners who ensure that its operations are in conformity with its statutes and with the Charities' Acts. By 1918 the Trust had declared a large acreage inalienable. Over some of this it was clearly desirable to grant leases. However the Commissioners held that special legislation was necessary for this purpose and accordingly in 1919, after consultation with the Trust, they promoted the National Trust Charity Scheme Confirmation Act. On the passing of the Act it became possible, subject to the sanction of the Charity Commissioners, for the Trust to grant leases of inalienable land for so long and at such rents as seemed desirable. Since the Charities Act of 1960, leases for less than twenty-two years do not require approval, but those of longer duration are still referred to the Commissioners who must ensure that the proposals are in the best interests of the Trust as a charitable body.

FURTHER LEGISLATION

Apart from the specific difficulty met by the Charity Scheme Confirmation Act of 1919, the Act of 1907 stood up remarkably to the years. However with the passage of time and in particular with the launching of the Country House Scheme (see Chapter 12), it became clear in the late thirties that some redefinition of purpose and some extension of powers were called for. In 1936 the Annual General Meeting empowered the Council to promote further legislation.

A Bill, which was unopposed in both houses, became law as The National Trust Act 1937. It was of importance in four respects. Firstly, it extended the general purposes of the Trust. The Act of 1907 had referred to the preservation of buildings 'of beauty or historic interest'. After 1937 buildings qualified for preservation on grounds of 'national interest or architectural, historic or artistic interest', a change which in part reflected an increasing preoccupation with architectural values and their expression in the tradition of the country house. The Act, logically enough, also empowered the Trust to protect and augment the amenities of its land and buildings and of their surroundings. At the same time it included among the purposes of the Trust—and this was a new departure—'the preservation of furniture and pictures and chattels of any description having national or historic or artistic interest'. The clause relating to chattels has had far-reaching results and has led to the acquisition of great collections.

The section of the Act dealing with the Trust's purposes also mentioned access to, and enjoyment of, its property by the public. These had always been among the Trust's avowed aims, but no specific reference to them was inserted in the Act of 1907. Their inclusion in 1937 was appropriate and timely. After the Second World War, with increased means and leisure, millions were to visit and enjoy Trust property.

Secondly, the Act of 1937 permitted the Trust to acquire and hold land, buildings, and securities purely as investments for the upkeep of its property or for its general purposes. This provision enabled the Trust to accept endowments in property or securities when, soon after, it came to acquire mansions such as Blickling under its Country House Scheme.

Thirdly, the Act empowered Local Authorities, subject to the consent of the appropriate Minister, to vest land or buildings in the Trust, and to contribute to the acquisition and maintenance of Trust properties. These powers have been frequently used and have led to fruitful co-operation with local authorities (see Chapter 7).

Lastly, the Act of 1937 afforded a new, though subsidiary, means of protecting land and buildings. It enabled the Trust to accept from an owner protective covenants over his property and to enforce such covenants in perpetuity and against all succeeding owners. The right of enforcement was stipulated to exist even where the Trust could be shown to have no interest in land adjacent, such an interest being in law normally essential to the validity of a covenant. Covenants do not involve any change of ownership, and it must be emphasised that covenants with the Trust offer, like other covenants, a merely negative protection. An owner may covenant *not* to develop his park for housing, *not* to cut timber, or *not* to alter the elevations of an historic building. He is unable to covenant to maintain his parkland in good heart, to plant trees, or to keep a building in repair. Though covenants can never be positive, they have the advantage of flexibility. The restrictions that an owner may be ready to impose on land or buildings can be varied to suit the circumstances. Exceptionally covenants may be valid only for a limited number of years. While they necessarily restrict the development value of an owner's land, this fortunately will be reflected in a reduced liability for death duties. The Trust's standard forms of covenant are no more than suggestions based upon experience and can be modified to suit the wishes of an owner and the character of the property to be protected. The Trust today holds covenants over some 60,000 acres and a number of houses, thus affording a useful safeguard for landscape and buildings in private ownership. The degree of protection is of course not comparable to that enjoyed by inalienable land. Covenants, though they will deter, cannot always prevent compulsory acquisition by the authorities. On the other hand they do not entail a right of public access, and many owners understandably prefer privacy with limited protection to the complete safeguard offered by Trust ownership.[3]

Since 1937 further legislation has twice been required to deal with specific points and two Acts of Parliament have been promoted. Trustees wishing to make over entailed estates found it impossible to do so, even if the transaction seemed in the best interest of the heirs. To meet their predicament, a Bill was drafted to enable the Trust under clearly defined conditions to accept, and declare inalienable, settled lands and a mansion house with an endowment to support it. The Lord Chancellor considered that the measure, though unopposed, introduced such an important legal precedent that he insisted on its submission to a Select Committee, the normal procedure only for opposed Bills. The measure became law as the National Trust Act 1939, and since that date has achieved the preservation of properties subject to entail, such as Coughton Court and Hatchlands.

The first National Trust Act had fixed the minimum subscription at ten shillings. When prices rose following the last war, this sum ceased to be realistic. The gap between the yield from subscriptions and the costs of the Trust's administration widened. Power to increase the subscription was conferred on the Council by the National Trust Act 1953. In the same year the minimum subscription was raised to £1, and following the further inflation of the ensuing decade was increased to £2 in 1965. These changes seemed justified to members; resignations were few and membership of the Trust continued to increase. The passing of the 1953 Act also provided a convenient opportunity to bulwark the Trust against inflation by permitting the investment of funds in non-trustee securities.

GENERAL STATUTES

In addition to the privileges and exemptions of the National Trust Acts, the Trust has acquired others under General Statutes. Some of these are of the first importance and received preliminary consideration in Chapter 7.

The Finance Acts of 1910 and 1947 respectively gave concessions in regard to stamp duty on gifts *inter vivos*, and on conveyances and leases. The concession in the 1910 Act followed representations made by the Trust to the Chancellor in the previous year. Of greater significance was the provision in the Finance Act of 1931 which accorded exemption both from death duties, and from aggregation with other property in assessing the rate of duty, of land and buildings given to the Trust provided they were declared inalienable. In 1936 the Finance Act (Northern Ireland) extended the same exemption to Trust land in Ulster. The need for such legislation had been apparent since 1925. In that year, following Lord Curzon's death, the question of duty arose at Bodiam and Tattershall Castles, properties which he had given to the Trust. In 1926 and 1930 the Chairman of the Trust had made representations to the Chancellor of the Exchequer on the subject.

The Finance Acts of 1937, 1949, and 1951 extended exemption from death duty to cases in which the donor retained a life interest in the property, to endowments in land or money given by the donor of a property to provide for its maintenance, and lastly to chattels in a building given to the Trust. These significant measures offered owners a tax incentive for the transfer of property to the Trust. By enabling them to reconcile private advantage with public interest, the Finance Acts have led to the preservation of buildings and of fine country which might otherwise have fallen into decay or been lost to development.

Realisation that death duties were inevitably and persistently leading to the dereliction of historic houses and the break-up of unspoilt estates prompted successive Chancellors after the last war to introduce other legislation hardly less important to the Trust and the public. Since the Finance Act of 1910 the Revenue had possessed powers to accept land and buildings instead of cash in payment of death duties. After 1946, at the instance of Dr Hugh Dalton, these powers were effectively exercised. This was a development of vital consequence. Further Finance Acts in 1953, 1956, and 1958 enabled the Revenue also to accept chattels and works of art in satisfaction of death duty and to transfer them at their choice to the Trust and certain other bodies. The preservation of many of the greater properties and collections that have come to the Trust in the last decade has been ensured in this way. Given the present rate of estate duty it is to be presumed that this trend will continue. Owners, appreciating the financial advantage of the transfer of their estates to the Trust through the Treasury on their death, are likely to prefer this to a gift *inter vivos* or a devise. The Revenue's power to accept property in satisfaction of death duty is thus becoming a major factor in the preservation of buildings and unspoilt country.[4]

FURTHER AMENDMENTS

The law as it stands today is in general well adapted to the purposes of the Trust. The machinery of the 1939 Act relating to entailed property is perhaps unnecessarily cumbersome, and its form reflects Lord

Chancellor Maugham's extreme concern for the sanctity of entail. However the Act has only been called in use three times in the last twenty-five years, and is unlikely to be often invoked in the future. With the postwar tax structure entails have little to recommend them and their creation in the last generation has become a rarity. It is curious that the Act of 1939 did not make provision for the trustees of entailed estates to grant covenants. This omission and certain other minor matters it is hoped to rectify in an act consolidating existing Trust legislation. Possibly provision should also be made for the annual retirement of a proportion of the Council, on the pattern of the Scottish National Trust, so that the Annual General Meeting instead of electing twenty-five members each year will be required to fill only the vacancies caused by the retirement of one-fifth or one-quarter of the elected Council. As the result of recent events the Charity Commission is also considering new legislation to enable members to vote for the election of the Council by proxy and to change the regulations covering extraordinary general meetings and polls. When the Act of 1907 was passed there were 550 members and it was not unreasonable that thirty (5·4 per cent) could demand an extraordinary meeting and twenty (3·6 per cent) a poll. Today when there are 175,000 members thirty persons represent 0·018 per cent of the membership.

There is a further respect, and a major one, in which the progress of events has overtaken the Trust Acts. Reference has been made to the obligation—an obligation on which the Charity Commissioners insist—formally to oppose any considerable encroachment on inalienable land even when the encroachment, in the opinion of the Trust, is both in the public interest and would not materially damage its property. The obligation has become unrealistic in an age when development, particularly in relation to new roads, is taking place at a rate, and on a scale, not envisaged when power to hold land inalienably was conferred on the Trust by the Act of 1907. The conception of inalienability which the Act enshrines seems too inflexible in a time of rapid change. In coming years it is likely to put the Trust increasingly in the position of opposing developments which it thinks reasonable and desirable. Such opposition will harm its reputation.

There are grounds for promoting legislation to enable the Trust *at its sole discretion* to dedicate not only small strips of inalienable land for such purposes as road widening, but larger areas for new roads and public services. (It is not suggested that a new Bill should enable the Trust to dedicate for building). Power to dedicate in a wider but still restricted fashion would not impair the essential, and vitally important, ability of

the Trust to protect its inalienable property against undesirable development. A decision to dedicate would in every case lie wholly with the
Executive Committee. The Committee would be able to reconcile as
seemed best two differing but not always incompatible interests:
protection of the countryside and the needs of transport and other
services. If the Trust is not to become associated with obstructive rather
than constructive preservation, power to deal with this point may prove
necessary.

THE LEGAL DEPARTMENT

The link between the Trust and the law is, naturally enough, its legal
department. This consists at present of a legal adviser and two deputies.
Given the nature of the Trust, the work of the department is largely
conveyancing, but it is also the legal adviser's duty to ensure that
activity strictly conforms to the National Trust Acts, to offer guidance
on legal issues, and to act as intermediary between the Trust and the
Charity Commission.

Perceval Birkett, a solicitor friend of Sir Robert Hunter, had been
associated with him in the early struggles of the Commons Preservation
Society and on the formation of the Trust the firm of Horne and Birkett
were appointed honorary solicitors. As work increased it was natural
that the firm should be paid. It throws light on the spirit of cooperation
that informed the early Trust—while illustrating that its future scope was
not foreseen—that in 1902 the Executive Committee, in view of the cost
of the solicitors' charges, considered whether the 'legal work . . . might
be done by members and friends without charge, the work being
distributed among those willing to assist'. Sir Robert Hunter, from the
Chair, wisely opposed the idea, pointing out that legal expenses since the
formation of the Trust had averaged only £52 a year, that the solicitors,
whose fees were always reasonable, often made no charge at all, and that
the proposed change 'would not in the long run cost less and [the work]
would not be so satisfactorily done'. The firm of Horne and Birkett
were in fact to act as solicitors for nearly half a century and the young
Horne who had penned a fair copy of the draft Bill of 1907 in his father's
office was still conducting the Trust's legal affairs at the end of the
Second World War. By that time it had become clear that the scope of
the Trust's work warranted the creation of a legal department. A. A.
Martineau, who had joined the staff some time earlier, was appointed
legal adviser in 1945. During the twenty years in which he served in this
capacity, assistant legal advisers were appointed and the legal department
assumed its present form.

Chapter 17

Administration

As established by the National Trust Act of 1907, control and ultimate responsibility reside in the Council. Of its fifty members twenty-five are nominated by bodies such as the British Museum, the National Gallery, the Royal Academy, the Universities of Oxford and Cambridge, the Royal Horticultural Society, the Society for the Promotion of Nature Reserves, and the Society for the Protection of Ancient Buildings. These nominated members not only add authority to the Council's decisions but provide a permanent safeguard against the possibility of an irresponsible minority gaining control of the Trust. The other twenty-five places on the Council are filled each year by election at the Annual General Meeting. To this meeting the Council also submits its report on the Trust's activity during the preceding year.

A body as large as the Council cannot conveniently deal with day to day business, and its powers, as provided by the Act of 1907, are delegated to an Executive Committee whose members need not necessarily be members of the Council. This Committee from the inception of the Trust has directed its policy and controlled its affairs. Its chairmen understandably have played a decisive role in the history of the Trust.[1] The Committee meets once a month (except in September). It is established practice that members of the Executive Committee, and also of its sub-committees, are appointed for their personal qualities rather than as representatives of particular interests or organisations. None the less close links with bodies such as the Society for the Protection of Ancient Buildings, the Council for the Preservation of Rural England, and the Georgian Group tend to be reflected in the membership of Trust committees, while the custom has sensibly arisen of appointing to the Executive Committee a Conservative and a Labour member of parliament who can represent the Trust's views in the House when legislation affecting the amenities is under consideration.[2] Furthermore the chairmen of regional committees (see Chapter 8) are now appointed *ex officio* to the Executive Committee to ensure uniform policy throughout the country.

The members of the Executive Committee, though they have a

common concern for the preservation of the countryside and historic buildings, vary widely in their experience. Professional men, business men, and not least landowners with a lifetime's knowledge of the country and country problems, have their special contributions to make. The size of the Executive Committee has tended to increase with the growth of the Trust, but as early as 1899 the need for a smaller Committee for detailed business was apparent. In that year a Finance and General Purposes Committee was set up by the Executive. Meeting monthly, its terms of reference were:

(a) To control the ordinary office expenditure of the Trust.
(b) To deal with other financial questions, reporting to the Executive Committee when necessary.
(c) To deal with other matters, referred to it either by the Executive Committee or in pressing cases by the Chairman.

Its beginnings were modest, and at its first meeting the Committee considered such matters as the rent of the Trust's offices, legal charges, and the deeds of a newly acquired property at Ide Hill in Kent. But the Committee controlled the purse strings, and power tends to derive from the purse. After Sir Robert Hunter's death the Committee played an increasingly important role, and in 1915 it somewhat peremptorily recommended that 'the Executive Committee should make a standing order . . . that no decision of theirs involving expenditure of money should take effect until approved and endorsed by the Finance Committee or until the Committee has had an opportunity of submitting to the Executive Committee its reasons for disapproval.' Six years later the terms of reference of the General Purposes Committee were considerably widened. Among other changes, it was empowered 'to receive and give preliminary consideration to any matter relating to the work of the Trust brought before it by any of its members'. This was no more than recognition of its current practice. The Committee was in a fair way to becoming an inner cabinet. In later years it has habitually dealt not only with questions of finance but has given careful consideration to controversial issues and problems of policy before submitting them to the Executive Committee. This role has been valuable, but it had drawbacks when the chairmanship of the two Committees was held, as was usually the case, by different men, and when the members of the General Purposes Committee were not necessarily members of the Executive. These drawbacks disappeared in 1965. Since that date the chairman of the Executive has also been chairman of the General Purposes Committee, and the latter has become a true sub-committee, its members (eleven in 1966) all being members of the Executive.

The Executive appoints five specialist committees—the Estates, Historic Buildings, Gardens, Publicity, and Finance Committees—to advise on particular aspects of the Trust's work. They are predominantly committees of experts, and take decisions on technical or semi-technical matters. They also consider and refer to the Executive Committee issues of policy in the fields for which they are responsible. Thus the Estates Committee will forward to the Executive its views on the amalgamation of farm tenancies or the management of woodlands, and the Historic Buildings Committee its recommendations on country houses and their contents or on planning proposals affecting Trust buildings.

The Executive and its sub-committees are permanent in the sense that their members do not retire by rote and are eligible for re-appointment. This continuity is useful, for committee members are usually able to contribute to the Trust precisely in so far as they have visited its many and widely scattered properties and made themselves conversant with local problems. Chairmen of the Estates Committee, such as G. M. Trevelyan and Lord De La Warr, and of the Historic Buildings Committee, such as Lord Esher and Lord Rosse, have been valuable in direct ratio to the time which they have devoted over many years to visiting Trust properties and appreciating the diverse issues involved.

Even before 1914 the Trust's holdings were so widely distributed, and many of them so far from the centre of administration, that the Executive set up Local Committees to manage specific properties. This arrangement had the advantage of keeping the Trust in contact with local opinion and of enlisting local enthusiasm and knowledge. There are today over eighty local committees. Many, such as the Bodiam, Tattershall, Ashridge, Box Hill, Hindhead and Farne Islands Committees, have important properties in their care and more was said of their work in Chapter 9. Members of local committees hold office for three years, but are re-eligible.

With expansion after the Second World War, it became evident that a regional organisation was also necessary if the Trust was to avoid over-centralisation. Circumstances in Ulster had led to the establishment of a semi-autonomous committee there in 1936. Committees for the Lake District and Wales, where special conditions also prevailed, were set up in 1942 and 1945. More recently, as stated in Chapter 8, Northumberland and Durham (1964), Devon and Cornwall (1965), East Anglia (1966), and the Severn Valley (1967) received their separate Committees. The terms of reference and the responsibilities of the regional committees are laid down by the Executive. The head office of the Trust retains control of general policy, of finance, of negotiations with central as opposed to local government authorities, and of various other matters, such as the acquisition of properties and inalienability.

The members of the Trust's many committees serve in an honorary capacity. Service in many cases means far more than attendance at committee meetings. The chairman of the Executive Committee may devote as many as two or three days a week to the work of the Trust. Other chairmen also give generously of their time, and committee members with special knowledge travel up and down the country to advise on estate management, forestry, and historic buildings. Though committee members attending meetings may in certain circumstances charge their travel expenses, few chose to do so. Special advisory visits to properties are also chargeable to the Trust. The same voluntary service is given by the Trust's honorary advisers and honorary representatives (see Chapters 9 and 12).

The public spirit that finds expression in the committees of the Trust calls for comment. For seventy years people have come forward to undertake burdensome service that brings no material reward. Their satisfaction was to further work which they believed valuable. Whether the Trust in a changing society will be able indefinitely to rely on the same supply of voluntary talent is uncertain. The uncertainty confronts most charities. There may be no decline in public spirit, but a change of tempo and sharpening economic pressure make it difficult for men of goodwill to devote themselves to unpaid service. Fewer people have time and means. This is particularly true of the professional class which faces greater competition for less reward. The high average age of some of the Trust's committees and the difficulty of enlisting suitable young men to carry on is already causing concern. Young men and contact with new ideas are essential.

HEAD OFFICE STAFF

A committee can direct but it cannot run an organisation. The Executive Committee lays down principles and takes major decisions, but day to day management is the duty of the Trust's officers. The first of these is the Secretary. Such is the character of the Trust that his role resembles that of a director of one of the national museums rather than that of a company secretary. His responsibility is second only to that of the chairman of the Executive Committee and the health and tone of the administration reflect his influence. The secretary must possess not only organising ability, but the tact and persuasion to reconcile the many interests of the Trust and the sub-committees which represent those interests. He must be able to accommodate views as diverse as those of donors and local authorities, of ecologists and farmers, of philistines and art experts. He must be firm yet emollient, tractable yet determined. The Trust has been well served by its secretaries.[3]

With the growing diversity of the Trust's activities, the term director-general would more accurately indicate the secretary's duties.[4] His work is largely supervision and co-ordination, and the ability to delegate responsibility has become essential. The secretary has two immediate deputies, the Chief Agent and the Historic Buildings Secretary to whom fall the supervision of the two departments concerned respectively with the Trust's estates, and with its historic buildings and their contents. The secretary must also oversee the ancillary services essential to the functioning of any large organisation: departments dealing with law, finance, and public relations. The special nature of the Trust also requires a membership department. The detailed work of these departments is considered in other Chapters.

Chapter 18

Finance

The Trust like other charities enjoys the valuable privilege of exemption from tax on most of its income. This means not only that the yield on its endowments is gross, but that tax can be reclaimed on any payments, such as subscriptions, made under a covenant for seven years or longer. The special tax concessions allowed to the Trust, but not to all charities, in respect of devises, bequests, and gifts *inter vivos*, were outlined in Chapter 16.

The following figures show the steady growth of income, exclusive of legacies and donations, and its relation to acreage, over the last sixty years.

	Income	Acreage
1905	837	188
1915	2,022	5,908
1925	4,371	21,000
1935	27,451	43,537
1945	162,500	113,174
1955	590,700	225,374
1965	1,617,700	328,189

These figures, impressive though they may appear, reflect increased responsibilities rather than comfortable circumstances. The greater part of this income is strictly tied. In terms of money that may be freely spent, and in relation to the scope of its activities, the Trust is poor and likely to remain so.

SOURCES OF INCOME

Income derives from five sources.

1. *Membership subscriptions.* These in 1966 amounted to £204,000. It has always been hoped that annual subscriptions, with income from untied investments, would cover the costs of head office administration. Since the Second World War they have never done so, though in recent years the gap has been narrow and in 1965 was only £1,800.

2. *Income from the Trust's free invested monies*, usually referred to as the General Fund. The interest on this fund, which has slowly built up over the years, in 1966 amounted to £25,000.

3. *Free legacies and donations*. These are not placed to capital account but are usually treated as income. From 1960–65 they averaged £155,000 a year. Viewed over a long period they show a steady increase.

4. *Admission fees paid by visitors to properties*. In 1966 the receipts at some hundred and forty houses and gardens amounted to over £150,000. This figure is gross. At many properties the costs of showing are considerable. At a house which is little visited the outgoings attributable to the admission and supervision of the public sometimes exceed the money taken at the gate.

5. *Property endowments*. These, in the form of investments and rents, account for the greater part of the Trust's income, but the money is tied to the maintenance of properties, and often to a specific house or estate. Many properties are given or left to the Trust with a maintenance endowment in a Special Trust. If this produces a surplus, it must be credited to the property concerned and cannot be applied to the relief of another property or credited to free reserves. On the other hand if a Special Trust falls into debt, the deficit arising must be met by borrowing from the free reserve. By 1966 certain Special Trusts were in debt to the Trust for the sum of £656,000. In the same year other Special Trusts in credit had piled up a surplus of £211,000, which the Trust could apply only to the properties concerned. It is not always possible to calculate endowments with exactitude and a few Special Trusts produce an annually increasing surplus which the Trust cannot easily utilise.

Unfortunately in a greater number of cases endowments have proved inadequate. Year after year the Trust finds itself obliged to use free funds and legacies to meet maintenance expenditure which it was originally envisaged that endowments should cover. A number of properties show a substantial deficit which is likely to be permanent. These deficits make a recurring demand on the free funds of the Trust.[1]

A few were anticipated when the Trust took over the properties in question. Certain stretches of beautiful country, certain houses of unique interest, seemed of such national consequence that the Trust of set, and surely well set, purpose decided to meet the annual deficits which the donors could not fully cover by endowment. Knole is a notable example of a great house where the Trust took such a decision in the public interest.[2]

At other properties where annual losses were not anticipated, they are mainly attributable to three causes. First, the decline in the real value of fixed interest investments in a period of inflation. To this the Trust as a charity was of necessity exposed before the National Trust Act of 1953 permitted investment in other than trustee securities.

Secondly, a number of agricultural estates taken over in the forties were 'unimproved' (see Chapters 6 and 11). Though they conformed passably to the standards of the time, the postwar social and agricultural revolution overtook them. Modern farm buildings, water and electricity, bathrooms in cottages: these, once luxuries, have become necessities. Since 1950 the Trust has had to spend £1,700,000 on modernising farms and cottages. This expenditure was not foreseen when endowments were arranged twenty and thirty years ago. Further, most of the Trust's farms are held inalienably as land of outstanding natural beauty, and it follows that there is rarely the option, available to the ordinary landowner, of selling an outlying farm to raise capital for the modernisation of an estate. Similarly, the Trust is unable to borrow capital on inalienable land.

Thirdly, when a number of country houses with large estates were acquired during the last war or soon after, the Trust had no previous experience of such ownership. The calculation of endowments, particularly at such a time, presented great difficulties. The Trust learnt a costly lesson. Since 1958 a new formula has been used to establish the sums required for endowments. It makes provision for inflation, and for improvements whose precise nature cannot always be foreseen but which, in the context of the twentieth century, will certainly be necessary sooner or later.

The endowment required to maintain a property is normally furnished by the donor (see Chapter 12) or more rarely is raised by public subscription. In certain cases substantial contributions towards the endowment of properties have been made by other charities, and notably by the Pilgrim Trust to whose generous benefactions the Trust has frequently been indebted.

Endowments at some properties are supplemented by annual maintenance grants made by the government on the advice of the Historic Buildings Council for England, or by local authorities, or by both, under legislation referred to in Chapters 7 and 16. Furthermore, in a limited number of instances local authorities assume full financial responsibility for maintenance, either as tenants or under the terms of a management agreement. In such cases no financial problem confronts the Trust and any deficit that may arise is met by the authority concerned.

Endowment may take the form of income-producing land and buildings, or of cash and securities. If the Trust's estimates reveal that the maintenance of a property under negotiation will result in an annual deficit, the deficit is capitalised at a given rate of interest and the gross figure represents the endowment required in cash or farm rents. The rate of interest at which deficits are capitalised is related to the average return anticipated from the investment of endowment capital in a wide range of securities. In recent years the Trust has usually capitalised deficits at four to five per cent. At 5 per cent an anticipated annual deficit of £2,500 calls for an endowment of £50,000. 'Why', donors sometimes ask, 'should the Trust capitalise at 5 per cent, when my capital will earn as much as 6 per cent or more if invested in gilt-edged securities? At 6 per cent a lesser sum would cover the anticipated deficit on the maintenance of my property.' The enquiry is understandable, but is fully answered. 'If you wish the Trust to preserve your property not only in the immediate but in the unforeseeable future, it must be in a position to combat inflation. Your money must thus be invested in a wide range of securities. Only a proportion of these will be gilt-edged; many will be growth stocks, since the Trust must look ahead. Few of the latter are likely to yield 6 per cent'.

ANNUAL DEFICIT

This summary of the Trust's revenue has revealed the essential fact that there is an annual deficit on head office administration not covered by membership subscription income, and on property maintenance and improvement not covered by endowment. The adverse balance which in recent years has amounted to between £170,000 and £250,000 has been annually met for the greater part by free legacies and donations, by the income from the General Fund and, if necessary, by drawing on the capital of the fund. This indicates the vital part that legacies and donations play in the Trust's economy. They may be regarded as the lifeblood of the Trust. Upon them its healthy activity depends. Fortunately over many years these benefactions, the gifts of the living and the dead, have been little subject to fluctuation, and their growth has kept step with the growth of the Trust's work. None the less they are an imponderable, the one factor in the economy which cannot be forecast with certainty. Thus the Trust's dependence on free legacies and donations, and the essential part which they play in balancing the budget, is disquieting. The long-term aim of the Trust is so to increase the income from subscriptions, endowments and the General Fund, that its economy will no longer depend on benefactions. These will then become available for new ventures and for the extension of the Trust's work.

Porth Farm, Bohortha, Cornwall. Before Trust ownership

Porth Farm after acquisition by the Trust. The caravans have been re-sited and screened in the wood

Carved Rococo decoration at Claydon House, Buckinghamshire after removal of brown paint and varnish

Design by Rex Whistler (*circa* 1929) for an envelope to contain views of Trust properties

CAPITAL ASSETS

A statement of the income position has given by implication some idea of the Trust's capital resources. It seems hardly necessary to state that among these resources cannot be included the inalienable property which comprises by far the greater part of the land and buildings in Trust ownership. These can never be sold or used as security for loans.[3] Property endowments in the form of investments are in the same case. Though valued at over five and a half million pounds, these by their very nature can rarely be realised. The capital is tied to the Trust's properties and has a specific work to perform.

The only capital assets of importance that can be freely spent are the investments in the General Fund, standing at some £470,000, and such part of the Trust's alienable land as is not held for the endowment of specific properties. This land is valued at approximately £850,000. It is present policy to sell it when vacant possession can be obtained. The proceeds of sale, which since 1961 have amounted to about £140,000, are credited to the General Fund. By contrast, when alienable land held as endowment is sold the proceeds must be invested and credited to the property concerned.

In relation to income, reference has been made to free legacies and donations. The Trust also receives many benefactions for a specific purpose, most usually the purchase, and more rarely the maintenance, of land or buildings often in a particular county or region. Such specific purpose funds amounted in 1966 to £1,200,000. Though they are invaluable to the Trust in the extension of its work, it must be emphasised that they are in no sense *free* capital, since the purposes to which they can be applied are strictly limited.

The investment of capital funds, whether tied or free, is the responsibility of a small Finance Committee, a sub-committee of the Executive which is advised by a City finance house. Except where donors have expressed a positive wish that funds for specific properties should be treated separately, monies are invested with a wide spread. At the end of 1966 the invesments held were 24 per cent fixed interest securities and 76 per cent equities (of which dollar securities accounted for 17 per cent).

The following figures indicate the growth in Stock Exchange investments held by the Trust in recent years:

	Book value	Market value
1955	£2,811,000	£3,111,000
1960	£3,990,000	£5,178,000
1965	£5,203,000	£7,030,000

Though the above increases are due in part to the investment of additional funds over the ten-year period, there has been a substantial capital gain, and an improved return. An endowment of £1,000, invested in 1955, produced some £50 a year; by 1965 the value of the endowment was about £1,400, and the yield some £70 per annum.

INSURANCE AND ACCOUNTING

The Trust's insurance position may be appropriately dealt with here. For alienable buildings that can be sold and thus represent a realistic asset, the Trust takes out comprehensive cover, as a private owner would do. Inalienable buildings call for a different approach. If a great historic house were burnt to the ground, to rebuild would be to produce a fake. No one would contemplate totally rebuilding mansions such as Hardwick or Blickling. On the other hand some provision must be made to enable the Trust to restore a partially damaged building, if for instance a suite of rooms or a wing is gutted. In respect of an historic house the Trust therefore takes out insurance to cover that proportion of the whole which it would be reasonable to restore. This can best be illustrated by reference to a hypothetical case. Let it be supposed that to reconstruct Headlong Hall in the event of total loss would cost £500,000. The Trust would not contemplate such a reconstruction, and would not therefore insure for such a sum, but in this and similar cases it must decide precisely what degree of damage the house could suffer and yet merit restoration. At Headlong Hall it might be 50 per cent (£250,000). The Trust has thus far been fortunate in suffering only one major fire. This occurred in 1960 at Polesden Lacey which was insured for partial restoration at £150,000. In the event the cost of the damage fell well within the Trust's estimate.[4]

Pictures, furniture, and porcelain in Trust houses pose a similar problem. The collections are worth many millions and the cost of insurance cover would be prohibitive. Full insurance would also be inappropriate. Like historic buildings, works of art do not represent an asset the Trust would ever wish to realise, and like historic buildings they are unique. Once destroyed they are lost for ever. The Trust therefore, at a reduced cost, effects a partial insurance for reparable damage only. Thus if a visitor puts his walking stick through a Reynolds, or if the veneer on a Louis XV commode suffers as the result of fire, the Trust is covered for the cost of repair. It is not covered for the loss or total destruction of such objects. Since 1911 the greater part of the

Trust's insurance has been placed with the Yorkshire Insurance Company.

Investment accounting and the control of endowments and special funds are handled at head office. In 1946 a qualified accountant was appointed to the staff, and there are now a chief accountant and deputy, with a clerical staff. The auditing of the Trust's accounts has since 1895 been entrusted to Messrs. Price Waterhouse and Co.

For many years property accounts were also handled in London, though in a limited number of cases local committees were responsible for their own accounts and submitted annual figures. With the growth of the Trust after the Second World War and the establishment of area offices, this system led to a centralisation of property accounting that was inconvenient. It appeared simpler that the area staffs should be responsible for records of income and expenditure on their properties. Since 1954 each area office has had its own accounts department, staffed by one or more clerks. They receive guidance from internal auditors who visit each area office in rotation.

Appendices

Appendix 1

Presidents, Chairmen and Vice-Chairmen of the Executive Committee, and Principal Officers of the National Trust since 1895

Presidents
1895 Duke of Westminster
1900 Marquess of Dufferin and Ava
1902 Princess Louise, Duchess of Argyll
1944 H.M. Queen Mary
1953 H.M. Queen Elizabeth, the Queen Mother

Chairmen of the Executive Committee
1895–1913 Sir Robert Hunter
1914–1923 Earl of Plymouth
1923–1931 John Bailey
1932–1945 Marquess of Zetland
1945–1965 Earl of Crawford and Balcarres
1965–   Earl of Antrim

Vice-Chairmen of the Executive Committee (since 1910)
1911–1921 John Bailey
1922   John Bailey and Nigel Bond
1923–1927 Nigel Bond and R. C. Norman
1928–1945 R. C. Norman and G. M. Trevelyan
1946–1947 R. C. Norman and Sir Harold Nicolson
1948–1960 Sir Harold Nicolson
1961–   Lord Chorley and the Earl of Rosse

Treasurers
1895–1924 Miss Harriet Yorke
1925–1932 Honourable Sidney Peel
1933–1945 Cecil Lubbock
1945–   Edward Holland-Martin

Honorary Secretary
1895–1920 H. C. Rawnsley

Secretaries

1895–1896 Lawrence Chubb
1896–1899 A. M. Poynter
1899–1901 Hugh Blakiston
1901–1911 Nigel Bond
1911–1933 S. H. Hamer
1934–1945 D. M. Matheson
1945–1946 George Mallaby
1946–1949 Admiral Oliver Bevir
1949–1968 J. F. W. Rathbone

Appendix 2

*Graph showing the Increase in the Acreage of National Trust Land
1895–1965*

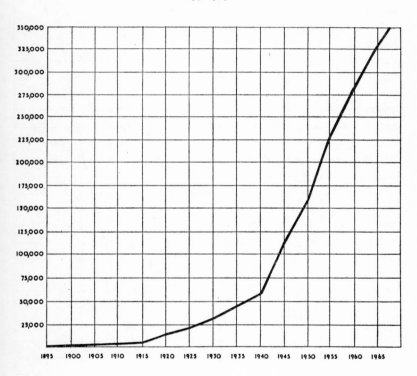

Appendix 3

Graph showing the Increase in National Trust Membership 1925–1965

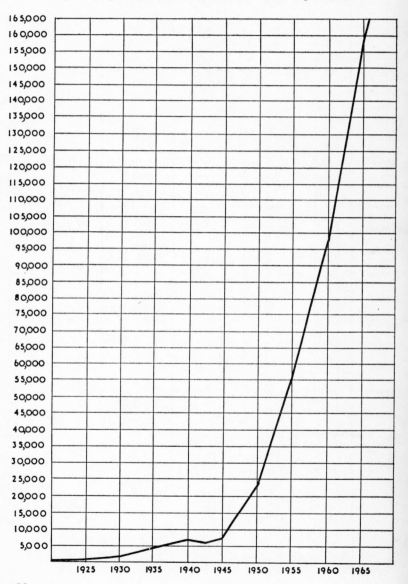

Appendix 4

New Members enrolled in 1966 Classified by Methods of Recruitment

National Trust publicity leaflets	2,224
Membership forms in Trust guidebooks, Annual Report, List of Properties and Calendar	1,547
Enrolled when visiting properties	1,462
Enrolled following visits to properties	152
Enrolled at Trust exhibitions	338
Enrolled at Trust exhibition van	333
Enrolled after lectures	135
Introduced by members and staff	618
Recruited at Area Offices	366
Recruited by Local Centres	149
Recruited by Local Committees	60
Overseas members recruited abroad	43
Enterprise Neptune appeal	2,588
Gift of membership	670
Press publicity and advertisement	48
Advertisement in the Historic Houses Guide	756
Sundry	37
No indication	1,995
Life and Honorary Members (various sources)	11
	13,529

Appendix 5

The National Trust Acts 1907 and 1937

I

An Act to incorporate and confer powers upon the National Trust for Places of Historic Interest or Natural Beauty.
[21st August, 1907]

Whereas the National Trust for Places of Historic Interest or Natural Beauty (hereinafter referred to as 'the Association') was in the year 1894 incorporated as an Association not for profit under the Companies Acts 1862 to 1890 with a liability of the members limited by guarantee:

And whereas the Association was incorporated for the purposes of promoting the permanent preservation for the benefit of the nation of lands and tenements (including buildings) of beauty or historic interest and as regards lands for the preservation (so far as practicable) of their natural aspect features and animal and plant life:

And whereas the Association in furtherance of those purposes have acquired considerable property comprising common park and mountain land and buildings and are or are reputed to be the owners of or interested in the properties specified in the First Schedule to this Act to the extent and in the manner therein specified:

And whereas the public are admitted to the enjoyment of the lands buildings and property held by the Association but no adequate powers exist for regulating the use of or protecting the property of the Association or for controlling the persons using the same or resorting thereto:

And whereas with a view to the continuance of the work of the Association for obtaining and preserving lands and buildings as aforesaid and for the permanent holding and maintenance thereof and for the preventing as far as possible their destruction or disfigurement and for promoting the permanent preservation of buildings places or property having historic associations or being celebrated for their natural beauty it is expedient that the Association should be dissolved and re-incorporated as in this Act provided and that the powers of this Act should be conferred:

And whereas the objects of this Act cannot be attained without the authority of Parliament:

May it therefore please Your Majesty that it may be enacted and be it enacted by the King's most Excellent Majesty by and with the advice and consent of the

Lords Spiritual and Temporal and Commons in this present Parliament assembled and by the authority of the same as follows (that is to say):

1. This Act may be cited as the National Trust Act 1907. Short title

2. In this Act unless the subject or context otherwise requires– Interpretation
'The Association' means the National Trust for Places of Historic Interest or
 - Natural Beauty incorporated under the Companies Acts 1862 to 1890 and
   dissolved by this Act;
'The National Trust' means the National Trust for Places of Historic Interest or
   Natural Beauty incorporated by this Act;
'The Trust property' means the property held by the National Trust for purposes
   of preservation;
'The council' means the council of the National Trust appointed by this Act.

3. From and after the passing of this Act the Association shall be dissolved and the Incorporation
several persons who immediately before the passing of this Act were members of National
thereof and all other persons who shall subscribe to or who shall hereafter become Trust
members of the National Trust in accordance with the provisions of this Act and
their executors administrators successors and assigns respectively shall be and
they are hereby incorporated for the purposes hereinafter mentioned by the
name of 'The National Trust for Places of Historic Interest or Natural Beauty'
and by that name shall be a body corporate with perpetual succession and a
common seal and with power to purchase take hold deal with and dispose of
lands and other property without licence in mortmain.

4. (1) The National Trust shall be established for the purposes of promoting the General
permanent preservation for the benefit of the nation of lands and tenements purposes of
(including buildings) of beauty or historic interest and as regards lands for the National
preservation (so far as practicable) of their natural aspect features and animal and Trust
plant life.
(2) Subject to the provisions and for the purposes of this Act the National
Trust may acquire by purchase gift or otherwise and may hold without licence in
mortmain lands buildings and hereditaments and any rights easement or interests
therein or thereover and any other property of whatsoever nature and may
maintain and manage or assist in the maintenance and management of lands as
open spaces or places of public resort and buildings for purposes of public
recreation resort or instruction and may accept property in trust for any public
purposes and may act in any trusts for or as trustee of any property devoted to
public purposes and may do all acts or things and take all such proceedings as they
may deem desirable in the furtherance of the objects of the National Trust and
they may upon or with respect to any property belonging to them or in which
they have any interest do all such things and make all such provisions as may be
beneficial for the property or desirable for the comfort or convenience of persons
resorting to or using such property and may exercise full powers of ownership
over their lands and property according to their estate and interest therein not

inconsistent with the objects for which they are constituted and may apply their funds to all or any of such objects.

National Trust not to divide profits among its members

5. No dividend bonus or other profit shall at any time be paid out of the income or property of the National Trust to any member of the National Trust.

Present property of Association vested in National Trust

6. Subject to the provisions of this Act all the lands buildings rights and easements which immediately before the passing of this Act were vested in the Association or any person in trust for them or to which the Association are in any wise entitled or which immediately before the passing of this Act were the property of the Association and all moneys securities credits effects and other property whatsoever which immediately before the passing of this Act belonged to the Association or to any trustee on their behalf and the benefit of all contracts and engagements entered into by or on behalf of the Association and immediately before the passing of this Act in force shall be and the same are hereby vested in the National Trust to the same extent and for the same estate and interest as the same were previously to the passing of this Act vested in the Association or any trustee on their behalf and may subject and according to the provisions of this Act be held and enjoyed sued for and recovered maintained dealt with and disposed of by the National Trust as they think fit.

Memorandum and articles of association of Association to be void

7. Subject to the provisions of this Act the memorandum and articles of association of the Association shall as to any prospective operation thereof be wholly void and the National Trust and the members thereof shall be exempted from all the provisions restrictions and requirements of any Act which applied to the Association and the members thereof as such. But nothing in this Act contained shall release or discharge any person from any liability or obligation in respect of any breach of the provisions of the said memorandum or articles of association incurred before the passing of this Act but such liability or obligation in respect of any such breach shall continue and save as in this Act otherwise provided may be enforced by or on behalf of the National Trust as nearly as may be in like manner as the same might have been enforced by or on behalf of the Association if this Act had not been passed.

Nothing to affect previous rights and liabilities

8. Except as is by this Act otherwise expressly provided everything before the passing of this Act done or suffered by or with reference to the Association or the members thereof as such shall be as valid as if the National Trust had not been incorporated and the said memorandum and articles of association had not been avoided by this Act and such incorporation and avoidance and this Act respectively shall accordingly be subject and without prejudice to everything so done or suffered and to all rights liabilities claims and demands both present and future which if the National Trust were not incorporated and the said memorandum and articles of association were not avoided by this Act and this Act were not passed would be incident to or consequent on any and every thing so done or suffered and with respect to all such rights liabilities claims and demands the

National Trust and the members and property thereof shall to all intents and purposes represent the Association and the members thereof as such and the property of the Association as the case may be and the generality of this enactment shall not be restricted by any of the other sections and provisions of this Act.

9. Except as is by this Act otherwise specially provided all purchases sales conveyances grants assurances deeds contracts bonds and agreements entered into or made before the passing of this Act by to or with the Association or any trustees or persons acting on behalf of the Association or by to or with any other person to whose rights and liabilities they have succeeded and now in force shall be as binding and of as full force and effect in every respect against or in favour of the National Trust and may be enforced as fully and effectually as if instead of the Association or the trustees or persons acting on behalf of the Association the National Trust had been a party thereto.

Contracts prior to Act to be binding

10. Nothing in this Act contained shall release discharge or suspend any action or other proceeding which was pending by or against the Association or any member thereof in relation to the affairs of the Association or to which the Association or any member thereof in relation to such affairs were parties immediately before the passing of this Act but such action suit or other proceeding may be maintained prosecuted or continued by or in favour of or against the National Trust (as the case may be) in the same manner and as effectually and advantageously as the same might have been maintained prosecuted or continued by or in favour of or against the Association or any member thereof if this Act had not been passed the National Trust and the members thereof being in reference to the matters aforesaid in all respects substituted for the Association and its members respectively.

Actions &c. not to abate

11. From and after the passing of this Act and except as is by this Act otherwise expressly provided the National Trust shall in all respects be subject to and shall discharge all obligations and liabilities to which the Association immediately before the passing of this Act were subject and shall indemnify the members council officers and servants of the Association and their respective representatives from all such obligations and liabilities and from all expenses and costs in that behalf.

National Trust to satisfy liabilities of Association

12. All documents books and writings which if the dissolution of the Association and the avoidance of its memorandum and articles of association had not taken place would have been receivable in evidence shall be admitted as evidence in all courts and elsewhere notwithstanding such dissolution and avoidance.

Books &c. continued evidence

13. The dissolution of the Association and the avoidance of its memorandum and articles of association shall not affect any deed or other instruments or any testamentary disposition of or affecting any property in or to which the Association would but for such dissolution and avoidance have been interested or become entitled.

Saving to National Trust of benefits of deeds &c. in which Association interested

14. The members of the National Trust shall be divided into (A) ordinary subscribing members (B) life members (C) honorary members and (D) local corresponding members:

> (A) *Ordinary subscribing members shall be annual subscribers to the funds of the National Trust of ten shillings or more;*
>
> (B) Life members shall be the persons who were life members of the Association and any persons who shall hereafter pay to the funds of the National Trust the sum of twenty pounds or such other sum as the council may from time to time specify in that behalf;
>
> (C) Honorary members shall be the persons who were honorary members of the Association and any persons who shall give to the National Trust any property which or any part of which in the opinion of the council is proper to be preserved for the benefit of the nation or who shall give to the National Trust such sum of money or other property as shall appear to the council to entitle such persons to be distinguished as honorary members;
>
> (D) Local corresponding members shall be the persons who were local corresponding members of the Association and any persons who without pecuniary contribution undertake to further the objects of the National Trust in any parish district or place in such manner as to the council may seem meet.

15. *Every ordinary subscribing member shall be liable for the amount of his subscription and the subscriptions of such members shall be payable on the first day of January in each year;*

Provided that any such member may at any time previously to the thirty-first day of December in any year resign his membership and cease to be a member by sending his resignation in writing to the secretary of the National Trust but subject to such resignation in writing every such member shall be liable for the amount of his subscription in respect of the ensuing year.

16. No member of the National Trust shall be liable for or to contribute towards the payment of the debts and liabilities of the National Trust beyond the amount of the annual subscription of such member or of any contribution agreed to be given and remaining unpaid.

17. The first general meeting of the National Trust shall be held within six months after the passing of this Act and the future general meetings shall be held once at least every year at such time and place as the council may appoint and the general meetings shall be called and held in accordance with the regulations contained in the Second Schedule to this Act.

18. (1) The affairs of the National Trust shall be administered by a council to be called 'the council of the National Trust' consisting of a president of the council and fifty members of whom twenty-five shall be elected annually from among the members at the annual general meeting of the National Trust.

(2) Any of the bodies or persons hereinafter named may appoint a member or members to the council of the National Trust as follows (that is to say):

Two members may be appointed by each of the following bodies or persons:

> The Trustees of the National Gallery;
> The President of the Royal Academy of Arts; and
> The Trustees of the British Museum;

And one member may be appointed by each of the following bodies or persons:

> The Youth Hostels Association (*in place of The President of the Royal Society of Painters in Water Colours*);
> The President of the Society of Antiquaries of London;
> The President of the Royal Institute of British Architects;
> The President of the Linnean Society;
> The President of the Entomological Society;
> The Royal Horticultural Society (*in place of The President of the Royal Botanic Society*);
> The Vice-Chancellor of the University of Oxford;
> The Vice-Chancellor of the University of Cambridge;
> The Vice-Chancellor of the Universty of London;
> The National Trust for Scotland for Places of Historic Interest or Natural Beauty (*in place of The senate of the University of Edinburgh*);
> The National Museum of Wales (*in place of The senate of the University of Glasgow*);
> The Ramblers Association (*in place of The senate of the University of Saint Andrew's*);
> The Governor of Northern Ireland (*in place of The senate of the University of Dublin*);
> The chairman of the Commons Preservation Society;
> The Society for the Promotion of Nature Reserves (*in place of the chairman of the Kyrle Society*);
> The Selborne Society;
> The County Councils Association;
> The Society for the Protection of Ancient Buildings; and
> The Trustees of Public Reservations Massachusetts United States of America.

(3) Any annual general meeting of the National Trust may determine that a member or members of the council shall be appointed by or on behalf of some body or persons other than those hereinbefore mentioned either by way of addition to or by way of substitution for any one or more of the bodies or persons so mentioned or by way of increase or reduction of the number of members appointed by or on behalf of any of the bodies or persons so mentioned but so that the number of appointed members shall not exceed twenty-five.

(4) The council shall be deemed fully constituted and all acts and proceedings of the council shall be deemed valid in all respects if and so long as twenty-five members shall have been elected to the council as by this section provided.

Supply of
casual
vacancies in
council

19. If any elected member of the council dies or resigns the council may appoint in his place another member to be a member of the council and any member appointed under this section shall continue a member of the council until the next annual general meeting after his appointment and the acts of the council shall not be deemed invalid by reason of the death or resignation of any member or members thereof.

Powers and
proceedings
of council

20.—(1) The entire business of the National Trust shall be arranged and managed by the council who may exercise all such powers of the National Trust as are not exercisable only by the National Trust in general meeting and no regulation made or resolution passed by the National Trust in general meeting shall invalidate any prior act of the council which would have been valid if such regulation or resolution had not been made or passed.

(2) The council shall have power to make such regulations as to the procedure of the council (including the quorum required at its meetings) and for the conduct of the business and affairs of the National Trust and for the despatch of business at meetings as the council may deem necessary provided that such regulations do not contravene any of the provisions of this Act.

(3) The council may elect a president for such periods as they may from time to time fix by their regulations and may appoint such officers and servants as they may from time to time think desirable and fix their salaries and wages and the conditions of service including the provision of pension on retirement and determine their respective duties and the tenure of their offices.

(4) The council may also elect any number of honorary vice-presidents but the persons so elected shall not by reason of such election be members of the council.

(5) The council may exercise the powers of borrowing on mortgage which are by this Act conferred on the National Trust.

(6) The council shall appoint from their own number an executive committee and may add to any such committee for such length of time and with such powers of voting or otherwise as the council may think fit any member of the National Trust or other person whose aid they judge useful to forward the objects of the National Trust and such committee shall exercise and enjoy all the powers conferred upon the council by this Act except the power of electing a president and except any other power which the council expressly withholds from the committee. But the council may impose conditions and limitations as to the exercise of any of the powers enjoyed by the committee.

(7) The council may also appoint from their own number any committee for any special purpose and may add to any such committee for such length of time and with such powers of voting or otherwise as the council may think fit any member of the National Trust or other person whose aid they judge useful to forward the objects of the National Trust.

(8) The executive committee shall have power of appointing sub-committees for special purposes similar in all respects to the powers hereby conferred upon the council of appointing committees for special purposes. The executive committee may also appoint a chairman to hold office during such period as the

committee may specify and may make such regulations as to the procedure of the committee as the council is hereby empowered to make as to the procedure of the council.

(9) No act or proceeding of the council the executive committee or of any committee or sub-committee shall be questioned on account of there being at the time of such act or proceeding any vacancy or vacancies in the council executive committee or in any committee or sub-committee.

(10) No defect in the qualification or election of any person or persons acting as members or members of the council the executive committee or of any committee or sub-committee shall be deemed to invalidate any proceedings of such council executive committee committee or sub-committee in which he or they has or have taken part in cases where the majority of members parties to such proceedings are duly entitled to act.

(11) The council the executive committee and all committees and sub-committees appointed as aforesaid shall cause minutes to be made of all proceedings at any meeting thereof respectively and the council shall at all times cause to be kept minutes of the meetings of the National Trust and a register of the members of the National Trust with their respective last-known places of abode.

(12) Any minute made of proceedings at a meeting of the National Trust the council the executive committee or of any committee or sub-committee respectively if signed either at the meeting at which such proceedings took place or at the next ensuing meeting by any person purporting for the time being to be the president of the council or the chairman of the executive committee committee or sub-committee as the case may be shall be receivable evidence of such proceedings in all legal proceedings without further proof and until the contrary is proved every meeting of the council the executive committee or of any committee or sub-committee shall be deemed to have been duly convened and held and all the members thereof to have been duly qualified.

(13) Any instrument which if made by private persons would be required to be under seal shall be under the seal of the National Trust. Any notice issued by or on behalf of the National Trust shall be deemed to be duly executed if signed by the chairman the deputy-chairman or the secretary but subject as aforesaid any appointment made by the National Trust and any contract order or other document made by or proceeding from the National Trust shall be deemed to be duly executed either if sealed with the seal of the National Trust or signed by two or more members of the council authorised to sign by a resolution of the council or executive committee but it shall not be necessary in any legal proceedings to prove that the member signing any such order or other document were authorised to sign and such authority shall be presumed until the contrary is proved.

21.—(1) The property specified in the First Part of the First Schedule to this Act so far as the same is vested in the National Trust shall be held by the National Trust for preservation for the benefit of the nation in accordance with the objects

Certain property of Trust to be inalienable.

Extended
N.T. Act
1919
Sch. (1)
N.T. Act
1939
Sec. 12

of the National Trust and shall not be chargeable with any debts or liabilities of the National Trust and shall be inalienable.

(2) Whenever after the passing of this Act any lands or tenements (including buildings) shall become vested in the National Trust the council may by resolution determine that such lands or tenements or such portions thereof as may be specified in such resolution are proper to be held for the benefit of the nation and such lands or buildings shall thereupon be held so by the National Trust and shall be inalienable.

Power to raise money

22. The National Trust may raise money by borrowing on the security of any of their property (not being property specified in the First Schedule to this Act or in any such resolution of the council as proper to be held for the benefit of the nation) by way of specific mortgage thereof and by charging or appropriating as security for money borrowed the rents profits or income derivable from any of the lands and properties of the National Trust including the rents profits and income arising from any property held for the benefit of the nation.

Incorporation of certain provisions of Companies Clauses Consolidation Act as to mortgages

23. The provisions of sections 45 and 47 to 55 (both inclusive) of the Companies Clauses Consolidation Act 1845 shall so far as applicable extend and apply to the raising of money by the National Trust under the provisions of this Act and to the mortgagees of the National Trust and to the mortgages or other securities granted or given by the National Trust and in those sections any reference to the company shall for the purposes of this Act be deemed to be references to the National Trust.

Appointment of receiver

24. The mortgagees of the National Trust (other than mortgagees of specific properties with a power of foreclosure and sale) may enforce payment of arrears of interest or principal or principal and interest due on their mortgages by the appointment of a receiver. In order to authorise the appointment of a receiver in respect of arrears of principal the amount owing to the mortgagees by whom the application for a receiver is made shall not be less than one thousand pounds in the whole.

Accounts

25. Proper accounts shall be kept of all sums of money received and expended by the National Trust and of the matters in respect of which such receipt and expenditure take place and of the property credits and liabilities of the National Trust and subject to any reasonable restrictions as to the time and manner of inspecting the same that may be imposed in accordance with the regulations for the time being of the National Trust such accounts shall be open at all reasonable times to the inspection of the members.

Audit

26. Once at least in every year the accounts of the National Trust shall be examined and audited by an auditor or auditors being a member or members of the Institute of Chartered Accountants and such auditor or auditors shall be elected annually at the annual general meeting and any previously elected auditor or auditors shall be eligible for re-election.

27. The council shall apply all money received by the National Trust under this Act except money borrowed and money received from the sale of lands or other moneys received on capital account as follows (that is to say): Application of revenue Varied N.T. Act 1937 Sec. 10

First. In payment of the working and establishment expenses of the National Trust and the cost of management maintenance upkeep and improvement of the Trust property; Extended N.T. Act 1953 Sec. 4

Secondly. In payment of the interest on moneys borrowed under the powers of this Act and of the instalments (if any) of principal money so borrowed: And the balance if any shall be applied in furthering the objects for which the National Trust is established in such manner as the council may from time to time direct and may if the council see fit be invested in *securities in which trustees are by law entitled to invest trust funds*. Extended N.T. Act 1937 Sec. 4, N.T. Act 1937 Sec. 14

28. All moneys received by the National Trust on capital account shall subject to any conditions attached to any gift be applicable in or towards the repayment of moneys borrowed or otherwise in furthering the objects for which the National Trust is established. Capital Further extended N.T. Act 1953, Sec. 4

29. By virtue of this Act there shall be imposed upon the National Trust with respect of any of the Trust property which consists of common or commonable land the following duties and the National Trust shall (subject to the provisions of this Act) have with respect to the same property the following powers (namely): Powers exerciseable over certain Trust property

(A) Except as in this Act otherwise provided they shall at all times keep such property unenclosed and unbuilt on as open spaces for the recreation and and enjoyment of the public:

(B) They may plant drain level and otherwise improve and alter any part or parts of such property so far as they may deem necessary or desirable for the purposes of this sub-section and for the purpose of protecting or renovating turf and for protecting trees and plantations:

(C) They may make and maintain roads footpaths and ways over such property and may make and maintain ornamental ponds and waters on such property:

(D) They may on such property erect sheds for tools and materials and may maintain and repair such sheds:

(E) They shall by all lawful means prevent resist and abate all enclosures and encroachments upon and all attempts to enclose or encroach upon such property or any part thereof or to appropriate or use the same or the soil timber or roads thereof or any part thereof for any purpose inconsistent with this Act:

(F) They may set apart from time to time parts of such property upon which persons may play games or hold meetings or gatherings for athletic sports.

30.—(1) The National Trust may make such reasonable charges for the admission of the public to any of the property of the National Trust or any part or parts Power to charge for admission to

Trust property

thereof or for the use by the public of any such property as they may from time to time determine.

(2) The National Trust shall not make charges for admission to any common or commonable land or to any other property of the Trust to which the public had a right of access at the date when such property was acquired by the National Trust or the Association except such part or parts of such common or commonable land as may be from time to time set apart under the provisions of and for the purposes specified in sub-section (F) of the section of this Act of which the marginal note is 'Powers exerciseable over certain Trust Property.'

Arrangements with local authorities and others

31. The National Trust may act in concert with and make any arrangements and agreements with any local authority now or hereafter constituted or with any residents or committee of residents in the neighbourhood of any land or property of the National Trust or with any other persons for giving effect to the objects of this Act.

Bye-laws
Extended.
N.T. Act
1937
Sec. 12.
N.T. Act
1939
Sec. 14

32. For the regulation and protection of and for prevention of nuisances and preservation of order upon any lands or property of the National Trust held for the benefit of the nation the National Trust may make revoke and alter bye-laws for any of the following purposes (that is to say):

(A) For prohibiting any person without lawful authority from digging cutting or taking turves sods gravel stone sand clay or other substance on or from such lands or property and from cutting felling or injuring any gorse heather timber or other tree shrub brushwood or other plant growing thereon:

(B) For prohibiting or regulating the lighting of any fire on such lands or property:

(C) For prohibiting or regulating the firing or discharge of firearms or the throwing or discharge of missiles on such lands or property without lawful authority:

(D) For prohibiting the deposit on such lands or property or in any pond thereon of road-sand materials for repair of roads or wood or any dung rubbish or other offensive matter:

(E) For prohibiting the injury defacement or removal of any building structure or other thing upon such lands or property or of seats fences notice boards or other things put up or maintained by the National Trust:

(F) For prohibiting or regulating the posting or painting of bills placards advertisements or notices on trees or fences or notice boards on such lands or property:

(G) For prohibiting any person without lawful authority from bird catching setting traps or nets or liming trees or laying snares for birds or other animals taking birds' eggs or nests and shooting driving or chasing game or other animals on such lands or property:

(H) For prohibiting or regulating the drawing or propelling upon such lands or property without lawful authority of any carriage cart caravan truck motor car cycle or other vehicle and the erecting or permitting to remain on such lands or property without the consent of the National Trust or other lawful authority any building shed tent fence post railing or other structure whether used in connection with the playing of games or not and for authorising an officer of the National Trust to remove therefrom any vehicle drawn or propelled thereon and any structure erected thereon in contravention of the bye-laws and for prescribing any roads other than public roads upon which motor cars and cycles may be used:

(I) For prohibiting or regulating the placing on such lands or property of any photographic cart or of any show exhibition swing roundabout or other like thing and for authorising an officer of the National Trust to remove from such lands or property anything placed thereon in contravention of the bye-laws:

(J) For regulating games to be played and other means of recreation to be exercised on such lands or property and assemblages of persons thereon:

(K) For regulating the use of any portion of such lands or property temporarily closed or set apart under this Act for any purpose:

(L) For prohibiting or regulating horses being exercised or broken in on such lands without lawful authority:

(M) For prohibiting any person without lawful authority from turning out or permitting to remain on such lands any cattle sheep or other animals and for authorising an officer of the National Trust to remove therefrom any cattle sheep or other animal being thereon in contravention of the bye-laws or suffering from disease:

(N) Generally for prohibiting or regulating any act or thing tending to injure or disfigure such lands or property or to interfere with the use and enjoyment thereof by the public:

(O) For authorising an officer of the National Trust after due warning to remove or exclude from such lands or property any person who within his view commits an offence against the bye-laws made under this Act:

(P) For prohibiting the hindrance or obstruction of an officer of the National Trust in the exercise of his powers or duties under this Act or under any bye-laws made thereunder.

Extended
N.T. Act
1937
Sec. 11

33. The National Trust may in respect of any building forming part of the Trust property and being open to the public whether on payment or not make bye-laws for the purposes specified in section 3 of the Public Libraries Act 1901 in respect of such building as if they were a library authority under that Act and the provisions of section 2 of the Libraries Offences Act 1898 shall apply to any such building.

Bye-laws as
to buildings

34. Copies of the bye-laws for the time being in force shall be put up by the National Trust on the Trust property at such places and in such manner as the National Trust think best calculated to give information to persons resorting to such property.

Bye-laws to
be exhibited

Provisions
applicable to
bye-laws

Repealed
N.T. Act
1937
Sec. 12(2)

35. *The provisions of sections 182 183 184 186 and 251 of the Public Health Act 1875 shall apply to bye-laws to be made under this Act as if the National Trust were a local authority:*

Provided that in section 184 (Confirmation of bye-laws) of the said Act the Secretary of State for the Home Department shall for the purposes of this section be deemed to be substituted for the Local Government Board and in the said sections for the purposes of this Act the expression 'this Act' shall mean this Act.

Restriction
on digging
gravel &c.
from
commons

36. Any common or commonable land the soil of which is vested in the National Trust shall be deemed to be a common to which the provisions of section 20 of the Commons Act 1876 apply.

Saving of
rights

37. All rights of common commonable or other like rights or rights of way in over or affecting the Trust property shall remain and be unaffected by the provisions of this Act and save as in this Act expressly provided nothing contained in or done under or in pursuance of this Act shall take away abridge or prejudicially affect any estate vested in or any right belonging to and previously to the passing of this Act exerciseable by any person.

Copy of Act
to be
registered

38. The National Trust shall deliver to the Registrar of Joint Stock Companies a printed copy of this Act and he shall retain and register the same and if such copy is not so delivered within three months from the passing of this Act the National Trust shall incur a penalty not exceeding two pounds for every day after the expiration of those three months during which the default continues and any member of the council of the National Trust who knowingly and wilfully authorises such default shall incur the like penalty. Every penalty under this section shall be recoverable summarily.

There shall be paid to the registrar by the National Trust on such copy being registered the like fee as is for the time being payable under the Companies Act 1862 on registration of any document other than a memorandum of association.

Costs of Act

39. The costs charges and expenses of and incidental to the preparation obtaining and passing of this Act or otherwise in relation thereto shall be paid by the National Trust.

THE SECOND SCHEDULE

Regulations Governing the Calling and Holding of General Meetings of the National Trust

1. The annual general meetings shall be called ordinary meetings and all other general meetings shall be called extraordinary meetings.

2. The council at each ordinary meeting shall lay before the meeting a report of the work done in the preceding year.

3. The council of the executive committee may whenever they think fit and the executive committee (or in their default the council) shall upon a requisition made in writing and signed by any thirty or more members convene an extraordinary meeting.

4. Any requisition made by the members shall express the object of the meeting proposed to be called and shall be left with the secretary of the National Trust.

5. Upon the receipt of such requisition the executive committee (or in their default the council) shall forthwith proceed to convene a general meeting and if the executive committee or the council do not convene the same within fourteen days from the date of the receipt of such requisition the requisitionists may themselves convene a meeting.

6. A notice of every general meeting and of the agenda shall be given to the members at such time and in such form and manner as the council may from time to time prescribe.

7. Notice of any motion proposed to be made at a general meeting by any person not being a member of the council shall be sent to the secretary of the National Trust fourteen days before the general meeting. Such notice shall be signed by the proposer and two seconders being members of the National Trust and no motion made by any member other than a member of the council shall be entertained by a general meeting unless notice thereof has been given as aforesaid.

8. The non-receipt of a notice by any member shall not invalidate the proceedings of any general meeting.

9. Twenty members shall form a quorum for a general meeting.

10. If within an hour from the time appointed for a meeting convened upon the requisition of members a quorum be not present the meeting shall be dissolved. In any other case the meeting may transact such business as they think necessary notwithstanding the absence of a quorum.

11. At every general meeting all matters which come up for the decision of such meeting shall be decided by a majority of votes of the members personally present and voting by show of hands unless a poll be demanded as hereinafter mentioned.

12. The president of the council or in his absence the chairman of the executive committee shall take the chair at a general meeting.

13. If neither the president or the chairman of the executive committee be present the meeting shall elect a chairman. The chairman shall in case the votes at any general meeting or in the case of a poll are equally divided have as well as his own vote a second or casting vote. The chairman may with the consent of the meeting adjourn any meeting from time to time and from place to place but no business shall be transacted at any adjourned meeting other than the business left undisposed of at a meeting at which the adjournment took place unless in pursuance of a notice and agenda given to the members as hereinbefore prescribed.

14. At a general meeting one-third of the members of the executive committee or any twenty members of the National Trust may demand a poll in respect of any resolution and on such demand being made a poll of the National Trust shall be taken accordingly by voting papers in such manner as the chairman may direct and the result of the poll shall be deemed to be the decision of the general meeting on the resolution.

15. Every member shall have one vote only with the exception of the chairman's casting vote.

2

Act of 1937   An act to confer further powers upon the National Trust for places of Historic Interest or Natural Beauty and for other purposes.
[1st July 1937]

7 Edw. 7
c. cxxxvi

Whereas by the National Trust Act 1907 (in this Act called 'the Act of 1907') the National Trust for Places of Historic Interest or Natural Beauty (in this Act called 'the National Trust') was incorporated:

And whereas the National Trust was established for the general purposes of promoting the permanent preservation for the benefit of the nation of lands and tenements (including buildings) of beauty or historic interest and as regards lands for the preservation (so far as practicable) of their natural aspect features and animal and plant life:

9 & 10
Geo. 5
c. lxxxiv

And whereas by the National Trust Charity Scheme Confirmation Act 1919 (in this Act called 'the Act of 1919') a Scheme of the Charity Commissioners for the application or management of the National Trust was confirmed:

And whereas the National Trust with the generous support of landowners donors subscribers and others has acquired by purchase gift and otherwise considerable property including lands and buildings and funds for the upkeep and preservation thereof:

And whereas the use by the public for purposes of recreation resort and instruction of the lands and buildings held by the National Trust has increased and is increasing:

And whereas with the objects of promoting the preservation of buildings and chattels of national interest or of architectural historic or artistic interest and places of natural interest or beauty and of protecting and augmenting the amenities of such buildings and places and of facilitating access by the public to such buildings chattels and places it is expedient that the purposes and powers of the National Trust should be extended as by this Act provided:

And whereas in furtherance of the said objects it is expedient to make provision for the assurance of property to the National Trust subject to the reservation in favour of the assuror of an interest for life or other limited interest:

And whereas it is expedient that the other powers contained in this Act should be conferred on the National Trust and that the other provisions contained in this Act should be enacted:

And whereas the objects of this Act cannot be attained without the authority of Parliament:

May it therefore please your Majesty that it may be enacted and be it enacted by the King's most Excellent Majesty by and with the advice and consent of the Lords Spiritual and Temporal and Commons in this present Parliament assembled and by the authority of the same as follows:

1.—(1) This Act may be cited as the National Trust Act 1937.

(2) The National Trust Act 1907 and the National Trust Charity Scheme Confirmation Act 1919 and this Act may be cited together as the National Trust Acts 1907 to 1937.

Short and collective titles

2. In this Act unless the subject or context otherwise requires–
'The National Trust' means the National Trust for Places of Historic Interest or Natural Beauty:
'The Act of 1907' means the National Trust Act 1907;
'The Act of 1919' means the National Trust Charity Scheme Confirmation Act 1919;
'The Scheme' means the Scheme set out in the Schedule to the Act of 1919;
'The Trust Property' includes all property from time to time vested for a legal estate in the National Trust;
'Assurance' 'assure' and 'assuror' have the same respective meanings as in the Mortmain and Charitable Uses Act 1888;
'The Council' means the Council of the National Trust.

Interpretation

15 & 52 Vict. c. 42

3. The purposes of the National Trust shall be extended so as to include the promotion of–
  (a) The preservation of buildings of national interest or architectural historic or artistic interest and places of natural interest or beauty and the protection and augmentation of the amenities of such buildings and places and their surroundings;
  (b) The preservation of furniture and pictures and chattels of any description having national or historic or artistic interest;
  (c) The access to and enjoyment of such buildings places and chattels by the public;
and all such purposes shall be deemed to be purposes of the Act of 1907.

Extension of general purposes of National Trust

4. The powers of the National Trust shall be extended so as to include–

(a) The acquisition in any manner (including acquisition by purchase out of any funds applicable for the general purposes of the National Trust or liable to be invested in the purchase of land) and retention of any lands buildings and hereditaments and any rights easements or interests therein or thereover which in the opinion of the Council it may be desirable to hold as investments with a view to the provision out of the rents and profits thereof of funds applicable for the maintenance and preservation of any other part of the Trust Property or for any particular purpose of the National Trust or for its general purposes;

(b) The acquisition in any manner and retention of any investments (being at the time of acquisition of a nature authorised by *Section 4 (Powers of investment) of the National Trust Act 1953* or of a nature authorised by the Trusts imposed by the donor of the same or of the funds out of which the same shall be acquired) the income whereof shall be applicable (subject to any trusts imposed by the donor or otherwise affecting the same) at the discretion of the Council for the preservation and maintenance of the Trust Property or any specified part or parts thereof or for any particular purpose of the National Trust or for its general purposes.

5. Notwithstanding Section 5 (National Trust not to divide profits among its Members) of the Act of 1907 it shall be lawful for any Member of the National Trust (not being a Member of the Council or of any Committee of the Council) by agreement with the National Trust to reside in or occupy any of the Trust Property either at the best rent that could reasonably be obtained or (in the case of any property other than property acquired and held as an investment under paragraph (a) of section 4 of this Act) at a less rent or gratuitously and on such other terms and conditions as the Council shall think fit to approve.

6.—(1) Part II of the Mortmain and Charitable Uses Act 1888 and so much of Section 5 of the Mortmain and Charitable Uses Act 1891 as requires land assured by Will to be sold within one year from the death of the Testator or the extended period referred to in that section shall not apply to an assurance of land of any quantity or of personal estate to the National Trust for any purpose for which the National Trust is authorised to hold the same.

(2) For the purposes of Section 55 of the Settled Land Act 1925 (which empowers tenants for life to grant land for public and charitable purposes) any grant or lease of settled land to the National Trust shall be deemed to be made for the general benefit of the settled land and for a charitable purpose in connection with the settled land and in the application of that section to grants or leases made to the National Trust five acres shall be substituted for one acre.

7.—(1) The Council of any county or borough or urban or rural districts or parish or two or more of them may with the consent of the Minister of Health and of any other Government Department or authority whose consent would be required if the intended transaction were a sale by deed assure to the National

206

Trust any land or building vested in them which the National Trust has power to acquire and hold and such land shall thenceforward be held by the National Trust accordingly subject nevertheless to any trusts covenants or restrictions affecting the same.

(2) The Council of any county or borough or urban or rural district or parish may with the consent of the Minister of Health contribute to the expenses of acquisition by the National Trust of any land or building wholly or partly within or in the neighbourhood of the district of such council or to the expenses of maintenance and preservation of any land or building wholly or partly within or in the neighbourhood of such district vested or proposed to be vested in the National Trust provided that the consent of the Minister of Health shall not be required in respect of any contribution by the London County Council under the provisions of this sub-section.

8. Where any person is willing to agree with the National Trust that any land or any part thereof shall so far as his interest in the land enables him to bind it be made subject either permanently or for a specified period to conditions restricting the planning development or use thereof in any manner the National Trust may if it thinks fit enter into an agreement with him or accept a covenant from him to that effect and shall have power to enforce such agreement or covenant against persons deriving title under him in the like manner and to the like extent as if the National Trust were possessed of or entitled to or interested in adjacent land and as if the agreement or covenant had been and had been expressed to be entered into for the benefit of that adjacent land. *[Power to enter into agreements restricting use of land]*

9. Separate accounts shall be kept of all sums of money received or expended by the National Trust and not applicable at the discretion of the Council to the general purposes of the National Trust. *[Accounts]*

10. Notwithstanding the provisions of Section 27 (Application of Revenue) of the Act of 1907 the Council may from time to time by resolution determine that the expenses of and concerning any one or more purposes of the National Trust shall (subject to any trusts imposed by the donor or otherwise affecting the same) be defrayed exclusively out of any specified part or parts of the Trust Property or the capital or income of any particular fund or funds and such determination (unless and until modified or abrogated by a like resolution) shall be binding. *[Application of Trust Property]*

11.—(1) Section 32 (Bye-laws) of the Act of 1907 shall be read and have effect as if at the end thereof the following paragraph were added: *[Bye-laws]*

'(Q.) For permitting the public or any specified persons or person to view and to make copies or reproductions of or extracts from any chattel vested in the National Trust on such terms in all respects as may be from time to time prescribed by the Council.'

(2) Section 33 (Bye-laws as to buildings) of the Act of 1907 shall apply in respect of any building notwithstanding that the same may be open to the public at specified times or for specified periods only.

Provisions
applicable
to
bye-laws

23 & 24
Geo. 5. c. 51

12.—(1) The provisions contained in subsections (2) (3) (4) (5) (6) (7) and (10) of Section 250 and in Sections 251 and 252 of the Local Government Act 1933 shall apply to bye-laws made by the National Trust under Section 32 (Bye-laws) or Section 33 (Bye-laws as to buildings) of the Act of 1907 as amended or extended by this Act as if the National Trust were a local authority within the meaning of those sections and the secretary of the National Trust were the clerk to such local authority. The confirming authority for the purpose of that application of the said sections shall be the Secretary of State.

(2) Section 35 (Provisions applicable to bye-laws) of the Act of 1907 is hereby repealed.

13. Paragraph 2 of the Scheme is hereby annulled.

Amendment
of Section 27
of Act of 1907

14. Section 27 (Application of Revenue) of the Act of 1907 shall be read and have effect as if the word 'investments' were substituted for the word 'securities.'

Extent
of Acts

Repealed by
Sec. 16 of
N.T. Act
1939

15.—(1) *The National Trust Acts 1907 to 1937 shall extend to the Isle of Man:*

Provided always that the powers of the Trust shall not be exercised with reference to any property situate in the Isle of Man without the approval of Tynwald and that nothing in the said Acts shall extend to prejudice or affect the rights and powers of the Manx Museum and Ancient Monuments Trustees.

(2) *This Act shall not extend to Northern Ireland.*

Costs of
Act

16. The costs charges and expenses of and incidental to the preparation applying for obtaining and passing of this Act or otherwise in relation thereto shall be paid by the National Trust and may in whole or in part be defrayed out of revenue.

N.B. The Council (1967) has in mind the promotion of an amending Act to cover some of the points mentioned on pp. 169-171 and such other matters raised by the Advisory Committee (see p. 72) as may seem to call for legislation.

Appendix 6

The National Trust's Standard Form of Covenant

THIS DEED OF COVENANT is made the   day of   19
BETWEEN
of

(hereinafter called 'the Covenantor') of the one part and THE NATIONAL TRUST FOR PLACES OF HISTORIC INTEREST OR NATURAL BEAUTY whose office is at Number 42 Queen Anne's Gate in the City of Westminster (hereinafter called 'the Trust') of the other part

WHEREAS:

(A) THE Covenantor is seised for an estate in fee simple free from incumbrances of

(hereinafter called 'the said land') and delineated on the plan annexed hereto and thereon coloured

(B) THE Trust is by Section 8 of the National Trust Act 1937 empowered to accept restrictive covenants in respect of any land notwithstanding that it may not own adjacent land

(C) THE Covenantor has agreed with the Trust that the said land shall be made permanently subject to the restrictions and stipulations hereinafter mentioned

NOW THIS DEED WITNESSETH as follows:

1. In pursuance of the said agreement and by virtue of Section 8 of The National Trust Act 1937 the Covenantor with intent and so as to bind the said land into whosoever hands the same may come (but not so as to render the Covenantor personally liable in damages for any breach of covenant committed after he shall have parted with all interest in the property in respect of which such breach shall occur) HEREBY COVENANTS with the Trust that he will at all times hereafter observe and perform the restrictions and stipulations contained in the Schedule hereto

2. Any dispute or question which may arise between the Covenantor or his successors in title and the Trust as to the construction of this Deed or the covenants herein contained shall be referred to a single arbitrator to be appointed by the President for the time being of the Lands Agents' Society and such reference shall

be deemed to be a reference to arbitration within the meaning of the Arbitration Act 1950 or any statutory modification or re-enactment thereof for the time being in force

IN WITNESS whereof the Covenantor has hereunto set his hand and seal and the Trust has caused its Common Seal to be hereunto affixed the day and year first above written

THE SCHEDULE *above referred to: The Restrictions and Stipulations*

Restrictions affecting Covenanted Land

1. No act or thing shall be done or placed or permitted to remain upon the said land which in the opinion of the Trust shall materially alter the natural appearance or condition of the said land or which in the opinion of the Trust shall be prejudicial to the amenities of the said land or of the neighbourhood or to the Trust

2. No alteration shall without the previous written consent of the Trust be made in the present lay-out and design of any garden situated on the said land

3. No new building or other erection shall without the previous written consent of the Trust at any time be erected or allowed to remain upon any part of the said land

4. No mine or quarry shall be opened or worked upon any part of the said land without the previous written consent of the Trust

5. No timber or timberlike trees shall without the previous written consent of the Trust be felled lopped topped cut removed or replaced by other species or by a different mixture of species or any different distribution of species

PROVIDED ALWAYS that nothing in the foregoing stipulations shall prevent the cultivation of the said land or any part thereof in the ordinary course of agriculture or husbandry in accordance with the custom of the country

THE SCHEDULE *above referred to: The Restrictions and Stipulations*

Restrictions affecting Covenanted Buildings

1. Not without the previous consent in writing of the Trust to make or permit any alteration in or addition to the front side or rear elevations of the building situate and being on the restricted property

2. Not without the previous consent in writing of the Trust to make or permit any alterations in or additions to the roofs parapet or cornices of the said building or which may affect the external appearance of any of the window frames sashes architraves hoods to doors or doors railings or steps thereof

3. Not to treat or permit to be treated with tar creosote paint varnish or any other form of preservative whatsoever any part of the exterior of the said building which as not been heretofore so treated

4. Not in any way to clean paint or otherwise treat or permit to be cleaned painted or treated any of the external timber brickwork stonework or plasterwork

of the said building except at such times and in such manner as the Trust may from time to time approve in writing

5. Not to permit any of the internal walls or partitions panelling stairs or fireplaces of the said building to be destroyed interfered with or removed without the previous consent in writing of the Trust

SIGNED SEALED and DELIVERED by the
said
in the presence of:

Appendix 7

Books about the National Trust

J. DIXON SCOTT, *England Under Trust*, Maclehose 1937

JAMES LEES-MILNE, ed., *The National Trust: A Record of Fifty Years Achievement*, Batsford 1945

B. L. THOMPSON, *The Lake District and the National Trust*, Kendal 1946

CLOUGH WILLIAMS-ELLIS, *On Trust for the Nation*, 2 vols., Elek 1947–49

JAMES LEES-MILNE, *National Trust Guide: Buildings*, Batsford 1948

D. M. MATHESON, *National Trust Guide: Places of Natural Beauty*, Batsford 1950

COMPTON MACKENZIE, *I Took a Journey*, Naldrett Press 1951

MARCUS CROUCH, *Britain in Trust*, Constable 1963

Notes

Chapter 1

1. It was printed by the Society under the title *A suggestion for the Better Preservation of Open Spaces.*

2. Among those present at the meeting were Lord Dufferin, Lord Carlisle, Lord Rosebery, Lord Hobhouse, Sir John Lubbock, Thomas Huxley, Sir Frederick Leighton, G. F. Watts, Holman Hunt, Walter Crane, and Mrs Humphry Ward.

3. Westminster, Carlisle, Hobhouse, G. Shaw Lefevre, James Bryce, Robert Hunter, Octavia Hill, G. E. Briscoe Eyre, Hardwicke D. Rawnsley.

4. Had the founders been able to foresee the economic and political developments of the twentieth century, and the connotation that nationalisation would in due course give to the adjective 'National', the Trust would no doubt have been christened differently. In the light of subsequent events the title has proved unhappy and has led in the last generation to much misunderstanding. That the Trust is 'national' often conveys to the uninstructed the idea that it is a government organisation. As the Prince of Wales said at the Fortieth Anniversary dinner in 1935; 'It should be made more widely and better known that, in spite of its name, the National Trust is a purely private body.' But knowledge spreads slowly and it requires constant publicity to combat an ever-recurring misconception.

Chapter 2

1. See Appendix 1 for the Principal Officers of the Trust since 1895.

2. The office was moved in 1902 to 25 Victoria Street, and thence in 1924 to 7 Buckingham Palace Gardens. In 1944 Mrs Murray Smith left the Trust 40 and 42 Queen Anne's Gate, once the home of Jeremy Bentham, and the office was established there in the following year. The adjoining house, No. 44, was bought in 1964.

3. The manor was ultimately acquired by trustees, the Sulgrave Manor Board, and formally opened to the public in 1921.

4. The history of the National Trust for Scotland is considered in Chapter 15.

Chapter 3

1. It was many years before the pattern of subscription changed. In 1930 when membership had more than doubled the percentage of Honorary and Life

members was still astonishingly high, and only about one quarter of the Ordinary members were paying less than a pound. One in thirteen was paying between £3 and £10. The subscription was still 10s. The figures for 1930 are as follows:

Hon. Members	228
Life Members	443
Ordinary Members paying £3 to £10	105
Ordinary Members paying £1 or £2	906
Ordinary Members paying less than £1	362

Chapter 4

1. Gutted in one of the worst of the 'Baedeker' raids in 1942, the Assembly Rooms were reduced to an empty shell. The interior was faithfully restored after the war.

Chapter 6

1. Some of the problems created by public access to the Trust's houses are further considered in Chapter 12.

2. Author's italics.

3. As early as 1897 the Executive Committee had considered the division of the country into districts under the supervision of regional secretaries.

Chapter 7

1. In 1957 the Land Fund, despite representations by the Trust and other bodies, was arbitrarily reduced to £10 million.

2. Some of the properties transferred were not financially self-supporting. By 1966 property acquired through the Treasury had produced a cumulative deficit of £229,000. This deficit has been met by the General Fund of the Trust.

3. Among the more important collections of works of art exempted from death duty and transferred to the Trust as a gift by the donors since the 1951 Act are those at Attingham Park, Fenton House, Tatton Park, The Vyne, and Waddesdon Manor. The last, one of the most splendid collections in Europe, was a truly munificent bequest.

4. During the same period a total of £5,175,842 was allocated to owners, on the recommendation of the Historic Buildings Council for England, for the repair and maintenance of historic buildings and their contents. Grants amounting to some £5,500 have been made to the Trust for Powis Castle on the recommendation of the Historic Buildings Council for Wales.

5. See Chapter 11. The Commission's dedication scheme makes grants for planting and management available to owners who devote woods to sustained timber production and manage them systematically and to the satisfaction of the Commission.

Chapter 8

1. The establishment of regional committees for Wessex, the West Midlands, and Yorkshire is under consideration.

Chapter 9

1. From 1953–55, when Lord De La Warr was Postmaster-General, the late Lord Fortescue became Chairman.

2. The Estates Committee went into abeyance on the outbreak of the Second World War, but was revived in the summer of 1944.

3. A sixteenth area, Northern Ireland, where a regional committee was set up in 1936, has developed on rather different lines.

4. An office such as that of the Cornwall and South Devon Area, where the Trust owns a large number of properties, has a considerable staff. The area establishment in 1967 consisted of an agent and assistant agent with an office staff of fourteen that included secretariat, accounts department, clerk of the works and assistant clerk. Sub-agents looked after three Special Trusts (see Chapter 18), and at two properties with great houses, Cotehele and Saltram, there were separate administrative staffs. Two building and maintenance gangs were responsible for West and Central Cornwall (15 men) and East Cornwall and South Devon (12 men). The coast, divided into five stretches, was under the supervision of as many Head Wardens, helped by numbers of voluntary and paid assistants.

5. A charge for access is made at only four open spaces: Lydford Gorge in Devon (to meet the cost of maintaining the gorge-side paths and the special safety precautions that are necessary), Brownsea Island, the Farne Islands and Watermeads in Surrey.

6. After the Second World War when there was a shortage of glass, the sale of jettisoned bottles from Box Hill regularly brought in £100 a year.

7. People have sometimes been surprised that picnicking is not allowed in some of the Trust's deer parks.

Chapter 10

1. Exceptions prove the rule. With the recent gift of Anglesey Abbey the Trust acquired one of the few boldly conceived parkscapes of the twentieth-century. The achievement at Anglesey Abbey is the more remarkable as the park is set in the unrelieved levels of Cambridgeshire. Park planting today, it may be noted, is often as much a matter of screening development as of creating vistas.

2. The work, largely carried out by Junior Seamen from H.M.S. Ganges is a notable example of the voluntary help which the Trust receives. Contribution has also been made by the Conservation Corps of the Nature Conservancy and by Cambridge graduates and students.

3. This may happen despite farm policy. The future of hill-farming depends on the willingness of a younger generation to accept the hard conditions that it often entails.

Chapter 11

1. Major waterworks in recent years have been carried out at Buscot Park, Farnborough Hall, Hardwick Hall, Stourhead, and The Vyne.

2. A further 9,000 are leased to the Forestry Commission.

3. Appointed in 1954. Part-time advisers on forestry had advised the Trust since 1930.

4. The general increase on lowland farms may be illustrated by reference to rents on two or three of the larger agricultural estates in 1956 and 1966: Attingham Park, Shropshire (1,159 acres), £8,930–£20,107; Buscot and Coleshill, Berkshire (7,473 acres), £12,096–£29,122; Blickling, Norfolk (4,857 acres), £10,707–£21,453. The return on Trust land varies to an unusual degree. Sixty-seven farms in and about the Lake District, many of them on marginal agricultural land, yielded in 1966 an average rent of 9s 4d per acre, while in Cornwall land let for market gardening realised as much as 200s an acre.

Chapter 12

1. Until 1945 it was known as the Country Houses Committee.

2. Family occupation also represents a substantial saving to the Trust. In almost every case it costs the Trust far less to run houses with donors living in them. The latter not only act as unpaid curators but they meet many outgoings, such as contributions to rates, lighting and heating, which would otherwise fall on the Trust.

3. The list excludes a limited number of historic buildings subject to a life-interest or in occupation as farm houses or farm cottages.

4. Shortly before the Second World War the Trust published some thirty descriptive guides and pamphlets to its properties. There are now over 150.

Chapter 13

1. One of the first tasks to which the Committee addressed itself was the presentation, with the help of a government grant, of five Trust gardens that were specially opened in connection with the Festival of Britain in 1951.

2. Four other gardens of horticultural importance have been accepted on the recommendation of the Gardens Committee: Mount Stewart (1955) and Rowallane (1956) are managed by the Regional Committee for Northern

Ireland; Glendurgan (1962) by the Regional Committee for Devon and Cornwall; and Wakehurst (1965) by the Royal Botanical Gardens.

3. The National Trust for Scotland in 1960 set up the Threave School of Practical Gardening in Kirckudbrightshire (see Chapter 15).

Chapter 14

1. Until 1935 the Annual Report and List of Properties were issued as a single volume.

2. In Northern Ireland the Trust's headquarters virtually act as a regional centre, providing a social focus and a programme of activity for Ulster members.

3. Jointly with the Kyrle Society and the Metropolitan Gardens Association.

4. Official cooperation has often reflected personal contacts. The late Lord Esher was for many years chairman both of the Society for the Protection of Ancient Buildings and the Trust's Historic Buildings Committee; and the present chairman of the Society, Lord Euston, was for some years on the staff of the Trust and is now chairman of its East Anglia Committee. Other members of the committees and staff of the Trust serve on the committees of the Society for the Protection of Ancient Buildings, and Rex Wailes, a member of the Executive of the Society for the Protection of Ancient Buildings is the Trust's Honorary Adviser on Industrial Monuments.

5. Approximate membersip: Council for the Preservation of Rural England, 7,500; Commons Preservation Society, 2,400 (including 1,200 local authorities); Ancient Monuments Society, 2,000; Society for the Protection of Ancient Buildings, 3,500; Georgian Group 2,000; Victorian Society, 1,500.

6. Since 1966 Europa Nostra has enjoyed consultative status within the Council of Europe, and is thus able to make its views known to the Council on all matters affecting historic buildings and their sites. There are now twenty-four member organisations (of which the largest is the Deutscher Heimatbund with some half-a-million members) and twelve associate members. The President (since 1966) is the Hon. Hubert Howard, the Trust's Representative in Italy. The Trust is also represented on the Executive Committee of Europa Nostra.

Chapter 15

1. In the same year the National Trust in London relinquished its powers in Scotland but suggested, perhaps ill-advisedly, that the new body should adopt a name other than the National Trust for Scotland as less likely to cause confusion.

2. The Act otherwise differed only in minor respects, such as the right of the Council to co-opt up to four members.

3. The National Trust for Scotland Confirmation Acts of 1938, 1952, and 1961 cover between them almost the same ground as the National Trust Acts of 1937 and 1953.

4. *Chairmen of Council*
   1931 Sir Iain Colquhoun, Bt.
   1946 The Earl of Wemyss and March.

Secretaries
   1931 A. W. Russell.
   1933 E. D. Stevenson (later Sir Edward Stevenson, K.C.V.O.) whose duties were temporarily assumed by Arthur Russell during the Second World War.
   1947 J. Grimond (later Leader of the Liberal Party).
   1949 J. C. Stormonth Darling.
   5. The survey by Mr W. H. Murray was published by the Trust in book form in 1962 as *Highland Landscape*. The survey distinguishes twenty-one areas of outstanding importance, and examines the major threats to Highland scenery. It is characteristic of the situation in Scotland that these threats derive rather from government and its agencies (e.g. hydro-electric schemes, afforestation, and new roads) than from private development and the pressure of population.
   6. An account of this interesting development is to be found in the National Trust for Scotland's publication *Preservation at Stenhouse*, n.d.

Chapter 16
   1. In drafting both the National Trust Act of 1907, and the earlier Articles of Association, Sir Robert Hunter found a useful model in *An Act to Establish the Trustees of Public Reservations*. Passed in 1891 by the General Court of Massachusetts, the Act created trustees 'for the purpose of acquiring, holding, arranging, maintaining, and opening to the public, under suitable regulations, beautiful and historic places and tracts of land', and empowered them as a corporation to 'acquire and hold by grant, gift, devise, purchase, or otherwise, real estate such as it may deem worthy of preservation for the enjoyment of the public'. The Massachusetts Trustees are the senior holding trust for the conservation of land and buildings.
   2. For the text of the National Trust Acts see Appendix 5.
   3. For the National Trust's standard forms of Covenant see Appendix 6.
   4. In Ulster the transfer of property to the Trust through the Ministry of Finance is made possible by the Finance Acts (Northern Ireland) 1936 and 1948.

Chapter 17
   1. See Appendix 1.
   2. A Labour member was first appointed in 1922.
   3. See Appendix 1.
   4. The Secretary has in fact been given this title as from March 1st 1968.

218

Chapter 18

1. Four houses and one agricultural estate show deficits of over £20,000 which have been met by loans (from the free funds of the Trust) which are likely to be irrecoverable.

	£
a. Knole	41,900
b. Gunby	34,400
c. Hatchlands	32,700
d. Farnborough Hall	24,900
e. Dolaucothi (2,400 acres)	45,100

2. At Knole the Historic Buildings Council (see Chapter 7) now recommends a substantial grant in aid.

3. Chattels cannot be declared inalienable and legally the Trust could dispose of the contents of many of the houses committed to its care, thus realising vast sums. To do so would be an unthinkable breach of trust. On the rare occasions when the Trust has sold chattels the circumstances have been exceptional and the sale has been in accordance with the wishes of the donor or his heirs.

4. Unhappily since this chapter was written the Trust has suffered another serious fire. In November 1967 Dunsland in Devon was gutted.

Index